BAD
ANIMALS

BAD ANIMALS

a father's accidental education in autism

JOEL YANOFSKY

VIKING
CANADA

VIKING CANADA

Published by the Penguin Group
Penguin Group (Canada), 90 Eglinton Avenue East, Suite 700, Toronto, Ontario, Canada M4P 2Y3
(a division of Pearson Canada Inc.)

Penguin Group (USA) Inc., 375 Hudson Street, New York, New York 10014, U.S.A.
Penguin Books Ltd, 80 Strand, London WC2R 0RL, England
Penguin Ireland, 25 St Stephen's Green, Dublin 2, Ireland (a division of Penguin Books Ltd)
Penguin Group (Australia), 250 Camberwell Road, Camberwell, Victoria 3124, Australia
(a division of Pearson Australia Group Pty Ltd)
Penguin Books India Pvt Ltd, 11 Community Centre, Panchsheel Park, New Delhi – 110 017, India
Penguin Group (NZ), 67 Apollo Drive, Rosedale, North Shore 0632, Auckland, New Zealand
(a division of Pearson New Zealand Ltd)
Penguin Books (South Africa) (Pty) Ltd, 24 Sturdee Avenue, Rosebank, Johannesburg 2196,
South Africa

Penguin Books Ltd, Registered Offices: 80 Strand, London WC2R 0RL, England

First published 2011

1 2 3 4 5 6 7 8 9 10   (RRD)

Author representation: Westwood Creative Artists
94 Harbord Street, Toronto, Ontario M5S 1G6

Excerpt from *Worstward Ho*, copyright © 1983 by Samuel Beckett. Used by permission
of Grove/Atlantic, Inc.

LIBRARY AND ARCHIVES CANADA CATALOGUING IN PUBLICATION

Yanofsky, Joel, 1955–
Bad animals : a father's accidental education in autism / Joel Yanofsky.

ISBN 978-0-670-06510-3

1. Yanofsky, Joel, 1955–. 2. Yanofsky, Jonah. 3. Parents of autistic children—Canada—Biography.
4. Autistic children—Canada--Biography. 5. Autistic children—Family relationships—Canada.
6. Authors, Canadian (English)—20th century—Biography. I. Title.

PS8597.A559Z53 2011   C813'.54   C2010-906650-2

Visit the Penguin Group (Canada) website at **www.penguin.ca**

Special and corporate bulk purchase rates available; please see
www.penguin.ca/corporatesales or call 1-800-810-3104, ext. 477 or 474

For all those parents in the same boat

To Cynthia, with love, always

To Jonah, a most awesome guy

Contents

Vacation

BAD
ANIMALS

PROLOGUE
September

There have always been too many books. When I was seventeen a shelf over the desk in my bedroom collapsed, more or less, on top of me. A three-foot plank of dark wood-stained laminate, supported by two flimsy metal brackets, which were, in turn, supported by four tiny plastic anchors, gave way under the weight of my evolving literary taste. The shelf was arranged alphabetically—authors from M to P—and my latest purchase, Thomas Pynchon's *Gravity's Rainbow,* proved too weighty. The avalanche of paperbacks—Penguins, Pelicans, Bantams, Signets, Dells—stunned me more than anything else. Some landed in my lap; most dispersed like shrapnel, taking out a lamp, a turntable, and a tennis trophy I won when I was eleven. I never imagined *Remembrance of Things Past, Volume One,* could cause so much collateral damage.

I should have taken the incident as a sign, a warning. Even then, I should have realized that my so-called library was conspiring to teach me one of literature's most enduring lessons—there's a price to pay for precocity, for our reach exceeding our grasp. And while I may have harboured a secret ambition to write at the time, I was young and oblivious to irony and metaphor. Who knew this was precisely the kind of stuff—stuff you couldn't make up if you tried— you were supposed to remember, take note of, cherish even? These silly, seemingly insignificant moments were, in lieu of something more dramatic or meaningful, what you were given as a writer and you better learn to make the most of it—lemons into lemonade. My mother heard the crash from the kitchen, gasped, and came running. Once she realized I was unhurt, only embarrassed, she covered her mouth to stifle a laugh. It was as if she'd walked in on the aftermath of some slapstick routine and was reconstructing it in reverse, as if she'd discovered someone lying on their back next to a banana peel. She could afford to draw her own conclusions. She wasn't complicit in this oddball preoccupation of mine.

My mother had been a serious reader once. That was when she still entertained dreams of finishing high school and attending college. Before she had to drop out and work for her older brother pressing shirts, she'd ordered a complete set of novels by the American social realist Sinclair Lewis—*Babbitt* and *Main Street* and *Elmer Gantry*. (I asked her once: Why Lewis? But she no longer had a clue. "There must have been a reason," she said.) And while you could still find the occasional bestseller on her night table—*Mila 18* or *A Stone for Danny Fisher*—they remained mainly unread. My father didn't read at all, not even the newspaper. So, naturally, both of them were a little bewildered by my bookishness. They assumed it was a phase and I let them think so. But they must have wondered where it came from and, more important, when it would end. I wondered myself. (They must have also thought what all parents think eventually—*Whose kid is this?*) Our four television sets—one in each of our suburban bungalow's three bedrooms as well as one in the kitchen—were always playing in our house: soap operas, quiz shows, baseball games, old black-and-white movies. I watched as much TV as I wanted. Back then, no one could see the harm. My parents never read to me when I was a child either. As far as I know, they never considered it. Even if they had, there were no children's books around to read. I didn't discover the kidlit classics—Lewis Carroll, Dr. Seuss, *The Wind in the*

Willows, Where the Wild Things Are, Shel Silverstein—until my son was born.

It didn't help that at the suburban high school I attended all my friends wanted to be dentists or, failing that, chartered accountants. Plans A and B. I seem to remember them just showing up one September determined to be solid citizens. Rather abruptly, they stopped wrestling in the halls and giving each other wedgies. It was like *Invasion of the Body Snatchers.* In the meantime, I was betting that my high-minded taste in books would make me unique, which it did—unique and isolated. As my must-read list grew longer, my social life dwindled, or perhaps vice versa. I didn't care about school either. I cared about life and love and literature. And it hardly mattered which came first—my chicken-hearted pomposity or my egg-headed awkwardness.

I'd spend entire summer vacations wrapped up in novels that were so far above my head I practically had to translate them line by line— from English into English. Still, on the last day of school, I trudged off to a neighbourhood bookstore (they had those then) where I'd had my eye on a copy of James Joyce's *Ulysses.* I agonized over the enormous cost, nine bucks for a paperback, but then finally bought it. I'd spend all of July and August immersed or, more precisely, drowning in Joycean prose. I read and reread Molly Bloom's final monologue, never realizing it might be dirty. By the time school began again, I would be confused for weeks by my English teacher's comparatively simple assignments. I kept searching for layers of meaning that no one else cared about.

In university, my friends, who were studying commerce or science, teased me about never carrying a schoolbag. The only books I was ever seen with were ones that slipped easily into my pocket. It was the 1970s, a time for thin, revelatory, pretentious fiction: Herman Hesse, Richard Brautigan, *The Crying of Lot 49,* Pynchon in a brief though no less bewildering mood. Why Pynchon? You could ask me that now and I would be, like my mother, hard-pressed to come up with a reason.

At home, I was spending more and more time banging out term papers with pretentious subtitles—*Resignation and Despair in the Comedies of Samuel Beckett*—on my manual typewriter. "What's he doing?" my father would ask my mother constantly. A sign painter, my father worked at home, in the basement, and the constant clacking noise from one floor up must have been unbearable. I can't know what he was thinking, but I'm in a better position now than ever to guess. Something like: *Is this why you have children? So they can drive you crazy and turn into someone you don't recognize?*

I was, in my own low-key way, weird; saving my money to acquire six-foot-high bookcases as though they were precious collectibles. (Why didn't I want a car? Or a guitar? Or a girlfriend? Why didn't I backpack through Europe?) When I ran out of space for any more bookcases in my bedroom, they ended up in the basement. I spent long, lonely weekends assembling them. I became an expert with an Allen key. There are still dozens of those useless things lying around.

In her memoir *Ruined by Reading: A Life in Books,* novelist Lynne Sharon Schwartz describes her transformation in college into a proselytizing pain in the neck. She was appalled that her parents had never studied the great works of Western literature. Without them, no life could be complete, she pronounced. If she'd had a bumper sticker, she writes, it would have proclaimed, "Lit Saves." My own expectations of literature were more modest and self-involved. I wanted it to save me, only me. From what exactly? Who knows? Likely it was a nagging concern about being average, typical, heaven forbid, normal. Literature honours the offbeat, the oddball; it thrives on idiosyncrasies. What would Captain Ahab be without his OCD? A regular, grumpy seafaring guy—think the Skipper on *Gilligan's Island.* Even writers who claim to devote their careers to championing ordinariness have their limits. John Updike talked a good game about his intention "to transcribe the middle"—middle-class, middle-of-the-road, middle-America—but in the *Rabbit* books, Harry "Rabbit" Angstrom is always going off the deep end or on the verge of doing so. Over the course of four novels, Rabbit remains a notable narcissist. "Harry, you're not actually the centre of the universe," his ex-wife tells him in *Rabbit at Rest,* "it just feels that way to you." Imagine Joseph K without his paranoia, Jay Gatsby without his self-delusion; or how about a happily married Anna Karenina, a well-adjusted Miss Havisham? What would they be? Good company at a dinner party or on a long road trip, and who's looking for that in a novel?

I didn't realize it then but I had nothing but time. So how come I always felt rushed? The extra Lit courses I took later in graduate school only made my sense of urgency worse. I began to realize I'd never be done, as one newly discovered author invariably led to another: Joyce to Flann O'Brien to Flannery O'Connor; Cheever to Updike to Anne Tyler to Alice Hoffman to Richard Ford. There was no end to the Russians and their doorstoppers. The same for the Brits, who, thankfully, were more succinct: Evelyn Waugh begat Anthony Powell who begat Henry Green who begat Graham Greene. I made a resolution to get through the Old Testament, but kept finding myself stuck early in *Genesis*, on Abraham's decision to sacrifice Isaac. He was not the first inept asshole father, I'm guessing, but he blazed the trail.

Still, I was fondest of the writers I stumbled across on my own, non-household names like Stanley Elkin or Peter De Vries. I sucked up important literary and life lessons by osmosis. From De Vries's *The Blood of the Lamb,* I learned you could be irreverent and sad at the same time, as De Vries's usual clowning around and wordplay—"The only thing that keeps me from killing myself is the will to live"—morphed into a heartbreaking, barely fictionalized account of his daughter's death from leukemia. "The future is a thing of the past," another father in the novel with a dying daughter says. And I laughed, though there's no chance I got this dark joke. Not then.

I went through my snobby phase, too. I remember auditing a course by renowned Canadian novelist Hugh MacLennan and dropping it before the poor man's lecture was ten minutes old. I knew I'd never read *Two Solitudes* or *Barometer Rising*. It was the kind of snap judgment I would repeat often—later in print, in the book reviews I regularly wrote for newspaper book sections. Readers and writers have their pet peeves. Vladimir Nabokov detested italics. Elmore Leonard refuses to read any book that begins with a description of the weather. I had my own rule about dumping novelists who didn't crack a joke by the end of the first chapter. Whatever else he was, MacLennan was no kidder.

Later, when I did begin reviewing books on a regular basis for whoever would pay me a tiny, unchanging sum to do what I increasingly realized was the only thing I was qualified to do—read—I discovered new books. Brand new, I mean. These were books with pub dates and press releases tucked inside their dust jackets; books with authors in town, waiting to be interviewed. Books lined up on my desk, like widgets on an assembly line. They never stopped coming, nor did my hurried, slapdash opinions of them. Somehow, I found something to say about everything. Imagine that. I also discovered I didn't like the vast majority of the books I reviewed, but I read them anyway, right to the end. Every six months or so I gathered up a pile of review copies and sold them at a second-hand bookstore across the street from the newspaper I freelanced for. The owner of the store found the practice—mine and other reviewers'—morally dubious but good for business. There was no more room on my shelves. Besides, I wasn't an amateur any more. I'd gone pro.

I've been a book reviewer, now, for almost three decades. I've also interviewed and profiled several hundred authors. And while it's not the kind of work that makes you rich or famous or especially fulfilled— "Nobody needs to spend his life telling the world that this not very good book is not very good," as Richard Ford once put it—there are worse jobs. I've been able to justify how little book reviewing pays and how little respect it has earned me by thinking about the ongoing education I've received from the books I've read and the writers I've encountered. "The important books will come to you when you need them," said Joseph Epstein, an American essayist and critic, and, until recently, this seemed true. I wasn't just devoted to literature; I depended on it. I filled up memo pads with passages from famous and obscure authors: my own *Coles Notes* of how to live a good, self-aware life. "Ambivalent love, the only love worth writing about"—John Updike. Or: "The tragedy of the man not set up for tragedy—that is every man's tragedy"—Philip Roth. I played hunches, too, guessing that one day I would understand George Bernard Shaw's aphorism about there being two tragedies in life: not getting your heart's desire and getting it. One day, I would understand.

Anyway, I must have believed everything I read then. I don't any more. My bookcases are in *my* basement office now, and sometimes I find myself staring at what is, at the moment, the unalphabetized chaos of my life. Sometimes, I flip through the books that were once important to me to see my scribbled notes in the margins, to wonder what I was trying to tell myself, what message I was sending. Maybe Joseph Epstein was wrong and the important book he promised isn't on its way. Maybe there aren't enough books, after all.

In any case, who has the time to wait around? Who has the energy or faith for clever quips or highlighted passages any more? Not me. I haven't for a while. Not since strangers, with their theories and their degrees in the social sciences, began telling my wife and me there was something wrong with our son Jonah; not since we finally noticed something was wrong; not since our world turned upside down; not since one word, not a metaphor or a turn of phrase or an illuminating passage, just one impenetrable word, *autism*, changed everything.

Now I'm clearing shelf space for a new set of books: manuals and memoirs and diet books, all with the same subject. I can't read them all; I certainly can't finish all of them. They infuriate me, bore me, make me scoff, make me cry, inspire envy, strike chords, ring bells, miss the mark, make no sense, make too much sense. Still, there are times I wonder if there might be one that might also make a difference, by which I mean an important difference. Nothing else is useful any more. I also wonder what would happen if I dismissed a certain book because the author was, let's say, a pretentious blowhard, or because he or she said something worth saying but said it ineptly. I'm preoccupied with my son and with autism now, not with prose style. I used to think the great advantage of studying literature was that no matter what, you could never be wrong. Your opinion was as good as anyone else's. The trouble is: I need to be right now. I need answers, not more questions.

Jonah is ten and starts grade five in a few days. We have bought his school supplies in bulk. We have stocked up on the grey jerseys and sweatpants that constitute his nondescript uniform at the public school he attends. We have talked to his teachers in advance. (That is, my wife, Cynthia, has.) We have a meeting scheduled with his principal. (Cynthia, again.) We've gotten up to speed, going over his previous Individualized Educational Programs, or IEPs, compulsory for special-needs children, as well as his previous report cards in case someone at the school misses some detail about him that might be helpful. They always do. And when we remind them of this detail, they will label us oversensitive, interfering parents, code us troublemakers, helicopter types, and we will be off again on the wrong foot, learning to be solicitous, diplomatic, subtly manipulative. Autism is an education, a crash course.

As each school year begins, Jonah's world, and ours as well, becomes more challenging, and I can't help thinking this is the year the other shoe drops. This is it—grade five—the year autism beats us in a landslide. The year we can't overlook this impossible-to-overlook fact and can no longer keep clinging to the small, incremental victories, the two-steps-forward-one-step-back life (or could it be the other way around?) we are now expected to live.

Jonah and Cynthia are better at challenges than I am. It should come as no surprise to my teachers in elementary and high school, particularly my math and science teachers, that I've turned out to be a bad student, often grumpy and unprepared, behind in my reading, tardy on crucial assignments, either unwilling or unable to learn anything new. Except I have to now, and have to hope it's not too late. Lucky for me, for all of us, it's only September.

First Term

Oh that my words were now written! oh that they were printed in a book!

—THE BOOK OF JOB

When [the animals] got to school, they worked and worked in math.... They worked on addition. They had lots of fun. They got a prize for doing well! They were never bad again. The End

—JONAH, AGED 10, FROM *BAD ANIMALS*

ONE

What You Need

"What's our motto, Jonah, our motto? Say it with me: 'You can't always get what you want,'" Cynthia says. She's speaking deliberately. Her voice is calm—better yet, neutral. I marvel at its neutrality and always have. *It's nothing you can't do, too, sweetheart.* My wife's words are always in my head. That "sweetheart," the slightly cloying inflection I give it, is hardly fair to her. It diminishes the soundness of the advice I imagine her giving me, the heartfelt concern I know is real. She's not being sarcastic when she says it, even in my head; still it's sarcasm I hear. I guess I never expected marriage to be like this—so intimate, so unnerving. Incidentally, Jonah is having a meltdown in the back of the car. This is not unusual, but that doesn't mean I'm used to it. We're twenty minutes from home. Or less, since I'm driving significantly above the speed limit. Even so, it seems as if we're barely moving, as if we're stuck in one of those interminable traffic jams that have you craning your neck out the window to see just a little farther ahead. Or if that's not doing the trick, maybe you put the car in park, step out, and commiserate with your fellow drivers, all the while searching for a better vantage point, as if there really might be some explanation for what caused this mess in the first place.

Jonah's latest tantrum started when he asked for a chocolate ice cream cone and Cynthia said he'd have to wait until after dinner. It has escalated from there. Now he's teary-eyed and practically hoarse in the backseat, carrying on an argument we are doing our best to ignore. The crying and the petulance I can just about tune out, but it's the whining that's so unrelenting I catch myself in awe, almost envious, of the sheer force of will required to sustain it. So when Cynthia tries to explain to Jonah that there is such a thing as limits and that a limit is when you can't have what you want at the exact moment you want it, like when you're driving in a car, Jonah is unappeased. "What's a limit?" he keeps asking, getting more and more worked up. He will keep asking the same question or some variation on it—his impatience rising and mine with it—until he will settle for nothing less than our full confession that we are deceiving him. Better still, that we are wrong and that ice cream before dinner will, from hereon in, become a new family policy. I worry, too, that if I were alone with him I would confirm this belief and capitulate. I would head for the nearest Dairy Queen or backtrack to find one, anything to make him stop. Now, I can only daydream about doing that. His mother is more effective at ignoring him at times like this, so his question is invariably directed at me. "Daddy, what's a limit?" "A limit is a bummer," I say and Cynthia gives me a sideways glance.

Jonah is too old to be having this kind of fit, but, still, I try to remind myself that it was worse when he was younger. He used to scream and kick, too, often until he gagged, sometimes threw up. Or he used to say, "I'm mad; I'm not mad. I am; I'm not," launching into what was, at the time, his standard self-contradictory soliloquy. It was the kind of thing that if you weren't stuck in a car with him or at a holiday dinner, if you were in the right mood, could be funny. Like a bit right out of the Marx Brothers or Abbott and Costello. The kid would agree to nothing, not even how he felt.

Jonah was first diagnosed with autism when he was almost four, and back then we were still not sure what we were dealing with. We were on a waiting list at the hospital for a second opinion and there were days I tried to put anything to do with autism on hold until this appointment. Some days my strategy proved more successful than others. Mostly, we were in a daze. *Speak for yourself, sweetheart, some of us were depressed.* We were never sure, for instance, if his latest tantrum was just one of those times when Jonah was acting like any other kid not getting his way. Back then, it could be difficult to distinguish between autistic behaviour and typical four- or five-year-old behaviour. (I should say neurotypical since that's the politically correct term now. It's used these days to describe, well, everyone who doesn't have autism.) Though, looking back, I suspect we were kidding ourselves. I suspect we understood or were beginning to understand our situation.

When I first learned what was wrong with Jonah I looked up the word *autism* in the dictionary. "A mental disorder characterized by self-absorption," it said, and I remember walking around for days thinking, *That sounds like me.* Then thinking, *That sounds like everyone.*

I know better now. I know the look in my son's eye, the sound of his voice, when he's gone somewhere else, somewhere deep and nearly impenetrable inside himself. I know why those tantrums were so fierce and unfathomable when he was younger, and why they continue to come and go, fade, return, disappear, mutate. Jonah has gone through a variety of overlapping phases, if you can call them phases. He has lost his temper with us and others, acted aggressively, stared off into space, mumbled, chattered, scripted, perseverated, echoed, and distorted words. Whatever he does, though, he does incessantly. At least, he would if we let him. He would, for instance, read the same books— even at ten, animal alphabet books remain his favourite—over and over again. He is intolerant of change, any change. "An overwhelming preservation of sameness," that's what Leo Kanner identified as the primary marker of the disorder. (Kanner was the Austrian-born American psychologist who first identified infantile autism in 1943; a year later another native Austrian, Hans Asperger, gave his name to Asperger's syndrome, a milder form of the disorder.) And so we, Jonah's family as well as the people—the experts and educators—working with him, are not only preventing him from retreating to that place where nothing changes, we are *conspiring* to prevent him. Every action we take, every person we hire, every theory or therapy we purchase, everything we do is designed to keep him from doing what he most wants to: to stay just the way he is. *Who are you talking about, sweetheart? Because that sounds like you.*

Autism is a spectrum of disorders (commonly referred to as ASD), and within a broad range of symptoms and deficits, Jonah is generally considered high-functioning. The first psychologist to diagnose him told us this in one session, a not-quite-two-hour introductory class in autism. He will likely have problems with communication and social interaction, she explained. He will be prone to repetitive behaviour, also known as self-stimulatory behaviour, or stims. Take, for instance, the way he lines up his toys, she said, referring to one stim she'd already observed. He will have trouble with empathy, too, with what's called theory of mind. For neurotypical kids, empathy is a natural, progressive part of development—not for Jonah. He will have to be taught that just because he feels something, it doesn't mean other people feel it too and in the same way. Right now, he is inclined to believe that whatever he experiences other people must be experiencing. In individuals with autism, that's called mind-blindness. *That's called yours truly*, I thought. Down deep, I always think everything is happening to me and only me. All *this*, for instance. The psychologist was a chubby, cheerful young woman with a framed bachelor's degree in psychology a little askew on her freshly painted but otherwise unadorned office wall. "Any questions?" she'd repeat every so often. *Were we supposed to raise our hands?* She couldn't have been more than twenty-five and she delivered the news matter-of-factly, as if it couldn't possibly come as a surprise to anyone since it wasn't a surprise to her. She got up from her chair, then smiled and said, "Have a nice drive home." *Talk about mind-blindness.* Still, when we didn't respond or even move, she glanced at Jonah and then at us, at our evident worry and desperation, and summed up her diagnosis with an improvised pronouncement.

"He has a whiff of autism," she said, nodding her wide face slowly and deliberately. I nearly hugged her; the phrase sounded so quaint. *A whiff? What's a whiff? Nothing. Hardly noticeable. Like a mole, a lisp. Like being left-handed.*

At first, I assumed Jonah's development would just be slower than that of other children. He'd be a few years behind; that's all. For instance, when he was ten, as he is now, he'd be more like an eight- or a six-year-old. He'd be held back a year or two in school. So what? By this same reasoning, I figured that by the time he was twenty-one, well, what would it matter? We were playing catch-up, that's all. Who cared? Instead, what we're playing is a whole other game with a whole other set of rules. I find myself dreading Jonah's birthdays, thinking: *He can't really be turning eleven this year.* Or dreading another September: *He can't really be in grade five.*

As it turns out, Jonah's developmental delay is not just a delay. It's not just a disability or a disorder or a condition either. It's something else entirely, something the mental health care profession or the educational system would never dare call it these days. Something I am well aware I shouldn't be calling it either. But there are moments when I, a reluctant but diligent student of my son's behaviour, can't think of any other word to describe him than strange. Sometimes, no P.C., no neutral, no other word will suffice.

I have also learned what any parent of a child with autism eventually learns: there's no such thing as "a whiff of autism." It's true there are kids worse off, and some better off, than Jonah, but that has not made the gulf between my son and the world he has to work so hard to understand and engage with any narrower. It has not prevented me from noticing that it appears to be growing wider every day.

"MOTTO, JONAH?" Cynthia prompts again. She is holding up *Forty Licks*, a compilation of Rolling Stones hits we keep in the car for this kind of occasion. Jonah, who is barely catching his breath, listens and grudgingly says, "Number six: 'You Can't Always Get What You Want.'" Jonah is not a child for whom logic will ever be simple, but somehow the simple logic of Mick Jagger's line appeals to him. That's why we need to be careful not to overuse it, Cynthia says. It's a feature of autism that anything that begins as if it's going to be a good thing—like an interest in classic British rock or knock-knock jokes or animal alphabet books—is bound to turn bad, which is to say turn into a fixation. So Cynthia saves the Rolling Stones lyric for moments of crisis or those moments of crisis we can no longer deal with. Which is another thing you learn when you have a child with autism: everything is a potential crisis.

Cynthia and I both used to avoid the A-word, as we called it, though we did so for different reasons. Cynthia because she believed, down deep, that with hours and hours of ABA or applied behavioural analysis therapy, with luck, with dedication, determination, and a positive, proactive attitude, autism was something we could overcome or at least battle to some kind of uneasy but workable truce. She believed that one day Jonah would be "indistinguishable" from any other neurotypical kid.

"Indistinguishable" was the word she repeated, mantra-like, every chance she got in the first few months after Jonah's diagnosis. It was the promise implicit in the course of action we were embarking on— ABA therapy. Indistinguishable implied Jonah would not be like everyone else but that he would almost be. At the very least, he would appear to be. We might always know the difference, of course, but there was a chance other people—friends, teachers, store clerks, future girlfriends, and employers—might not. We were determined to fool them all, now and in the future; we were depending on it. There was still no guaranteed treatment for autism, certainly no cure, but there was reason to be hopeful. Cynthia was reading everything she could about ABA back then and finding examples of kids who were doing fine, all things considered. *All things considered.* What a preposterous phrase to apply to a child, *my* child. It made me want to scream or, better yet, punch a wall or throw something, something heavy. I never needed qualifications for Jonah before. In fact, he was the only thing in my life I never needed them for. Now, I was learning that qualifications were all I had. I would have to take solace in them, but that would take time. *How much time, sweetheart?* Cynthia, meanwhile, met with the mother of another boy, a few years older than Jonah, who was in a private school where no one, not his classmates, not the teachers, not the administrators, knew he had autism. "It's true," Cynthia said when she got home, her tone lighter, less ominous than it had been for weeks. "No one can tell."

During their meeting, the other mother had recommended one of her son's therapists to Cynthia. This therapist had recently started her own practice and become a consultant. She was a slight, no-nonsense woman in her late-twenties when we first met her. She had long black hair and wore nothing but black; even so, it was hard to tell what look she was going for—Zorro or Morticia. Her job was her life and she undertook it with a zeal and self-assurance that was, for us, irresistible. Autism was and still is a seller's market and The Consultant, one of the kinder nicknames I would come up with for her, knew it. This was exactly what we wanted: someone who knew everything. We were more than willing, then, to believe in her methods, to believe in her as much as she believed in herself. The Consultant had only a bachelor's degree in psychology but her credentials were impressive nevertheless. She was only two degrees of separation from the California clinical psychologist O. Ivar Lovaas, an iconic, sometimes controversial figure in the world of autism treatment. What distinguished Lovaas—who began his research in the 1960s when autism was still considered a psychosis, a variation on childhood schizophrenia—was his belief that children with autism were both treatable and teachable. That was the real breakthrough in the model of behavioural therapy he used: his acknowledgment that children with autism should be treated like human beings and not locked away like animals. (When Cynthia first began reading about Lovaas, she was so grateful to have come across his research she wrote him what can only be described as a fan letter. She thanked him for providing us with something we could do for our son and enclosed a photograph of Jonah. He wrote back to wish us luck and to tell her he had shown her letter and Jonah's photograph to everyone working in his institute. He said he knew it would encourage them. His letter went up on the cork bulletin board in our kitchen and has remained there.)

By 1987, Lovaas had almost two decades of research studies to support his conclusion that in a good percentage of cases the children he and his team of therapists had treated had gone beyond "indistinguishable"—that "recovered" was, in as many as half those cases, a more accurate description of the results achieved.

The Consultant had also met Bridget Taylor; she'd even brought Taylor in as a supervisor once for one of her clients. Taylor had studied under Lovaas and was also legendary, mainly for the role she plays in Catherine Maurice's memoir *Let Me Hear Your Voice: A Family's Triumph over Autism*. Maurice's 1994 chronicle of how her daughter and then her son were "recovered" is an uplifting advertisement for unconditional parental love, but also for the almost miraculous effectiveness of ABA. Maurice's memoir also provides a kind of template for many autism narratives to come. First, it reveals what doesn't work—in Maurice's case, some cockamamie, parent-blaming hug therapy she initially swears by only to repudiate by the end of the story. Then it provides the antidote—namely ABA.

"You should read it," Cynthia said. I promised to. But it would take me years to finally get around to *Let Me Hear Your Voice* and my expanding shelf of similar books. You see, back then, I couldn't bear to read anything about autism, not all the way through anyway. The stories I was coming across tended to be front-loaded with catastrophe: head-banging tantrums, vacant stares, grim prognoses, bogus therapies. Invariably, I couldn't make it past the first twenty-seven pages of *Let Me Hear Your Voice*. It's there that Maurice writes: "We are catapulted into a future that has suddenly become menacing, terrifying." Similarly, on page forty of another classic autism memoir, *The Siege: A Family's Journey into the World of an Autistic Child*, author Clara Claiborne Park writes: "But autism? What was autism? How could we adjust to an unknown? To live with autism would be like living under water. We might never come up, yet we had not the option of drowning." Likewise, the title essay in Oliver Sacks's *An Anthropologist on Mars: Seven Paradoxical Tales* has an early passage that stops me cold: "Most people (and, indeed, most physicians), if asked about autism, summon up a picture of a profoundly disabled child ... almost inaccessible: a creature for whom very little future lies in store." Even if I knew consolation was coming, as dust-jacket blurbs invariably promise, as is the case in *Let Me Hear Your Voice*— both Maurice's children fully recover— or as happens in Sacks's story of Temple Grandin and her remarkable life and achievements, it didn't matter to me. There was no chance I was going to make it that far in either book.

Eventually, we hired The Consultant, though *hired* is not the right word. We pleaded with her to take Jonah on, to take all of us on really. In the beginning, The Consultant was encouraging but made no promises. She also made it clear from the start that she was the boss. It would be her way or the highway. Any suggestions we had would be noted but most likely ignored. From the moment she began, The Consultant was the person who knew what was best for our son. Her first recommendation was that we take Jonah out of daycare immediately. She'd observed him there and told us bluntly that he was lost. He's happy there, we maintained. "No, he's not,"

The Consultant assured us. He has friends there, we insisted. "No, he doesn't," she replied. Cynthia made a case for taking him out gradually, for reducing his days per week, then his hours per day. By then, Cynthia had realized herself that Jonah didn't belong in daycare, that the daycare should have told us as much at least a year earlier. But she also wanted time to accept what this change in Jonah's life and ours signified. How irrevocable it was. "Once he was out of daycare it meant he was out of the world of 'normal' for good," Cynthia would explain years later. Back then, we also believed we could put quotation marks around "normal," as if the word itself existed on some kind of sliding scale of behaviour, as if it could be graded from A to F. What you learn when your child has autism is that normal is simply normal, a separate category; pass/fail.

Still, there was no point in appealing to The Consultant on emotional grounds and no point arguing. There wouldn't be time for daycare in any case. Jonah's ABA therapy was going to be intensive, as close to forty hours a week as we could manage. Our son, barely four, was going to have a busier schedule than either his mother or I had or, for that matter, ever had. Cynthia worked part-time as an art therapist. I was a freelance literary journalist, reviewing books and writing author profiles. I hadn't had a raise in thirty years. "ABA will be demanding," The Consultant said, taking more trouble to warn us than I'm guessing she took with other parents, parents who probably seemed to her to have full-time grownup jobs and responsibilities. Her clients were usually lawyers or doctors, professionals of some kind, or executives, businessmen and women. Therapy like this was costly, after all, and they tended to be the only ones who could afford it. (We obviously couldn't, but we were lucky in this regard: Cynthia's parents volunteered to pay for everything related to Jonah's therapy and did so with no second-guessing, no questions asked, no regrets or recriminations. It was at the time a remarkable act of love and faith. It remains so. An act I know they would probably prefer I didn't mention here.)

ABA could also be uncompromising, and the decree that we take Jonah out of daycare was our first inkling of that. Was it a test? Even if it wasn't, it was an indication that from here on everything would feel like a test. What would really be required of us with this new therapy, The Consultant pointed out, was consistency—and not just in Jonah's program or the team of therapists The Consultant would eventually train and hire for his program, but in Jonah's everyday life. She was talking about us. *Consistency.* The word sounded, as did so many other words in those days, less like a prescription than a threat. Like something that was beyond my comprehension and capacity.

Which is the reason I avoided the A-word back then; because I believed, down deep, that words like *indistinguishable*, like *recovery*, like *consistency*, like *autism* were beyond all of us. What was being asked of me simply felt like too much to ask. I was also afraid that whatever progress Jonah made was not going to be enough. By which I mean—and was as deeply ashamed to admit this seven years ago as I am now—enough for me. When Jonah was diagnosed, Cynthia dealt with the devastating news by springing into action, developing a game plan, researching, networking, badgering government agencies and, later, school boards, doing battle with teachers and principals, researching ABA, finding The Consultant, hiring her, hiring therapists in consultation with her, talking to strangers, other families in similar circumstances, joining online listservs and chat rooms, borrowing and begging money, holding out hope, reading books, magazine articles, blogs, whatever she could. To-do lists and memo sheets littered the house back then; you'd come across book titles and strange phone numbers on Post-it notes, calendars, and pads by the telephone.

My primary game plan was to sulk. And sigh or mutter to myself every so often, not loudly, just loud enough for Cynthia to hear and, on occasion, come running. Mostly, though, she tried to ignore my bad behaviour the way you would ignore the behaviour of a disobedient household pet. In other words, she tried not to take my sulking and muttering personally. She tried to tell herself that I couldn't help myself. You wouldn't get into an argument with a cat, for example, for clawing up the sofa, or a dog for peeing on the carpet. As a result of this kind of thinking on her part, we didn't get into nearly as many fights back then as we might have. Cynthia also knew, thanks to her early training in ABA, that ignoring bad behaviour was the most effective way to deal with it, to deal, that is, with Jonah *and* me. We were both seeking attention, after all, and she had already learned, from a behavioural point of view, that the worst thing she could do was provide it.

CYNTHIA NEVER DOES complete the chorus to "You Can't Always Get What You Want" for Jonah. She never goes on to the lyric about how if you try you can, at least occasionally, get what you need. She knows Jonah won't understand. Come to think of it, who would? Who ever does?

Want is easy, after all. Want is unambiguous. It knows no reason, accepts no excuse. It wants what it wants. Want is chocolate ice cream before dinner. Want is everything the way you expected it. It's your son typical, intact, yes, normal. As it turns out, our family motto doesn't suit my son or me. Both of us want precisely what we are not permitted to have.

As for need, that's something else entirely. The song gets it wrong, as it happens. It makes need sound uncomplicated when, in fact, it's trickier. It's about striking a bargain. What can you make do with? Minimum: you better grow up. Absolute minimum: you better figure out how to accept what's happened so you can be the father your child is going to need.

"Please, Daddy, number three?" Jonah says, holding up *Forty Licks*, making his spluttering request from the back of the car. I turn to glance at him and Cynthia frowns and points ahead, at the road. This is a significant difference between us. She recognizes there are worse things than autism—not taking notice of an oncoming truck, for instance—while I have a hard time imagining anything worse. So as she turns to pat Jonah's leg, I lower my rear-view mirror just enough to see his bottom lip quivering, his eyes welling up. I also see the strain in Cynthia's profile, the effort she's making at staying neutral and comforting our son, the effort that is always there whether I acknowledge it or not. When she turns back to look at me her expression is no longer neutral. She is silently communicating what I should already know. I should see the problem is not that Jonah is asking for a song—that's good, that's him problem-solving—it's the way he's asking. We can't give in to that. We can't reward his continued fussing. *Not now, sweetheart. We're almost home. Be consistent. Stick to the plan. Breathe.* But Jonah is fussing and pleading, headed for another tantrum, when I accidentally run a stop sign. That's when I see my wife relent. She can't ignore me any longer. I have made it dangerous to do so. She is also tired, finally, of being the only adult in the car. She exhales and nods. The third track on *Forty Licks* is "Satisfaction": more tantrum than tune, Jagger in a rawer mood, less philosophical, more animalistic, less mature, more demanding. I glance at Jonah's suddenly beaming face in the rear-view mirror. He is giggling, out of the blue. It must be an inside joke. He has this capacity, my son, to turn on a dime, not only to forget the past, but to act as if it never existed. It is a strange gift but a gift nevertheless. One he clearly doesn't get from me. "Shmatisfaction," he says, giggling. Cynthia places her hand on the back of my neck. "We'll be home soon," she says, whispering under the clamour of Keith Richards's unrelenting guitar riff.

I sigh and mutter what I know she's heard me mutter countless times before: "Then what?"

TWO
Weltschmerz

When Cynthia learned she was pregnant, we were not married. We weren't really a couple. We'd met just three months before on a blind date, both of us more or less clear of relationships that had ended badly—hers, a couple of months earlier; mine a couple of years. I was forty-two, she was thirty-eight, and neither of us had, by then, any expectation of becoming parents. So our subsequent decision to get married and have a child together, albeit not in that order, came as a surprise to everyone, especially us. I remember announcing our plans at the start of a long-standing poker game with some old friends, and it took me till the end of the evening to convince them the news wasn't just another elaborate bluff.

Despite that, the decision to go ahead and have the baby proved simple for me, which explains why I was the one who ended up making it. Cynthia wanted the baby, in theory. However, she wouldn't have it if she was going to have to raise it on her own. On this point, she was adamant. She wasn't going to be a single parent. In case I thought she was bluffing, she intended, she said, to go to an abortion clinic by the end of the week. This was what's called in poker a put-up or shut-up situation. I had to ask myself: could I be counted on to stick around?

"If nothing happens, it's not a story," Flannery O'Connor once said, and one reason I was keen to become a father was because *I* was waiting for something to happen. It didn't matter how it happened—planned, unplanned—I just wanted my life to have the kind of narrative structure and coherence it had always lacked. And abortion, whatever else you want to say about it, is a story-killer. Looking back now, I can see I was rationalizing like crazy. How else could I have told Cynthia, just a few hours after she told me she was pregnant, that everything was going to be all right? How else could I mean it? Of course, I knew nothing of the sort. But if this was a lie, it didn't feel like one.

If Cynthia had known me better, she would have known that what I do best is stick around. Sometimes to complain; sometimes out of inertia; occasionally to the point where a person might find herself wishing I wouldn't. But then she didn't know me well nor I her. So we navigated our way around our ignorance of each other and of what we were likely getting ourselves into. She cried; I consoled her. I made jokes; she reluctantly laughed. After a few hours of negotiating over a wedding date—May for her; the following May for me we were engaged and booking a rabbi for early July.

After Jonah was born, I watched him day and night—out of the usual new parent's mix of worry and awe, but mostly out of unending interest. "The kid's better than cable," I repeatedly told friends and colleagues. Sometimes even complete strangers had to put up with my expositions on the unexpected and unending entertainment value of a newborn. I went on about the most insignificant, unseemly things: his boogers, his bowel movements.

I had a weekly book column in the *Montreal Gazette* at the time, and, more often than not, I would manage to squeeze some anecdote about Jonah into a review or an author profile I happened to be writing. In fact, I chose books that would give me the opportunity to comment on my current state of fatherhood—like Toronto writer Dave Eddie's *Housebroken: Confessions of a Stay-at-Home Dad*. And while I managed to keep my review free of any resentment I might have felt towards Eddie for pitching his book idea about the joys of fatherhood before I had time to think of something similar, I still squeezed in an anecdote about my efforts at teaching Jonah to do a spit take. (He was, at ten months, a natural, though it was, I realize, more of a drool take.) The editor of the book section was a friend, but eventually his journalistic instincts kicked in. "That's it," he finally said, announcing a moratorium on infant-related anecdotes. "The kid is off-limits for the next six months." I towed the line for a few weeks, but after that I couldn't help myself. Besides, I knew my editor was wrong. I couldn't imagine anyone not being interested in my baby or, more to the point, what I might have to say about him.

Now, it has become harder to remember what my life was really like back then. Was I that oblivious to everything? Was I really that happy all the time? I remember being tired, of course, and finding it difficult to get any work done. There's a photograph Cynthia took of Jonah and me sitting next to each other on our living room couch. A review copy is open in my lap, but my eyes are closed. Jonah's are closing. The truth is: once Jonah was born I couldn't read more than a few pages of any book without nodding off. Literature seemed beside the point anyway. Compared with whatever it was my son might be up to.

What I really don't remember from that time is doubt. Can you imagine it? Ambivalence out of my life, gone like a fever—not so much vanished as broken, dissipated. No wonder books were losing their appeal. Besides, I was an exceptional father or fast on my way to becoming one; I knew this with a kind of certainty I'd never experienced before. This was going to be a snap. Now, I wonder: could all this be true? Now, it's almost impossible to remember the way our lives were, to remember a time before autism.

A FEW WEEKS BEFORE Jonah was born I began telling jokes directly to Cynthia's belly. It was like being on the sidelines of a football game next to one of those oversized convex microphones the NFL Network uses to record the sounds of the game. I could imagine her belly picking up everything—not just my words but all my unexpressed hopes and fears as well. I'm aware, now, of how corny this sounds. But I wanted to give the kid a preview of how much fun we were going to have together. Some people play Mozart for their unborn children, read to them from Shakespeare, reel off math problems, or speak Italian, all on the off chance it will have an unquantifiable influence on the unpredictable future. I was giving my son the gift of shtick. Shtick is in my DNA, after all. Like the Yiddish I've never spoken but feel I could speak if forced to. Like my compulsion to make everything into a joke, everything palatable. Throw it all against the wall and whatever sticks—that's shtick.

"Here we go," I would say, snuggling up against the small of Cynthia's warm back. "Okay, kid, who's on first?" This was turning into such a persistent, irritating habit on my part that sometimes I would wait until Cynthia was asleep before I launched into the evening's routine. That way I didn't have to see the look of good-natured condescension on my wife's face when she heard me saying, "Knock, knock...."

At the time, my favourite joke was the one about the Jewish grand-mother who is entrusted with the care of her grandson for the day. She decides to take him to the beach and outdoes herself. Packs a picnic lunch, in one of those big wicker baskets, with all the little darling's favourite foods, peanut butter sandwiches with the crusts cut off, fruit scored into the shapes of stars, juice in a sippy cup, and more cookies than she knows is appropriate. But so what? She'll swear the kid to secrecy. Don't tell your mother. *Her daughter-in-law.* It so happens, it's a glorious day. Not a cloud in the sky. But she's prepared for that too. She's got suntan lotion on every inch of the kid, SPF 50. She bought him a new hat, the foreign legion kind with a flap that covers the sensitive area at the back of his neck. The hat is khaki, very snazzy. $29.95. No bargain, but money's no object.

The woman and the boy approach the beach holding hands. Meanwhile, she's on the lookout for stray dogs, broken glass, jellyfish, pedophiles, terrorists, falling asteroids, you name it. They sit under an orange-striped umbrella, the boy building an elaborate castle with a new set of sand toys. The grandmother is *qvelling*, beaming. She's thinking about all that she's going to teach him one day, about the chance to see him grow up to be who knows what: a movie star, prime minister, a brain surgeon, an orthodontist maybe? Did I mention it's a glorious day? Did I mention the hat?

Then, out of the corner of her eye, the grandmother sees a dark cloud approaching. She knows she should run. But she's an old woman with arthritis she wouldn't wish on Hitler and it's not so easy to get up. By the time she does, it's too late. The wind and water are swirling. One particular wave, malevolent and purposeful, picks up her grandson, just him, out of maybe one hundred and fifty other children on the beach, and carries him out into the now turbulent ocean. The grandmother is speechless. Then she screams. She thinks all the terrible things you might in that moment; how she's going to have to tell her son and his wife. *Her daughter-in-law*.

She thinks how her life will never be the same again, how this one moment—which isn't even her fault but who's ever going to believe that?—will change everything. So she drops to her knees, clasps her hands together, and prays out loud. Before long, she's shouting. She couldn't care less who hears. "Dear God," she screams over the rumble of the storm, "please spare my grandson, I'll do anything, just don't let him drown." Then she bows her head. An instant later, the skies clear and she can see the crest of another giant wave in the distance, and before she can believe what she's seeing, her grandson reappears, on the beach, beside her. He's unfazed, hardly wet. She hugs him hard, pinches him even, to make sure he's there, intact. Then she gets to her feet and looks up at the heavens, and addressing God, a God of infinite wisdom and mercy, she says, "He had a hat."

In retrospect, I can see there were probably better, more appropriate jokes I could have been whispering to my wife's belly: ones that didn't have the inevitability of dissatisfaction as their central theme; ones about not counting your chickens before they're hatched, for instance. I learned to be superstitious from my parents the same way they learned it from theirs. My mother and father were born in Montreal but that East European shtetl nonsense isn't easy to discard. My father never boasted; he believed in keeping a low profile. According to my sisters, my mother routinely attached a red ribbon to her bra strap to ward off the evil eye. She never would have dreamed of buying a baby gift, for instance, before said baby was born, before all his or her toes had been accounted for. *Don't hope for too much.* That's what I was brought up believing. Don't crow; don't *qvell*. Enough, you should be telling yourself, is enough. I was going to have a son.

WHAT I KNOW ABOUT loss I learned thirty-three years ago when my mother died of lymphoma. It seemed then and for a long time like all I needed to know. So much so that when my father died, also of cancer, a little more than a year after my mother, it felt as if there was nothing left to learn. It probably would have made sense for me to see a therapist then, according to Cynthia, but I'm guessing it never occurred to me. Instead, Cynthia theorizes, I came away from this experience at twenty-one incapable of believing things could get better. I developed a philosophy of hopelessness. I became an expert at expecting the worst. I learned to follow the path of least resistance: in other words, to give up, concede. I took solace in pessimism. It probably didn't hurt, Cynthia suggested, that I was young and impressionable and reading gloomy books all the time: Samuel Beckett, Thomas Hardy, Virginia Woolf. "But you were a kid then and you're not any more," Cynthia says. The point is well taken: despair is a luxury we can no longer afford.

Cynthia is a therapist, an art therapist to be exact, and she's passionate about what she does. She works with children, as young as three and as old as eighteen, who end up in Montreal's English-speaking youth protection system. She's a problem-solver. In addition to helping clients work through their challenges by making art—drawings, paintings, sculptures—she writes out personalized treatment plans. One of her methods is to assist her clients in externalizing what is often an internal issue. For example, a child is encouraged to fight her "Temper Monster" rather than her siblings.

And, yes, Cynthia sometimes takes her work home with her, where there is no shortage of problems to be externalized. This also explains why I sometimes find myself being analyzed more or less without my consent. Evidently, step one in my personalized treatment plan has me drawing a picture of a creature, a bear or gorilla, something hairy and chunky at any rate. Step two: I give this creature a name that sums up his personality. Let's call him the "Grumpy Monster," for example. "Never mind that it's too on the nose," Cynthia reminds me. "This isn't a literary exercise." Step three: I vanquish this creature in simple ways. No big showdowns. For instance, I could work on waking up in the morning in a good mood instead of having that automatically hopeless look on my face at the sound of Jonah babbling in his room about yaks and zebras. I could also, Cynthia suggests, ask her how she is feeling instead of asking her, as I invariably do, what's wrong? "You see the difference, don't you?" Cynthia says and then answers on my behalf. "One question expresses genuine concern for how I am feeling; the other expresses your concern about how I might make you feel. So why not just say, 'How are you this morning, my dearest darling?'" There are, evidently, many ways to slay a Grumpy Monster.

At our wedding reception, a friend joked about the upside of being married to a therapist. "Think of how much money you'll save on shrinks," he said. He was kidding, but he had a point. My treatment plan notwithstanding, when you first find yourself in a succession of waiting rooms, waiting for child psychiatrists and psychologists, occupational therapists and speech pathologists, the countless, escalating array of experts you never expected to consult, *not for your child*, when you are hearing opinions you never expected to hear, *not about your child*, it helps to have someone around to decipher what's being said. You need someone to cut through the bullshit because you can bet there will be an awful lot of it.

After my parents died I found a second-hand copy of Elisabeth Kübler-Ross's *On Death and Dying* in a university bookstore. This was the late 1970s and I didn't have to read the decade-old ground-breaking manifesto on loss to know what it said. Kübler-Ross and her bestselling five-stage theory were already famous by then. Like most of her readers who had experienced the death of a loved one, I applied her ideas retroactively. Like most readers, I appreciated that *On Death and Dying* came with a social science gravitas that trumped the clichés and platitudes I heard at my parents' respective shivas from a mix of well-meaning but obtuse relatives and friends. *Life goes on.* That seemed to be the best advice anyone had to offer. Not Kübler-Ross: she offered stages and who doesn't want stages? Five seemed like a reasonable number. Not too few, three, say, so you could dismiss the whole thing as simplistic feel-good advice. Not too many so you couldn't, with a little effort, memorize them. And once you did, you could check them off. Denial, you bet. Anger, sure: I'm pissed, it's true. Guilt, okay fine, not a problem, got that. Bargaining—do it all the time. Acceptance—that's done, more or less. Check and mate.

"People love the stages," Kübler-Ross acknowledged later, and, it's true, she was on to something: I'd felt all those things she said I should after my mother died and then felt them again after my father died. I rushed through those stages like a geeky teenager mastering a video game. I wasn't going to stop until I, what, won? Reached Level 5? I was good at it, too, so good I couldn't help feeling a little concerned about the ease and efficiency with which I'd advanced from anger to acceptance.

Kübler-Ross's stages would also become an all-purpose explanation for everything from a bad break-up to the loss of a pet. Cynthia and I heard it invoked a few years ago while sitting through yet another seminar aimed at the families of children with autism. We were a growing and suddenly sought-after demographic. We spent our weekends at conferences, lectures, potlucks, and get-togethers in the first year or two after Jonah's diagnosis. One psychologist at a conference told her small audience of mostly mothers that it was okay to mourn when you first learned your child had autism. This was a kind of loss, after all, a loss of expectations, of hope. The five stages appeared as part of her PowerPoint presentation, the tiny pink beam from her laser wand stopping briefly at each stage.

"Kübler-Ross was wrong, you know," I told Cynthia at home later, after I'd done some Googling. "I saw it on Wikipedia or somewhere. Anyway she admitted her doubts in a book she wrote when she was dying. It turns out her evidence was strictly anecdotal. You shrinks, I'm telling you."

"Kübler-Ross was a brilliant therapist," Cynthia said. "Obviously, her theory doesn't make sense in your case, sweetheart, but that doesn't mean she was wrong. It just means you've gotten stuck in a lower stage."

"Like a monkey?"

"What I mean is you've never accepted your mother's death, not really. You always say you got over it too fast, but it was thirty years ago and, ask yourself, are you over it yet? No. You're angry, sad, guilty. There's a part of you that doesn't believe it happened. Some part of you is still way back at those first stages—denial and anger."

"I wasn't asking to be analyzed."

"Of course, you were."

Grief can't be arranged in stages: at least not when it comes to autism. What is intended to be most comforting about Kübler-Ross's blueprint for overcoming loss—the predictability, the linearity, the end in sight—is not available to the parent of a child with autism. Yes, you experience anger and denial and bargaining and the rest of it, even acceptance, I suppose, but you experience it daily and in no particular order. With autism, forget stages, think revolving door: everything comes and goes. Think rollercoaster: you're up, you're down. In *On Grief and Grieving*, Kübler-Ross's long-anticipated 2004 sequel to *On Death and Dying*, she writes: "I now know that the purpose of my life is more than these stages. I have been married, had kids, then grand-kids, written books, and traveled. I have loved and lost, and I am so much more than five stages. And so are you."

JONAH WAS BORN nine days late. As Cynthia's due date came and went, there was time to think about the usual things, the important things—how our lives were going to change, what kind of parents we were going to be. But we were fixated, instead, on what Jonah was going to look like. We lay in bed that last week staring up at the light fixture on the ceiling above us. It was round and translucent and had a rather large, lumpy protuberance in the middle. With the room in shadow, it resembled an extremely goofy-looking person. We called it Ziggy—a nickname for zygote.

We had reason to worry. Just the thought of my nose and my wife's nose amalgamated in the middle of our poor, unsuspecting baby's face was enough to give us recurring and matching nightmares. There was also my height or lack of it to consider; and Cynthia's bad eyesight, her questionable taste in sweaters. We'd lie in bed, spinning out tales about how our beloved four-eyed pipsqueak would somehow manage to overcome his parents' *nebbishy* genes. How he would somehow not suffer through childhood and adolescence the way we had. How he'd make do with my self-deprecating sense of humour and Cynthia's implacable backbone. But all our musings ended the same way: with little Ziggy unable to find a date for the junior prom, with him being picked last for basketball. We couldn't have been more of a cliché.

A while back, Cynthia and I had a single session with a family therapist, a couples counsellor really—"Call me Jeff," he said, shaking my hand—who told us that the key to happiness was managing expectations. The problem was simple, according to Jeff: the more distance you allow between what you want and what you can reasonably expect, the unhappier you are bound to be. German philosophers had a word for this: *Weltschmerz*. Jeff was a nice fellow, about my age, the kind of guy I might have gone to school with or played softball with. But I was looking for a breakthrough—*In one session, sweetheart?*— not the kind of information I'd already read in a few thousand novels and poems, from Emily Dickinson to Philip Roth. Life is disappointment; expect less. That's it. "Can't they tell you something you don't know?" I asked Cynthia in the car on the way home.

The thing is, before Jonah was born, we'd done exactly what Jeff was suggesting; we'd managed expectations. In fact, we were experts; we were *Weltschmerz*-free. Or so we thought as we braced ourselves for an extraordinarily funny-looking kid. Then Jonah was born and he was beautiful. I know every parent feels this way and that every parent can't, objectively speaking, be right. There have to be mousy, unpleasant, irritating kids. Where do mousy, unpleasant, irritating adults come from? But we *were* being objective. (What I'd realize later is that physical attractiveness is made note of in most of the autism memoirs I've read. It is, Clara Clairborne Park writes in *The Siege*, "one of the inexplicable items" in the disorder, a way, she speculates, of making a family's burden lighter.) For weeks, maybe months after Jonah was born, Cynthia and I would look him up and down, then assess each other, and shake our heads. It wasn't just that he didn't look anything like either of us, he didn't look anything like the other newborn infants he shared the hospital nursery with, most of whom resembled aliens. Jonah had a full round face and an undented head. He was bigger than the other babies. He cried less. He seemed, when it came to baby behaviour, self-possessed, confident. I dubbed him the Mayor of Babytown.

The day Cynthia went into the hospital to have labour induced, I read a newspaper story about the movie-star couple Uma Thurman and Ethan Hawke and how they were about to have a baby, too. Our private joke, after Jonah was born, was that the infants, theirs and ours, had been switched at birth and that somewhere, in Hollywood or Martha's Vineyard, our real kid had a nanny and a pony and a swimming pool and was living a privileged, decadent life. He was destined for a career as a child actor, a series of rehabs, and a lifelong flirtation with Scientology. John Travolta would be his godfather. Quentin Tarantino his crazy uncle. We imagined, too, that Uma and Ethan loved him dearly even though they couldn't figure out how they, of all couples, had ended up with such a dweeb.

Jonah went from being a beautiful baby to an irresistible toddler to a handsome little boy. Put him on a motorcycle, in a leather jacket, I said the day he turned one, and there you have it: a young Steve McQueen—all right, extremely young. As he got older he only got better looking. It was almost embarrassing. There was no way to account for his exquisite cheekbones, his strong chin, his light brown hair, and his perfectly unobtrusive nose. The pale blue eyes were hardest to explain. So much so, Cynthia kept threatening to punch the next person who made some dumb comment about where exactly he'd gotten "those baby-blues" from.

In a few months, on Christmas Eve, Jonah will turn eleven. He is not tall for his age, though he will probably end up taller than both his parents. Cynthia and I still find ourselves staring at him and wondering how he ended up looking like he does. We're not the only ones. Jonah has an affinity for his own reflection, so much so we had to cover the two full-length sliding mirrors in our hall with contact paper and then put up a more discreetly located mirror in his bedroom. The Consultant advised us to designate it "the silly mirror," and Cynthia made a sign saying as much. This was where he would go, where he still goes sometimes, to make funny faces at himself or say funny words. It was initially intended to be an acceptable outlet, a substitute for the inappropriate bouts of face-making and staring at himself he was prone to—in department stores or the homes of relatives and friends. This has worked up to a point. Now, I'll catch him posing in the mirror, putting his hands in his pockets, cocking his eyebrow, and shooting himself a sweet, kooky grin. *Show time*, I think he's thinking. He can't seem to take his eyes off himself and won't until I push him on to the next thing. "Jonesy," I'll have to say, "enough cuteness." *But why?* In that instant, as he faces the mirror, I watch him and wonder what's going on in his head. I wonder how he can look at himself for so long and so uncritically. It's a strange gift, but a gift nevertheless. To not see a gap between who you are and who you hoped to be. Facing "the silly mirror," my son still looks extraordinarily self-possessed. As if he hasn't a worry in the world. Meanwhile, Cynthia and I cling to our shallowness, hoping Jonah will remain attractive, hoping too that his attractiveness will be his ace in the hole, one thing he will never have to worry about. "The world is unfair," Park writes in *The Siege*, "and in a pretty child the world will overlook a great deal."

JONAH TOLD HIS FIRST joke soon after he was born. Jokes are narratives in a nutshell, little bits of truth. They are uncomplicated. But even the dumbest ones, when they work, maintain their own internal logic. They are the purest form of storytelling: premise and punchline. You get it or you don't.

Jonah was lying on his back on his changing table when he sneezed. It shook his tiny body and left him startled by this new possibility. I looked down at him and immediately cracked up. After a few moments, I was laughing hard enough to attract Cynthia's attention.

"What is it?" she called from the other room.

"Come, quick," I said. We were new, first-time parents. It wasn't unusual for the other person to drop whatever they were doing—falling asleep, finishing a book, taking a shower, sitting on the toilet—and come running, invariably with a video camera.

"What?" Cynthia said, out of breath. "Is something wrong?"

"There. Look there," I said, pointing to a tiny trace of mucus on Jonah's forehead.

"That's disgusting," Cynthia said, reaching for a tissue.

"Wait, you're missing the point. Think about it: it came out of his nose and virtually did a one-eighty. It's a miracle of aerodynamics, at the very least. Better yet, it's a stunt, a prank."

"It's a booger," she said, wiping Jonah's forehead and leaving the room, shaking her head and rolling her eyes. In our relatively short time together, I was responsible for her having learned to do both simultaneously.

"You don't get it. It's his first sight gag. He's a natural. And," I said, leaning down to whisper the first rule of comedy in my son's ear, "it's funny, Jonesy, because it's true."

THREE
Bad Day

Has it made you a better father?

The question is put to me by a local CBC radio producer and it catches me off-guard, though I know it's something I should have considered by now. This is a pre-interview. It's the job of the young woman on the phone to help me figure out what I might say in advance of my live interview the following morning. I've been booked on this program because I've written a short personal essay about Jonah and me and autism. That would be the "it" she's referring to. In a way, I've been anticipating answering this question, aloud, in public, for a while. I've certainly had plenty of time to think about it and figure out what it presupposes. Now, here's my chance.

"Sure," I tell the friendly stranger on the other end of the phone, "it can be tough. But an experience like this teaches you what you're capable of. I've heard people, other parents, I mean, say that they're grateful for what they've come to see as an opportunity. I don't know if I'd go that far, but life gives you lemons and, well, you know."

Evidently, the proof of how well I've adjusted to this out-of-the-blue circumstance is in the fact that I have written about Jonah in the first place. No need to mention that it has taken me years or that it's only twelve hundred words. *What matters is you've done it, sweetheart. You've told part of our story anyway.* After the essay first appeared in a local magazine, I also received several supportive emails from acquaintances as well as a few phone calls from other parents of kids with autism. This essay, its hard-earned existence, is an indication of how someone like me, like any one of us, copes and is able to transform private trouble into a kind of public betterment. There is the possibility, because of it, for increased awareness, attention, and empathy. This essay, which won a minor prize and will, as a result, be broadcast on the radio, is a demonstration of my resilience. Lemons = lemonade.

I answer all the producer's questions quickly, easily. How did we find out about Jonah? His daycare complained he wasn't showing sufficient interest in gluing. How did we react? We thought they were kidding. My wife and I joked about it. *Can't glue? What did we do wrong? How will he ever survive in a world so dependent on a human being's ability to glue?*

I also jump at the chance to talk in the pre-interview about the book I am supposedly working on, the book which this essay is supposedly excerpted from. *Solace: A Father's Chronicle of Coping*, that's the title, I volunteer. "Why *Solace*? Good question. I guess because I feel as if the almost seven years since his diagnosis have been a kind of journey, you know, out of despair and towards acceptance. Autism is tragically misunderstood. Most people don't know what it is exactly or the toll it takes on families. That's one thing I hope I can help correct—here but also in the book eventually. How much have I written? Of the book you mean? Well ..."

The answer, again, is twelve hundred words, on the nose, but I manage to keep this to myself. The implication is that this book, when I finally finish it, will be upbeat, illuminating, ultimately helpful. It will provide, as advertised, solace. That's what I've managed to convey in all my grant applications anyway. All three of my successful grant applications, I should add. Meanwhile, I'm on a roll in the pre-interview. I can't seem to stop talking. *Why aren't we on the radio right now?*

"What people don't always realize is that autism is not just Dustin

Hoffman in *Rain Man*. No, it's a broad spectrum of developmental delays. There are children with all kind of deficits and all kinds of potential. The face of autism is also the face of my son, a beautiful, affectionate little boy who knows all about animals like the slow loris. Do you know what that is? It's a primate. Don't worry. I didn't know what it was either until he told me. My son also does long division, watches Katy Perry and Bing Crosby videos on YouTube. He rides a bike and loves joke books. He makes up his own jokes, too. Want to hear his latest? What do you call an animal with antlers who drinks too much?"

"I give up," the producer says indulgently.

"An elkaholic. He made that up himself. I mean, mostly. Not bad, huh? He loves language. He and I are also considering writing a book together. About animals, it has to be about animals, and, maybe, eventually, about autism, too, a kind of beginner's guide, maybe, you know, something that would be useful for both of us, maybe for lots of people."

No, the pre-interview could hardly be going better or going on longer. I haven't been this impressed with myself in years. I'm serious without being maudlin, funny without being glib. It's at moments like this I can almost convince myself that this project that's stagnated for nearly seven years is bound to open some minds and break some hearts. There is, however, one problem with what I'm telling the producer as well as what I'm going to say in the actual interview tomorrow morning. It's not true—not in any real way. My little essay isn't about potential or public awareness or, heaven help me, personal gratitude and growth. I couldn't be less grateful or have evolved less since finding out about Jonah. The essay is my tantrum, and my tantrum isn't likely to make anyone, no matter how they parse or misinterpret it, feel any better. Obviously, the woman interviewing me hasn't read the essay. But if she were to, if she read it backwards, forwards, sideways, it wouldn't matter. She wouldn't even need to finish it or search too far

between the lines to know that what I've written, my so-called triumphant, consoling tale of fatherhood, is a self-pitying rant, a primate
chest-thumping. It is, essentially, a bummer.

ALL I COULD THINK OF was the old joke. The one about the man
who's told he has six months to live. "I want a second opinion,"
he says. "Fine," his doctor replies, "you're ugly too." I laughed out
loud, an involuntary outburst in a crowded, gloomy waiting room.
All around us, parents, mothers mostly, hovered over their children,
boys mostly, shushing them, pulling their fingers out of their noses
or pants or out of the air, fighting a valiant losing battle against their
child's overwhelming inclination to fidget or babble or wander away.
I knew next to nothing about spectrums and stims back then, but I
still remember thinking: *What is normal behaviour for a four-year-old
and how do you recognize it?* By comparison, Jonah was calm. He was
seated beside me, immersed in an animal alphabet book he'd dug out
from a pile in the corner, doing what he always did then, what he still
does when he can get away with it. He was checking the final pages
to make sure the book ended as it should with a yak and then a zebra.
It's the equivalent of happily-ever-after for him. I patted him on the
head, a reward for his composure. *Reinforce, reinforce, reinforce*, as we'd
already been advised repeatedly by The Consultant.

"Ugly, too. That's the second opinion, get it? It's a classic punchline," I said, nudging Cynthia. She frowned and I did some fidgeting
myself, imagining the conversation she and I would be having if we
were alone.

Jokes, sweetheart, really? Here? Now?
I'm funniest when I'm most miserable. You should know that.

That may be true, but, under the circumstances, it wasn't unreasonable for Cynthia to expect I'd give it a rest for once. We were in The
Montreal Children's Hospital, after all, not some rinky-dink rookie
psychologist's office, the way we had been for Jonah's first diagnosis

a year earlier. This time there were teams of experienced specialists to meet, teams who had presumably dealt with autism and with the parents of children with autism for years.

"All right, then, a priest, a rabbi, and a psychiatrist ..."

Cynthia ignored me and returned to the magazine she'd discovered in the waiting room: *Exceptional Family: Canada's Resource Magazine for Parents of Exceptional Children*. "Listen," she said and began to read me a passage from the editorial page about "blessings in disguise." Now, it was my turn to suppress the urge to roll my eyes. *Quite the euphemism*, I almost said but restrained myself. You won't read this in any magazine, but when you are the parent of an "exceptional child" this is one of the first lessons you learn: try not to say what you're thinking. If you do, be prepared for the consequences because there will be consequences.

Dr. T. was a soft-spoken, smartly dressed woman in her early-fifties. She had red hair and a faint trace of freckles. A model of a concerned professional, she managed to balance kindness with detachment. It was a characteristic of the mental health care profession I had yet to get used to. There are probably sound reasons for this kind of practised impersonal compassion, but the only one I can think of, having now seen it too many times to count, is that it's because they know that no matter what they say they're only guessing; that when it comes to deciphering the vagaries of human behaviour and the human brain, in particular, the odds will always be against them.

I also couldn't shake the feeling that Dr. T. wanted to get this, likely her last appointment of the morning, over with. She kept glancing at the telephone on her desk like she was willing an interruption. In any case, there was nothing especially new she could tell us, which is what we suspected and feared just the same. She spent a few minutes examining Jonah, asking him his name, which he got right, and asking him to identify the colour blue, which he didn't. Mostly, though, there was a long list of questions for us.

"Does he rock back and forth?"

"No."

"Does he harm himself?"

"No."

"Does he flap his hands?"

"No."

"Have you had his hearing tested?"

"Yes."

"Does he mix up his pronouns—using *you* in place of *I*, for example?"

"Well …"

"Can he hop on one foot?"

"What?"

"When did you first notice a problem?"

"We have no idea—from daycare, probably."

We passed or, more likely, failed this test as Jonah bounced happily on a small trampoline in the corner of Dr. T.'s office. It was unusual for him to take to any toy or activity right away, but he did with the trampoline. (The next day Cynthia bought one for his therapy room.) Still, he'd stop bouncing sometimes to catch his breath, to assess the fun he was having before he decided it was time to have more. There is, in Jonah, a delight, a talent for it, that I hoped the teams of doctors and specialists would see, would take note of in their charts. But I was afraid they'd overlook it in the same way I so often did.

By the way, the trampoline wasn't there for Jonah; it was there so Dr. T. could talk to parents like Cynthia and me with a minimum of interruptions. Obviously, she knew the kind of kids, hard to quiet and distract, she was dealing with. Still, in that fluorescent-lit office, on that glum day, Jonah was impervious to judgment, to evaluation. For him, nothing seemed about to change.

"Mommy, mommy," he shouted, "give me a bad day."

Jonah's speech always made sense to us even if it didn't always make sense to other people. Dr. T. glanced at us and smiled sheepishly. Other people had no way of knowing, for instance, that what Jonah wanted when he said "give me a bad day" was a story *about* a bad day. He might also ask for a "bad sport" or a "broken promise." Typically, he wanted a story that he'd heard before, the more times the better, a story with multiple characters, animals preferably, getting into terrible trouble and acting badly as a consequence. He greeted the accumulation of bad news by pretending to cry, but his glum expression hid an adorably unsympathetic grin. He was always quirky, and we always loved his quirkiness. Now, it looked like it was about to become official: we were going to have to learn to call it something else. PDD NOS or Pervasive Developmental Disorder Not Otherwise Specified was the deliberately vague label the first psychologist had used.

I didn't understand then what I understand now, that adding the "not otherwise specified" served a purpose in diagnostic lingo. It covered a multitude of misinterpretations and miscalculations—sins, in other words. The British autism specialist Simon Baron-Cohen, a cousin incidentally of *Borat*'s Sacha Baron Cohen, refers to PDD NOS as "the part of the autism spectrum we understand the least." That tacked-on phrase—"not otherwise specified"—also served to underline for me that what the screenwriter William Goldman once observed about Hollywood applied as well to the fields of psychology, psychiatry, psychotherapy, social work, you name it: "Nobody here knows anything." With her second opinion, Dr. T. revised PDD NOS to the more encompassing but somehow also more specific ASD or Autism Spectrum Disorder. The label "high-functioning" came up again, though Dr. T. didn't mention what it meant in specifics. It was clear it could mean anything or nothing; it was almost as elusive as "NOS." What Dr. T. didn't tell us was whether Jonah would have friends, whether he'd hold up his end of a conversation. Or whether he'd be able to have a bar mitzvah, go to college, or even graduate from high school, drive a car, buy his own clothes, live his own life, be independent, be happy, stay happy. Dr. T. focused, instead, on what there was to be grateful for. Jonah talks. He makes eye contact. He is affectionate. He seems content. Delighted's *the word you're looking for doctor,* delighted. With luck and hard work, he could go to school, an integrated school if that's what we decided, though he might need support, a shadow or aide. She didn't recommend any treatments, but she mentioned acronyms like ABA, or Applied Behavioural Analysis, and RDI, or Relationship Development Intervention. And, of course, there were always new theories and therapies to explore. There were books we could buy, lots of them, diets we could try, medication we could consider—more experts we could talk to.

"I know, it's a great deal to absorb," Dr. T. said. "The learning curve can be steep."

Cynthia was taking notes and asking a few questions, even though she had begun her research a year earlier. The Consultant was already hired, and she, in turn, had hired and trained four therapists, three young women and a man, university students, pursuing degrees in psychology or teaching. Cynthia and I were trained, too, and Jonah's program—thirty-six hours of intensive ABA therapy—was under way. Our dining room had already been transformed into a cross between a playroom and a research laboratory. We weren't a family any more. We had become a team, a business, a lab experiment.

Before we left her office, Dr. T. reached into her drawer and handed Cynthia some literature to read as well as a photocopy of an article entitled "Welcome to Holland." I glanced at the title and the author's name—Emily Perl Kingsley—over Cynthia's shoulder. Meanwhile, Cynthia quickly tucked it into her copy of *Exceptional Family.*

On the drive home from the doctor's office, Jonah asked again for "a bad day" and he beamed when his mother, who was sitting in the back of the car with him, agreed. She usually saved this kind of treat for his bedtime. But that day was different, exceptional. That day, he was indulged. That day, if I remember correctly, we stopped for an ice cream before lunch. If we didn't, we should have. Cynthia was getting good at taking requests for these oddball narratives. She had a talent for escalating the badness in a story, transforming herself into a kind of Scheherazade of unhappy endings, regaling Jonah with an account of the worst things that could happen ever: the worst-dessert-ever, the worst-punishment-ever, the worst-animal-ever. And as Cynthia's story unfolded, Jonah braced himself in his booster seat, latching on to the downward spiral of events like he was holding on to the security bars on one of those amusement park rides. Free Fall: the ones that go up very slowly and come down super fast.

That day, Jonah was treated to the tale of Ellie the Elephant, who wakes up on the wrong side of the bed in the morning, puts on the wrong trousers, gets a cantaloupe stuck in her trunk, jumps on a trampoline which breaks, and is generally disappointed every hour on the hour. Jonah listened intently, mainly so he could correct any detail Cynthia got wrong, any word she omitted.

"Give me an 'instead of,'" Jonah said. By this he meant include the words "instead of" in the story. For instance, Ellie ordered blueberry pancakes with syrup, but "instead of" getting what she ordered she got "pickles with yucky mustard." So what did Ellie do? She stomped on every table in the restaurant, every table and every waiter, and every bit of food. There's a literary lesson in these stories Jonah demanded, still demands, and it's always the same. Jonah understands what some of us never manage to, what some of us have an unfortunate habit of forgetting: that to not get what you want is bad, truly bad, but it's nowhere near as bad as hoping for more than you get. You want to tell a really sad story, a crushing one, that's the component you're looking for.

In his own way, Jonah has always been a perfectionist, but a perfectionist forced to operate in an unapologetically imperfect world. A world that is, as far as he's concerned, in a constant state of chaos and upheaval. As a consequence, he's unnerved by change. He thrives, instead, on knowing only what he knows and knowing it perfectly.

This is, I realize now, how he makes sense of the world. It's why the questions he asks us, ninety-nine percent of the time, are questions he knows the answers to. In this respect, in his need for assurance and certainty, for meaning even, he is like all of us, only more so. He's making it up, the meaning, I mean, as he goes along.

Here's something else I've learned about my son: he deals with disappointment the same way I do—grudgingly. Our job then, as it is now, is to rescue him from isolation, to turn his attention to the outside world. To simply engage him has always required tremendous effort. I sometimes think that's because when it comes to the world and what it has to offer, Jonah has always been singularly unimpressed. It is yet another way in which we are more alike than different.

"SO LET'S SEE IT," I said to Cynthia once we'd returned home from Dr. T.'s office. There was no way to talk in the car with Jonah there, no way to analyze whether the second opinion we'd waited a year for and finally received was better or worse news than we had expected or exactly what we expected. We were, however, numb again, as we were after Jonah's first diagnosis.

"See what?" Cynthia said. She was busy preparing Jonah's lunch.

"The article—the one the doctor gave us ... gave *you* before we left. It looked like some kind of story."

"It's nothing, really, just what they give everyone, I'm guessing, when ..."

"When what?"

"I don't know ... when they don't know what else to say." Cynthia finally handed me the sheet of paper. Still, when I reached out to take it she hesitated, holding on to it for a moment, as if we were about to engage in a game of tug-of-war.

"Welcome to Holland" is intended as a pep talk for parents going through the same sort of experience its author went through. At worst, it's harmless, so how come I couldn't read it without stopping to sputter out some comment like: "Give me a break." Or: "You've got to be kidding." Eventually, I stopped reading. I couldn't finish it, not even a single page of helpful advice. Instead, I contemplated throwing something—a plate or vase seemed about right, but I'm a civilized man, if not an especially mature one, so I picked up an orange and threw it, as hard as I could, at our kitchen wall.

"She's comparing this ... this ... to Holland. We're not in fucking Holland." Cynthia glared at me. I forgot that Jonah was still in the room, waiting for his lunch. My wife patted him on the head and dragged me into the bathroom. She closed the door behind her and folded her arms across her chest. This was an argument I was going to lose; I just wasn't ready to lose it yet, which is to say not without a futile, hurtful fight.

"Don't you see how much this analogy sucks? Holland! Holland would be fine. Fucking fabulous," I said, trying, though not hard enough, to keep my voice down. "Holland has tulips ... wooden shoes ... windmills ... hashish ... hookers in the window. They used to anyway. I have news for you and the doctor and for Ms. Emily Perl Kingsley, whoever she is, this is not Holland we're in. Not even close. This is like thinking you're going to Italy and you find out you're in ... in ... hell."

"She is just saying you have to try to, I don't know, make the best of a bad situation, that's all."

"That's what she's got, that's what we get—the best of a bad ..."

"Yes, all right. Go ahead. Do what you do."

"What?"

"This is something to hold on to," she said, tearing the paper as she grabbed it back from me. "And, you want to know something, I appreciate that. I appreciate having something I can hold in my hand. Or put up on the kitchen bulletin board or I don't know what...."

"I won't have this in my house."

"You and your bitterness. I want *you* to tell *me* something," Cynthia said. "This self-pity—is it going to stop some time soon? What is it you *do* want? Do you want out? Then say so." She was close to tears, which I knew I could prevent if I made a gesture, if I put my arm around her, said a single kind word, simply apologized. Instead, I folded my arms tightly across my chest and rocked back and forth.

"You have to understand that the way you're behaving isn't helping me and it isn't helping our situation," Cynthia said. She was sitting on the edge of the bathtub now. It was as if she couldn't stand any longer, as if the only choice she had was between this uncomfortable bit of porcelain and falling down. "Because this isn't just about you, you know. Because I don't think you get it sometimes, and that's what scares me, really scares me. You need to know this is about our family, about our child."

But, at that moment, all I could think was, *She's wrong. She's finally wrong.* This *was* all about me, all about what was being done to *me*, about the catastrophe I felt descending upon me and my family. Incidentally, you may not know this, I certainly didn't at the time, but you can break an orange. You can do this by throwing it against the wall, hard. It will not bounce like an apple or splatter like a tomato, but a small fissure will appear in the peel and the inside will be damaged, almost imperceptibly.

HAS IT MADE YOU a better father, a better human being?

I have yet to answer the CBC producer's question, and now she's expanded it. I'm not usually good at sugar-coating things, but I can do it and have, countless times before, for family, friends, colleagues, acquaintances, teachers, doctors, therapists, social workers. Even, though less successfully, for Cynthia. So, yes, on occasion, I've managed to convince everyone, including myself, that, all things considered, I'm coping fine. Any kind of real prognosis is impossible to predict with autism so you have to learn to manufacture your own. And you do it, more often than not, day by day.

I also know that I have to be upbeat on the radio tomorrow morning for the interview to go well. If I can manage that, I'll end up feeling good about what I've written and about the possibility of giving someone listening a bit of hope or reassurance. So why am I not answering this straightforward question? I guess because what I have finally written isn't evidence of the triumph of narrative, but, instead, of its inevitable failure. My about-to-be-broadcast essay isn't so much an essay as the residue of all these years of planning to write a book I can't seem to write—a story I'm only now managing to make this tiny, almost imperceptible, twelve-hundred-word dent in. There is a message here. When life gives you lemons, lemonade isn't always the most probable outcome. Sometimes, you end up with a sourpuss.

So I finally tell the woman on the phone the truth; or something close to it. "Better father? God no," I finally say, which seems, even as I say it, like an inappropriate boast. "No, all this has made me a worse father."

I pause. This woman I've never met and I are sharing the same thought. We both know my uninspiring answer will never make it onto the air tomorrow. She'll make sure to tell the interviewer not to go near the question and I won't volunteer my insight, my revelation either. For now, though, I don't care. I'm glad to continue the pre-interview. "That's the thing," I go on. "It's made me worse, worse father, worse husband, worse primate—Jonah likes primates—worse across the board."

The producer is quiet for a moment, but then she's curious. She wants to know what happened. "I mean to you?" she says.

"I wish I could tell you," I say. "I used to be a good father." *Who am I kidding*, I think, *I used to be great.*

THE FUTURE IS what you are given when you have your first child. When you are a new parent you always have a sense of something coming—a sense so perpetual, so ordinary, you can't imagine you never felt it before. Except you never have; how could you? So you feel it and you do what people have always done: you choose names and wallpaper; debate disposable diapers versus cloth diapers; sign up for daycare; buy life insurance; daydream twenty years down the line about colleges and girlfriends. When you are told that your child has autism, it's the future that's taken away.

That evening, as Cynthia reread the handouts Dr. T. gave her, I put Jonah to bed and watched as he followed his usual routine, lining up his shelf of bedtime books so they stretched from one end of his bedroom to the other. He took on this seemingly pointless task with the deliberateness of a chess master. He weighed each move carefully, keeping his hand on the book he was placing in line until it was exactly where he wanted it. All I wanted, I gradually realized, was to stop him, distract him. "Jonah," I said, as he began the line, as usual, with Graeme Base's picture book *Animalia*. It occurred to me that here was something we could do together, a topic we could share—our own animal alphabet book. So I improvised a beginning. "Angry aardvarks are always after.... After what? Jonah. Go ahead, fill in the blank." But he didn't hear me or pretended not to and carried on.

What was suddenly clear to me was that, on this night anyway, I wasn't going to let him off the hook. I would intrude on his routine—somehow interrupt it. So I picked up a copy of *Green Eggs and Ham*, the book that always ended up at the end of the line, nearest the far wall, and opened it. Then I sat on his bed and lifted him into my lap as if I were going to read to him. Jonah wasn't pleased. Bedtime stories came later and usually from his mother. He scowled and muttered under his breath, "Put it back." When that tactic didn't work he tried to close the book on my hand. But the harder he tried the more tightly I held on to him, the more I bugged him. And so I read to Jonah about how, at first, nobody can stand Sam-I-am, how he is disliked everywhere he goes, on all manner of vehicles and animals, whether it's sunny or pouring rain.

Theodore Geisel, a.k.a. Dr. Seuss, wrote *Green Eggs and Ham* on a dare. After he'd written *The Cat in the Hat* using a vocabulary of two hundred and twenty-five words, Geisel's publisher Bennett Cerf bet him fifty dollars he couldn't write a book using only fifty words. Geisel won the bet easily. In fact, when the book came out in 1960 it barely contained fifty syllables. All the words in *Green Eggs and Ham*, except for "anywhere," are monosyllabic. The book has no exposition either and only the most unobtrusive narratives. It is a conversation really, a long, frustrating, one-sided conversation—at least, until the end of the story.

By the time I reached the end, I was gritting my teeth and squeezing Jonah so tightly, so desperately, I might have been hurting him and I would have never known it. *Green Eggs and Ham* is a battle of wills, too. It's about stubbornness, but also persistence. So I persisted. I made a pest of myself. By the time I finished the story, Jonah was crying softly. But when I gave him back the book to put in its proper place, he hesitated before taking it from me. For a moment, I could see how hard this was for him, how brave he was to make this simple gesture, this tiny concession to change. I could also see how hard things were going to be for him, how extraordinarily brave he would always have to be. There would be no miracles. There would just be the usual daily round of ups and downs, of despair followed by hope, and back again. I still forget that sometimes he's on the same rollercoaster we're on and that however hard it is for us, it's much harder for him. Because he hasn't learned yet that it is a rollercoaster he's on. No one can explain that to him yet, not even us. Finally, he handed the book back to me and got into bed. "Again, Daddy," he said. It was hard to tell if he was capitulating or if this was something else. Maybe he was just being a good sport. He'd had a bath before bed and his cheeks were still rosy from the hot water. His hair was wet, too, and sticking up in a variety of places. I smoothed the spots down. Then brushed his hair across his forehead with my hand, getting a glimpse of the big boy he was becoming. The expression on his face was uncharacteristically transparent. He was still a small boy, really, trying to decide whether or not he was ready for sleep. His decision was no—he'd stay awake a little longer if I had something interesting to offer. He sat up, clutched his pillow to his chest, and waited for me to read to him.

"Again, indeed, again!" I said, exclaiming like I imagined a triumphant Sam-I-Am might.

Cynthia was listening at Jonah's bedroom door and met me there after I'd tucked him in. "'I will hug you here and there and everywhere,'" she whispered in my ear, putting her arms around my neck. "In our bed. Wearing red."

"Give me a bad day," I said.

"Too late for that now," she said. "Maybe tomorrow."

FOUR

Let's Talk About Complaining

Last year, on the final day of school, Jonah came home with a book he'd spent all of his second term writing and illustrating in class. It was his grade four project. "It's called *Bad Animals*. He did it on his own," Jessica, his shadow at school, told us.

"He came up with the title, too?" I asked and couldn't help adding, "By himself?" I always seem to be asking this question or some variation on it. Yes, on his own, Jessica assured me again.

Jonah has always gone to a regular school, but he's always gone with an ABA shadow. Jessica is his latest. She's also been part of his team of therapists for several years. Like everyone who has worked with Jonah, Jessica was in her early twenties when she began. She's a keener, good-natured and hard-working, currently doing a graduate degree in education.

This is her second year as Jonah's shadow, a job for which she has been painstakingly trained. What she's not trained to do, however, is make things easier for the school, a fact routinely misinterpreted by overworked teachers trying to manage overcrowded classrooms. There can be as many as four or five kids in a class in need of special attention, so it's not surprising that the teachers have often expected Jonah's shadows to do everything for him when, in reality, it's their job to do the opposite. Jessica's job is to make herself unnecessary as soon as possible. Her job is to prompt Jonah and then fade her prompts, thus encouraging his independence. If he is dependent, it's the teacher he should depend on. *Just like the other kids, sweetheart, that's what we want.*

We had hoped that, by now, Jonah would be on his own. That while he needed a shadow in kindergarten, he would perhaps only need one part-time in grade one, and maybe only for a couple of hours in grade two. Grade three: that was going to be the limit, the year his shadow was gone for good. But he's in grade five now and none of our predictions have turned out to be reliable. There are still times he's lost at school. We know this from Jessica's notes, and we don't know what we would do without her or the other therapists who have worked with Jonah over the years. All have been reliable; all have come to care about our son. A few have become friends. A few we have missed desperately once they've moved on after a year or two as they invariably do. One confessed to me, "Even when it was a particularly tough session, I knew I was leaving after three hours and I always reminded myself that you and Cynthia weren't. You guys weren't going anywhere."

There are three main characters in *Bad Animals*: Deedee the Cow, Rooney the Camel, and Moe the Yak. Incidentally, the names are taken directly from the irritatingly upbeat CBC kids' show *The Doodlebops*. Fortunately, Jonah's story is not upbeat. There is, instead, a dark slapstick element to his narrative. Imagine *Animal Farm* meets *The Three Stooges*. There's also an autobiographical element. All three characters end up having to deal with the kind of problems Jonah may have recently encountered. Or, more likely, the kind of problems Jonah is anticipating and worrying obsessively about. A detailed account of Jonah's worries can be found in all his shadows' notes so far, along with a detailed description of how the worry is manifesting itself in his behaviour. How a surprise test, for instance, set him off on a downward spiral of anxiety. How something as minor as a disparaging comment from a teacher resulted in a week of Jonah biting his nails or giggling inappropriately. In *Bad Animals*, his characters are just as easily unnerved. The story begins with the three protagonists about to perform at Montreal's annual summer jazz festival. Jonah has drawn saxophones and drums on the margins of the page as well as the occasional musical note. His colouring is neatly inside the lines and shows considerable effort, an encouraging indication that he takes more care with such things at school than he does at home. The animals appear, at first, to be enjoying each other's company. Then a hurricane hits the city. As a result, the jazz festival is postponed. Next, the mall, where the animals decide to go to get dry, is closed. So is the Pizza Hut where they end up stranded in an empty parking lot. Disappointment accrues, as the ability of Jonah's alter egos to cope with it deteriorates. Eventually, they behave badly and, really, who can blame them?

> They felt mad. Rooney hit Moe's head. Moe punched
> Rooney's nose. Deedee kicked everybody. They all fought.
> Everybody was very angry. A policeman saw them. The
> policeman arrested them. He took them to jail. Poor
> Deedee, Rooney, and Moe! Poor them!

It was reading *Bad Animals* that made me think Jonah and I could collaborate on our own book. I don't know why I expected this kind of project would be different from all the others I'd begun with him and given up on or simply let slide. Like the time I taught him to swing a baseball bat but could make no headway teaching him the rules of the game. He kept running from home to third. Ditto hockey and basketball and poker. Or the times I've tried to teach him to talk on the telephone or to use a normal voice in public. *Bad Animals*, though, indicated that he could become involved in a story if it was one he cared enough about, if it was one that spoke directly to the day-to-day things bothering or besting him. That was his kind of story and, as it happened, mine too. The problem would be sticking with it. That would be the most important thing for him as well as me.

In retrospect, my mistake was telling Cynthia about the idea before I had properly thought it through. "We'll call it *More Bad Animals.* You know, a sequel. Everyone likes sequels," I explained one night as she and I were getting ready for bed.

I improvised a story about the further adventures of Deedee, Rooney, and Moe as well as two new characters, their father, who's a gorilla, and another son who's a monkey—"It's a blended family, okay?"—and I dreamed up a plot about how none of them get along. Still, they decide one day to, I don't know, bake a cake together and, guess what, it turns out terrible, they make an enormous mess, and that's it, that's all I've got so far, I told Cynthia. Except for the new characters, the father and son, who are inveterate troublemakers. I'm calling them The-Worst-Daddy-Ever and The Worst-Monkey-Ever. "Jonah will like that, don't you think?" I went on to explain how in each new chapter they mess up something else together—break a window playing ball or slip on a banana peel—and they always end up fighting with each other. They make up, eventually, but only once they've picked a fight with some other animal, a giraffe or hippo making a cameo appearance. And while there are no happy endings for this oddball bunch, the reader eventually realizes they're not bad exactly—Deedee, Rooney, Moe, and the new characters—only flawed, deeply, humanly flawed, for animals anyway. I was rambling now, barely coherent. I've had this experience before, teaching. Your mind suddenly goes blank but you keep on talking like you're stuck on a runaway treadmill. You can't get off and you can't stop either—because if you do, you're sure to go flying.

This needs work, I quickly realized; still, Cynthia was encouraging, though she did wonder out loud whether it's true that everyone likes sequels and whether a series of such resolutely unhappy endings are ideal for children. ("Non-happy," I corrected her, "not unhappy.") In the end, she said what she always says when it comes to my latest scheme to connect with Jonah. She said, "That sounds great, dear, really." Then she got into bed, turned out the light, and requested a story of her own, preferably happy and boring.

SHORTLY AFTER JONAH'S current school year began, Cynthia installed an exercise bar in the doorway connecting our vestibule to our dining room, or what used to be our dining room. It's the kind of item you see advertised on TV, targeted at viewers who believe they can lose weight easily and conveniently in their home doing ten minutes of chin-ups once a week. There's always a market for the self-improvement types: people willing to lay out a few dollars for the promise of the item as much as the item itself. In this case, the item itself is an eyesore, not to mention hazardous. While our family, Cynthia and Jonah and I, sail under it as if it weren't there, more than one guest above the height of 5′6″ has had to be warned to duck on entering our home.

The bar is there because Jessica informed us that Jonah doesn't seem able or willing to swing on the monkey bars in the school playground like the rest of the kids in his class. She has tried to encourage him to make the effort, but he is apprehensive, afraid of the height or of falling or, if I know my son, failing. The problem is, at school, swinging has become a favoured recess activity, the current craze, you could say. Like tether-ball or hopscotch in previous years. This year, for some reason, all the grade-fives are lining up at the jungle gym like army recruits at basic training. Meanwhile, Jessica, whose job is to make sure Jonah is integrated not just into his classroom but also into social situations, has come to the conclusion that his reluctance to swing is isolating him—isolating him even more, she means to say, though is careful not to. This is valuable information, the kind we wouldn't have without Jessica, the kind that makes having our own shadow in the school so important.

The first day our exercise bar went up Jonah eyed it suspiciously. He reasonably assumed that this change in the household decor had something to do with him—he always assumes that; he's usually right—and, as a result, avoided it. I had doubts, too. I wondered what purpose having a single exercise bar would serve. Didn't he need more than one to practise actual swinging, you know, from bar to bar? Wasn't that the point of monkey bars—the point of monkeys, for that matter? *And what, exactly, was the point of all this anyway? Did we expect Jonah to grow up to be a trapeze artist?* I wisely kept these complaints to myself; still, as if to prove my point, the first time we coaxed Jonah into hanging from the bar, that's all he would do. Hang from it limply and then only for a few seconds. Cynthia pushed his bum to get him going, but as soon as she did he released his hands and dropped to the floor.

"What?" Cynthia said to me the first time Jonah refused to swing his legs and then wandered away.

"Nothing. It just doesn't seem like this is the kind of thing we should have to teach him."

"We have to teach him everything," Cynthia said, not for the first time.

Now, we can't get Jonah off the thing. I'll call him to do his homework or to come to the kitchen for dinner, and when he doesn't show I always know where to find him. Now, I worry about him letting go of the bar in full swing and crashing through the nearest window, sticking a perfect landing somewhere in our next-door neighbour's backyard vegetable garden. Sometimes he beseeches us to push him. Other times, he drags over his small trampoline and positions it under the bar so he can vault onto it. This helps him gather speed. He's learned, with some coaching from Cynthia, who would be the first to admit she's no acrobat, to bend his knees and then fully extend his legs. He particularly enjoys the pendulum motion, the idea that you can only go so far forward before you inevitably end up going backward and, of course, vice versa. The gentle surprise of this as well as the constancy of it pleases him. Backward or forward, he is, on the bar, pure momentum. Sometimes, he'll belt out songs like "Swing Low, Sweet Chariot" or "Swinging on a Star"—he particularly likes the part about the monkeys not all being in the zoo. He's not so much being clever or cute but adding a soundtrack to his favourite new activity. Mostly, though, I hear him reciting the alphabet, attaching an animal to each letter. At first, he could only make it to "C is for Camel" on one swing. Now, he's up to "Q for Quetzal." Yes, quetzal, the national bird of Guatemala, in case you're wondering. Jonah's capacity for happiness is unlimited, and this is not always an unequiv-ocally good thing. It can turn, sometimes, into a kind of intoxication. Living with Jonah can be a bit like living with a little drunk—fun for a while but ultimately draining. But these days, on the swing, there's also a sober sense of pride and purpose. Cynthia suggests this has to do with the fact that Jonah is aware, more than I'm often prepared to acknowledge, that he has accomplished something he didn't believe he could. Jessica hasn't reported much progress in the schoolyard yet, but I'm willing to believe Cynthia is right. Even so, I suspect there's something else going through my son's head when he swings with this kind of abandon—something to do with gravity, with the sudden, conspicuous absence of it.

SOMETIMES I TRY TO imagine Jonah as a character in a novel. I know that if I can think of him that way, I'll have a better chance to understand him, figure out how he thinks. Isn't that what writers are supposed to do after all—get inside the heads of their characters? Negative capability: Keats coined the term. He used it to describe the uncanny aptitude a few extraordinary writers, like Shakespeare, had for empathy. Some writers, Keats said, were "capable of being in uncertainty, Mysteries, doubts without any irritable reaching after fact & reason." In other words, they became their creations. My problem is I'm always reaching for facts and reasons. I have a lousy imagination. Besides, you can't chase after empathy any more than you can after happiness or love. Either you have it or you don't.

In *Send in the Idiots: Stories from the Other Side of Autism*, author Kamran Nazeer, who is on the extremely high-functioning end of the autism spectrum, begins by telling the story of an unusually progressive school he attended in New York City when he was four and how, some twenty years later, he set out to find his classmates, also on the spectrum, to see how they fared. Nazeer, a successful policy adviser to the British government and an accomplished young writer, fared well. In fact, if he didn't remind us of his autism every now and then most readers would likely forget about it. He mentions some stims he still has, but they seem more like nervous tics. Even so, *Send in the Idiots* contains valuable insights about Nazeer's disorder, the kind only an insider could have. At one point, he explains that one of the reasons he was able to track down his long-lost classmates is because their parents had kept in touch with each other. The parents shared the same anxieties. "They knew ... there was unlikely to be a shining day when everything became fine," Nazeer writes and then takes a stab at putting himself in the parents' shoes. "What did that feel like, to have created a life that was so fundamentally different from their own? Not different interests, a different view about the importance of religion, a partner that you don't necessarily approve of, but a different sort of life."

A few years ago I was offered an assignment by *Canadian Geographic* to take Cynthia and Jonah, who was seven at the time, to Quebec City to write a travel article about the city's annual Winter Carnival. None of us had been before, and the idea was to view the trip through the eyes of a typical kid. I said yes because that's what you say when you're a freelance writer and someone offers you a job, especially a well-paying one for a national magazine. But the more I thought about the assignment the more I worried.

"I have to cancel," I complained to Cynthia, a week before we were to leave. She was unsympathetic. She was looking forward to getting away. This was an ideal chance to see a new place, have some new experiences. Not to mention be put up in a fancy hotel, all expenses paid. And Jonah will love it, she concluded. On this last point, she wasn't especially convincing. She knew what I was really concerned about. Jonah was going through a rough patch at the time, having more tantrums, more out-and-out meltdowns than usual, and we were all feeling the stress. None of us was coping well.

"You have to know how tough this is going to be. How do I explain that in an article like this? This is supposed to make people want to go on vacation." What I meant was how do I explain Jonah? *Canadian Geographic* wasn't looking for an article about autism.

"Maybe they are," Cynthia said. This was at least two years before I wrote the CBC essay, and I could guess what she was thinking: *Here it is. Your opportunity to do what you're always saying you're going to do—write about Jonah.* But all I could think about was the difficulty, the impossibility of seeing this so-called vacation through his eyes. All I could think was: *I have no clue how he sees anything.*

A week before the trip I called my editor at the magazine and blurted out that my son has autism and that might make this assignment problematic. I practically begged her to let me out of the job or at least send me by myself. I could go on the press junkets, which were already arranged and which I'd already declined. I could tag along with the other travel writers, see the sites, dream up another angle. I could stay in the famously bizarre ice hotel nearby—drink vodka out of ice cubes and sleep on a mattress of sleet, another option I had initially declined. There was plenty to write about. But the personal nature of the story was already approved, so was the family vacation theme. The magazine had assigned a photographer to follow Jonah around and

take an up-close look at his experience. My editor was sympathetic
and probably a little surprised at how much unsolicited information I
was sharing from the other end of the phone. (She wanted a personal
story but not that personal.) She told me to do my best. She also said
that if I felt I needed to mention Jonah's autism in the article then,
who knows, maybe it would work. She added that she would leave the
decision of what to write about to me.

The article turned out fine. There was no mention of autism.
Except when I look back at it now I can see all the gaps where it could
have, perhaps should have, been mentioned. An out-of-the-blue
reference, for instance, to Cynthia's capacity to make the best of a bad
situation; my insistence on holding Jonah's hand wherever we went;
Jonah's fondness for dawdling and singing random tunes over and over
again. The trip itself was a disaster. *That's a bit strong, sweetheart.* Jonah
didn't like the cold, for starters. None of us did. He stimmed constantly,
had frequent tantrums, and complained like, well, a travel writer. He
didn't like the pull-out sofa he was sleeping on or the fancy French
food in the hotel restaurant. He was afraid of the Carnival mascot,
a presumably friendly abominable snowman called Bonhomme. I
complained about everything, too. And Bonhomme is creepy. Cynthia
tried to remain upbeat but eventually stopped trying. The photographer, a seasoned professional, was also increasingly frustrated. He
couldn't seem to get a single shot of us that didn't reveal the strain on
our faces. We weren't having the kind of outdoor, rosy-cheeked fun we
were supposed to be having. "Joie de vivre," the Carnival's trademark,
was wasted on us. We all wanted to stay by the hotel pool.

Cynthia, our family photographer, also warned the magazine's
photographer about Jonah beforehand—about how she usually had
to take twenty tries to get a good one. Jonah was handsome, photo-
genic, too, at least when the shot worked out. When it didn't, though,
what you ended up photographing was something other than Jonah,
something additional, like autism. In the end, the only photo of

Jonah the magazine used was one of him sleeping. He was a hard kid to capture—in pictures. Or words. For my part, I focused mainly on Quebec City history and the Carnival's stoic philosophy. "When nature gives you ice, you make lots of ice sculptures," an organizer told me.

We were supposed to stay a week but we drove home on our fourth day. We barely spoke on the three-hour return trip. The only reference I made in the article to how miserable we were comes out as a joke, though it is, in retrospect, a veiled reference to what life with autism is like day after day. "The family vacation," I wrote, "is the triumph of hope over experience."

JONAH IS BALKING AT doing his homework, specifically reading *Let's Talk About Complaining*, a book he chose, admittedly at my urging, for Read and Respond—that's what his daily homework assignment is called. He's a little more than a month into the fifth grade so it's important he gets off to a good start and receives lots of positive reinforcement. We have to make sure he is taking on tasks that challenge him but that don't overwhelm or frustrate him. If it were up to Jonah he'd select a book with as little text as possible. He loves the brevity, not to mention the theme of Maurice Sendak's *Where the Wild Things Are*. In ten pages, Sendak sums up the childhood dilemma of having a parent who is always missing the point. Jonah is also drawn to Robert Munsch's sweet but subversive take on childhood and David Shannon's *No, David* books, which contain a multitude of misbehaviours. In *David Goes to School*, the sequel to *No, David*, the title character is berated by teachers and classmates on every page save the last. He's late. He won't sit down. He chews gum. He doesn't pay attention or wait his turn. And he does it all with a kind of mischievous glee that Jonah relates to. David *is* the worst-kid-ever. Even so, if Jonah were to choose a literary alter ego, I'm guessing it would be David. Another plus: there are seldom more than two words per page, usually just: "No, David!"

Let's Talk About Complaining is a compromise. It has enough text to require some time and concentration from Jonah but not enough to scare him off. For Read and Respond, all Jonah is required to do is jot down the author's name (Joy Berry), the number of pages (twenty-nine), read those pages, with my help, if necessary, and then write a few lines, also with my help, explaining what the book is about. ("I like *Let's Talk About Complaining* because …") As it happens, this isn't very different from my job most days. Sum up in a few lines—fewer and fewer now as book review sections dwindle and disappear—a new novel or memoir I just finished. Read, respond.

But if I feel an undue urgency about this time I'm spending beside Jonah at his desk in his therapy room, it's because I want him to have this part of his homework completed before Cynthia returns from work. She will have to do the harder subjects with him—math, French, social studies—subjects that will place the kind of demands on my son that might set him off into a paroxysm of self-doubt. Her part of his homework can take most of the evening to complete or, more precisely, not quite complete.

Read and Respond is how I can help. Even so, I have, as usual, managed to convince myself there's no way it is ever going to get done. Jonah is reading *Let's Talk About Complaining* slowly and in varying modulations of tone: loud then quiet, clear then muddled. He is, in short, screwing with me. We stop and start again. Sometimes he interrupts to tell me a knock-knock joke. Sometimes he wanders away from the desk to swing on his exercise bar. I let him go for a while but always have to call him back. *Follow through, sweetheart.* I find myself wishing for Cynthia to return, not just so she can take over but so she knows what I've been going through. The frustration is not just with Jonah's unwillingness to cooperate but with his inability to comprehend such simple books. He should not be so undone by them and I should not be so undone by his being undone.

A few months ago, Cynthia came across a stack of *Let's Talk About* books in a neighbourhood garage sale. Neither of us had heard of them before, but they cost practically nothing and the subject matter—teasing, feeling sad, expressing anger—seemed like a good fit for Jonah. According to author and publisher Joy Berry's website, her books are meant to cover every "raw emotion as well as emotionally-charged situation" a child will encounter. They are, in fact, self-help literature for kids. Berry's mission, as it also says on her website, is "to make available to children 1 to 13 years of age programs and material that can teach them the information and Living Skills they need in order to live their lives intelligently and responsibly." The conclusion Berry, originally an elementary school teacher, reached some thirty years ago was that the traditional message-laden narrative—fiction, she means—intended to help children understand their increasingly complicated emotions just wasn't doing the job. Her idea was to guide children in a straightforward, step-by-step format through this maze of feelings rather than mix them up with fairy-tale morals to untangle. Children don't need narrative, according to Berry, they need facts. This idea clicked. With the LTA series and other series like *Teach Me About*, *Help Me Be Good*, *Good Answers to Tough Questions*, Berry has more than two hundred and forty titles to her credit and has sold some eighty-five million copies.

Jonah is a competent reader and an excellent speller. His problems are with comprehension. The this-then-that aspect of narrative is often hard for him to grasp. It's hard too for Jonah to distinguish between the foreground and background in a story. The main idea sometimes escapes him as it sometimes escapes all of us. Still, we neurotypical types take this skill for granted—our ability to distinguish between what truly matters and what doesn't.

The advantage of the *Let's Talk About* books is that they are all main idea: example after example of kids behaving badly. "This should be easier for him," Cynthia said when she showed me what she'd found. "They have helpful illustrations, minimal text, and no story to speak of. They're meant for younger children, but I think they're a good place to start. You know he's going to love reading about bossiness and jealousy and breaking promises. He's a little contrarian."

Cynthia is right. He does love Berry's books, though not for the author's message, which is unwavering. No matter what situation she is "talking" about, the golden rule is Berry's answer to everything. If you don't want to be bullied, don't bully other people. If you don't like it when someone lies to you, don't lie to others. Break a promise, all right, let's see how it feels when someone breaks a promise to you. Jonah, despite being a sweet, gentle boy, doesn't get the golden rule. Autism and empathy seldom mix. What Jonah gets, instead, is a thrill from all the unrelenting discussion in Berry's books about bad behaviour and negative emotions. Every kid is good at being inappropriate; it goes with the territory. Jonah, however, is better. It's his trump card, and Berry's books, without intending to, play right into his hand. For Jonah, inappropriateness is always the main idea.

"Right here, bottom of the page, Jonah?" I put my forefinger on the place where we left off and coax him to read along with me, then alone. He's supposed to spend some of the time reading to himself, but I can hear him muttering Berry's heavy-handed message: "'Thinking about the bad things around you can put you into a bad mood. When you are in a bad mood you will be unhappy and most likely have a bad day.'"

"Jonah, come on, we have to finish this now. Try it again, quietly, to yourself. I can't believe we can't do this. Mommy is going to be home soon and she's going to be mad because you're not trying."

"Daddy, can I tell you something?"

This is taking too long. I should say no. I know what he wants. He wants to tell me the same joke he's been telling me ever since we started his homework a half hour ago. He wants me to play straight man, yet again: Abbott to his Costello. I also know I am not supposed to allow myself to be distracted again. *Ignore bad behaviour, sweetheart, reinforce good behaviour.* Still, there's something about this request that sounds reasonable, disarming even, and causes a tiny flutter of happy-go-lucky obliviousness in my chest. *This time*, I can't help thinking, *maybe he's going to initiate a conversation.* Maybe, he wants to tell me a story, tell me what happened in school today or try to explain his own tangled emotions. Something I can make sense of. Something we can genuinely discuss. This also takes me back to his baby days. To my memories of a time that was pure anticipation. When I couldn't wait to see what he might say or do next, when there were so many other ways—other than autism, I mean—to interpret his words and actions.

"Knock-knock ..." he says. I've been suckered again.

"No more, Jonah. This is homework time. You know what you have to do."

All parents fight with their kids over homework. I'm aware of this, but the fight doesn't inevitably turn into so much more, doesn't escalate out of all proportion, so instead of looking at a crabby, procrastinating child you find yourself staring down everything he might have been, everything he might not be. *The future is a thing of the past.* It should be enough to say that you are a parent and like every other parent you get tired and fed up. You worry. You lose your temper. Everyone has something to cope with and this is what you have. So, go ahead, cope.

"Think before you complain," Joy Berry writes. "Complain only if complaining will help to change something that needs to be changed. If things cannot be changed accept them the way they are ..."

"Daddy, knock-knock ..."

Stay calm, now. Be patient. Cynthia's instruction is so clearly audible in my head, I turn to the front door to see if she's arrived home and I've failed to notice. Or if maybe I've read this plain-spoken directive in an advanced reviewer's copy of Berry's yet-to-be-published *Let's Talk About Impatience.* Or *Let's Talk About Pessimism.* Or maybe *Let's Talk About Fucking Up.* In any case, it's too late for advice now.

"Jonah, for God's sake just read the damn book! This is for five-year-olds. You're not trying. Damn it, why do you have to be ... like ... like this?"

Tears accumulate in Jonah's eyes, and it will take all the patience and hopefulness I can call on to get him back on track. While he bravely tries not to cry, I know what I should do: I should leave the room. *Make yourself scarce, sweetheart, don't make matters worse.* Instead, all I can think is: *It's barely October and this is what we have in store for us—Read and Non-respond. For the next nine months.*

THE MORE I THINK ABOUT working with Jonah on the sequel to *Bad Animals* the more sense it makes, which is saying something around here, where making sense of things can be a full-time job. But writing has become one of the ways Jonah copes with stress. Some evenings, after he's fallen asleep, I find notes scattered throughout the house. Scraps of paper turn up everywhere: in his books, in the bathroom cabinet, in our bed, once even in the refrigerator. They aren't exactly stories; more like memos, negotiations, pleas, clues. Just this opening phrase, for example: "I'm so angry that _____" You fill in the blank.

Sometimes, the message is easy to decipher, as it is in *Bad Animals*. Other times, it can take a while to figure out what the accumulation of negatives adds up to: "I don't think I won't go to school no more. I don't think school will be no fun." Do the negatives cancel each other out? Does this mean he likes school? Or he doesn't? There are also arcane facts written down about animals I have never heard of before and I'm not sure exist; who knew, for instance, that the capybara is the largest rodent in the world? Or that the gharial, a crocodile native to India, is the longest-living of all crocodilians? Thanks to Jonah, I know.

It shouldn't come as a surprise to me that my son's writing requires decoding. All writing does. I'm a literary critic, after all—well, a book reviewer—and I should know this. So I read Jonah's stories critically, the same way I would read Philip Roth's latest Zuckerman novel, let's say, with foreknowledge of Roth's obsessions, but also on the lookout for a new thread, some new entry point into the mind of the author. In a way, this is hardly a new job for me. It's just never been essential before.

FIVE

Trouble Came

"*The Book of Job* is the only book," the late Stanley Elkin once said and proved repeatedly in his own writing. "I would never write about someone," he also said, "who was not at the end of his rope." Elkin understood what it meant to be hanging by a thread. He lived most of his adult life with a diagnosis of multiple sclerosis, and his work, while always brashly, blackly funny, was imbued with his awareness of the raw deal he'd been handed. In his most *Book of Job*–like work, *The Living End*, Elkin's hero, a good but otherwise unremarkable man named Ellerbee, dies, goes to hell, and can't figure out why. It's the question always at play in Elkin. Why me? So when Ellerbee is offered the chance to confront God, face to face, so to speak, he passionately pleads his case. He was a good man, seriously good. He never stole or bore false witness. "'Where were You when I picked up checks and popped for drinks all round? When I shelled out for charity and voted Yes on the bond issues?'" Ellerbee lobbies God.

The Almighty, being all mighty, has His own explanation for why things have gone so badly for His faithful servant, though it tends to make matters worse. God runs down a long list of Ellerbee's offences—like the time he opened his liquor store on the Sabbath; the time he said goddamn; the time he admired his neighbour's wife. "'You had a big boner,'" God reminds him. And there's more: "'You went dancing.

You wore zippers in your pants and drove automobiles. You smoked cigarettes and sold the demon rum.'" Ellerbee can't believe what he's hearing. This is God's cosmic explanation: a list of petty grievances, a sum total of nothing much. Here you have it: God's renowned and so-called mysterious ways.

I first read *The Book of Job* in earnest when I was twenty-one, not long after my mother died. At the time, I considered it research for a short story I was trying to write. That's what I told myself anyway—*research*. Really, I was looking, like Ellerbee and Elkin, for an explanation. My mother's death blindsided me. A year later, my reaction to my father's death couldn't have been more different. I was prepared for it. And I have been prepared for every bad thing that's happened in my life ever since: break-ups, betrayals, rejections, lost opportunities. Until Jonah's diagnosis: with that, I was blindsided all over again.

Of course, what keeps drawing me back to *The Book of Job* is not very different from what draws me to most literature—the central character. Job is my kind of hero, after all—passive-aggressive. He takes everything God can dish out—the devastation of his livestock and servants and children, not to mention his complexion, boils head to toe—with what appears to be heroic equanimity. Patience is the adjective so often ascribed to him. Read between the lines, though, and what becomes evident is that right from the start, Job's legendary patience is only skin deep. He is a fair-weather optimist, an unrepentant complainer. Sure, at first he tries to be a good sport, all the while thinking, *maybe this is just a mix-up.* Mistakes happen. Wires get crossed even now, so you can imagine how it was back then, with CNN, Google News, Facebook, and Twitter still several thousand years away. *So take a deep breath and relax, Job.* And, while you're at it, cut the Almighty some slack. Almighty is really just a nickname. In the first chapter, Job is still in a daze when he famously says: "The Lord gave and the Lord hath taken away; blessed be the name of the Lord." The words sound as if they were spoken by someone in deep denial, someone still waiting on a recount or, at the very least, a good reason. But one isn't forthcoming, and a few pages later Job changes his tune. Who can blame him? Job had it all: the camels and goats, the big, devoted family. What must he have been thinking when it finally sunk in that all of it was gone? Only one thing: *It wasn't supposed to be like this.*

THE RECORD OF JONAH'S earliest days is incomplete. My sisters bought a new video camera the day he was born and started filming. Often, they would leave the camera with us on the condition that we record every moment of potential cuteness. I'm pretty sure we had tape of that spot of mucus on his forehead. But one day they took the camera home with them and made the mistake of leaving it in plain sight on the backseat of the car. The next morning they found the car's back window smashed and the camera, along with its case, containing several other videos of Jonah as a baby, gone. I remember we kept expecting the tapes to be returned. That a classified ad would be placed in the community newspaper or that we'd receive an anonymous phone call saying we could pick up our valuable property at some out-of-the-way spot. We expected the thieves to go to considerable effort to find us. Maybe because they knew how much those early images meant to us and that we'd pay a ransom for their return. Or maybe because Jonah was so adorable and this record of his babyhood so endearing that they'd have to be utterly inhuman, in a way we hoped that penny-ante thieves weren't, to resist making things right again. The rightness of things—of which Jonah's birth seemed to be the main proof in those days—was out of whack, and the camera thieves would know, as we did, that it needed to be restored. No such thing happened. We took solace, instead, in old photos, but it wasn't the same as seeing Jonah in action, even if his actions were limited to sleeping or nursing or bathing. My sisters were heartbroken and, after that, became super-diligent. They bought another camera and took it with them everywhere, filming every move Jonah made for the next three years. The filming stopped abruptly then. Nobody can say why exactly, but I have a hunch. I'm guessing we didn't want to look at Jonah too closely, not once our complicated concern for him started to outdistance our simple pleasure.

I had forgotten about those videotapes until my older sister told me the other day she was thinking of transferring them to DVD so we could watch them more conveniently on our television set. She wanted to know what I thought of the idea, if I had any objections. Normally, she would have gone ahead and done this sort of thing without asking permission, the way, for instance, she and my other sister bought Jonah clothes. They are responsible for purchasing almost everything he wears, in fact. Cynthia and I trust them with those decisions. We trust their good taste and unrivalled shopping skills. But this decision about the DVDs was fraught, the way so many simple decisions are now. Besides, I'd blown up at my sisters more than once over the last seven years, launching into a rant about one thing or another to do with Jonah, a rant that invariably ended with me sounding ridiculously like Jack Nicholson delivering his "You-can't-handle-the-truth" speech.

It doesn't take much for the people you love to set you off. Their offence can be minuscule or imaginary. Like the way I imagine they're watching me watching Jonah when I am frustrated and out of patience. I sense their disappointment at my disappointment, their impatience with my impatience. And, once again, I end up thinking and sometimes saying aloud things I shouldn't: *You don't know how much I keep from you. You have no idea.*

Then again, I don't think a lot about what they're going through. How helpless they must feel; how hard unconditional love can be to sustain in the face of the confusing and contradictory facts I keep presenting them with. They are experts at explaining away all of their nephew's odd behaviours; all our worries seem overblown to them.

It's not that they refuse to acknowledge something is wrong, they refuse to acknowledge that it is wrong enough to change the way they feel about Jonah. So wrong that buying him a new argyle vest won't, somehow, make our situation marginally better. And they're right; it does. It makes it marginally better.

As for transferring those videos to DVD, I remained noncommittal, so I'm betting my sister has already gone ahead and done it. "It will be nice to have," she said, during her original pitch. "I've been looking at some of it on the video camera. We have his first birthday party. And the time he walked."

"The first time?"

"Could be."

Jonah walked at thirteen months. He hit all the marks, all the milestones set out for him in whatever unspeakably horrifying baby manual we happened to be reading. Late in Cynthia's pregnancy, she suffered from epic indigestion. Often, it would wake her in the middle of the night. She'd have a hard time getting back to sleep, so she would ask me to tell her a story, a boring one, if possible. After a while, I ran out of material so I started reading to her from *What to Expect When You're Expecting*. I did so dutifully for a while, trying to keep my voice steady and unaffected as I skimmed the endless catalogues of catastrophic occurrences to watch out for. All the things you never previously imagined going wrong; all the things you never imagined period. *What to Expect When You're Expecting* is not a book for the squeamish. Described in detail, the most innocuous ailments and conditions—cradle cap or colic—sound not only dire but inevitable. As I kept reading, night after night, I began to wonder if it were possible to have chosen a scarier bedtime story. Finally, it was Cynthia who gave the book away to a friend in her first trimester and replaced *What to Expect* with a jumbo-size bottle of Tums.

Even so, after Jonah was born, we felt compelled to buy a new set of manuals—*What to Expect: The First Years*, *What to Expect: The*

Toddler Years. We didn't read them exactly, but we kept them on hand to confirm that, yes, he's sitting up right on schedule. He's pointing on time, very important, pointing, the book said. He's talking when he should and standing when he's supposed to. He's leaning ahead of time. Actually, there was nothing about leaning, but Jonah looked so clever, so cool and deliberate doing it that I considered writing the *What to Expect* publishers with my own carefully considered observations: "For the truly advanced child: look for *the lean* at ten months."

Jonah started walking short distances right on cue, too, balancing himself on furniture, cruising, until he went solo, navigating the short, direct line between Cynthia's gentle nudge and my outstretched arms. Gradually, we increased the distance between us; gradually, his eyes straight ahead, he crossed the divide. Until one day, a day my sister apparently has on video and now I'm guessing DVD, he took an unexpected left turn and headed for the kitchen—uncharted territory. He walked maybe twenty feet, wobbled for a few more, but it was this image of him setting out on his own that made us all collectively hold our breath. It seemed we'd all inhaled together. He didn't make it to the kitchen. He fell on his diaper-padded behind, with a considerable thump considering his size. Still, he didn't cry. He simply waited for someone to help him up again and kept on walking in the same trailblazing direction. Someone, likely me, started singing "Sunrise, Sunset." At least that's how I remember the event. I suppose the DVD will confirm if my memory of any of this is accurate. That is, if I had any intention of watching the DVDs.

Here's what you want to avoid: comparisons, particularly between how things once were and how they are now. *Weltschmerz* lingers like indigestion. "You can't tell anything," my sister told me the other day, finally confessing the deed was done. She had the discs—twelve hours (so far). "I mean, you know what I mean. He looks just … like … he looks."

"THEREFORE I WILL NOT refrain my mouth," Job tells the three uninvited fair-weather friends who have come to comfort him but prove to be no comfort at all. God's little comic twist there, reminiscent of Kafka's deathbed complaint about his doctors: "So the help goes away again without helping." (Kafka was another writer always rewriting *The Book of Job*.)

Job also does what he vowed he wouldn't. He curses his fate: "I will speak in the anguish of my spirit; I will complain in the bitterness of my soul." Here, his suppressed anger at God is redirected inward—as he comes up with one reason after another why he'd be better off never existing. The guy could be poster boy for the passive-aggressive. "For the thing which I greatly feared is come upon me," Job says. "I was not in safety; neither had I rest, neither was I quiet; yet trouble came."

Blah, blah, blah. The whining continues, rising in intensity and bitterness, and you could argue that by the end of *The Book of Job*, even God can't take it any more. Maybe He's feeling a little guilty since He was the one who set all this in motion, who made a bet with Satan about Job's steadfast, incorruptible character. Remember, too, it's when Satan says in effect, "You call that trouble," that God turns up the heat and does so without a second thought. By the end of the story, after all Job's complaining, even God, the supreme practical joker, recognizes, as practical jokers occasionally do, that maybe He's gone too far. So in a rare Old Testament moment, God relents. Like *Punk'd* on rewind, He restores Job's wealth and gives him a new family. Job seems satisfied, but that only confirms the story as fiction. After all, it needs an ending, a quick wrap-up. So why not the old story-telling standby: *And they lived happily ever after?* Endings are difficult, and even the Bible can't get this one right. Who lives happily ever after? Who's naive enough to take a writer's word for that? We all know the score: Cinderella looks dreadful most mornings before her coffee and makeup; she's also too groggy to fix a proper breakfast for the prince. As for Charming, he can't find a real job. He's either over- or under-qualified. He watches a lot of daytime TV and drinks too much mead. His eye wanders. There are, he remembers from the good old days, other glass slippers to fill. Are we not supposed to wonder if Job ever picks at those old scabs on his skin, a reminder of his bad old days? Are we expected to believe he never thinks about his first family—all those dead kids? Is he—are we—supposed to just put that out of our minds?

And, by the way, why is Mrs. Job spared in the first place? I've seen this question raised in more than one Talmudic interpretation, a bit of Biblical exegesis offered in lieu of a Henny Youngman joke: "Taketh my wife ... please." No doubt, the patriarchal thinking goes that if you want this guy to suffer, truly suffer, let his wife stick around to dole out the I-told-you-so's. But maybe there's another, more enlightened, post-feminist way to look at it. Maybe his wife is there to keep Job from taking himself and his so-called suffering too seriously. Maybe she's there to say, "Sweetheart, we still have each other."

JONAH'S SCHOOL IS called Hillcrest. It's an inner-city primary school located, incongruously, in the centre of one of the wealthiest communities in Montreal. No one who lives in the immediate area attends the local school, not any more. Now, the children of residents attend private or parochial schools. Hillcrest caters, instead, to a wide variety of children with a wide variety of challenges. Many have transferred for the school's specialized SFA reading program. SFA, or Success for All, has lived up to its name and has succeeded in teaching the most recalcitrant students to read. Some other kids at Hillcrest have learning disabilities or behaviour problems or a combination of the two. Some are there because of difficult home environments or just because their parents, who come from South Korea or the Middle East, are in Montreal temporarily, employed in short-term jobs. Language is usually the issue: they have minimal knowledge of English and French and therefore fall through the many cracks in the system and land in Hillcrest. Other kids are on the spectrum. After a couple of months of observation, you start to have an eye for who's who. Look for boys, first of all, who are either almost indistinguishable or the reverse— just about impossible to miss. Jonah, I suppose, falls somewhere in between. I admit I have a problem with that word, *spectrum*, with its blend of psychobabble and cheery rationalization. It sounds to me like the work of an ad agency or PR firm. As if everyone who attends a school like Hillcrest is assigned, on entrance, a different colour and expected to love that colour simply because it's theirs. Welcome, class, to the SAF Rainbow—the Seriously All-Fucked-up Rainbow.

At Hillcrest, the parents stand out as much as the kids. I think of us as being on a spectrum too—ranging from cheerleaders (the my-kid-right-or-wrong crowd) to deadbeats (the couldn't-be-bothered gang). Mostly, though, we are a dispirited group. We are like members of a struggling sports franchise; we should have T-shirts printed with our team name on it: Last Resort. On those occasions when I attend meetings or fundraising events at Hillcrest, there is something palpable in the air, a kind of low-grade sadness. Let's just say, a lot goes unspoken whenever we meet with teachers or administrators. After all these years, I think I'm beginning to realize what it is: a pedagogical version of the "don't ask, don't tell" policy. If you agree not to ask how your child is doing and by that we mean *really* doing, we will agree not to tell you, not *really*.

Still, I admit Hillcrest has been good for Jonah. He's learned to behave there, to control his impulses, his everyday tantrums and frustrations. If he doesn't always fit in, he is still generally accepted by teachers and classmates. Cynthia, when she reads this, if she ever does, would insist on making this clear. She'd also point out that if I ever took the time to talk to some of the other parents I'd know I was wrong about them. They are not especially sad. *No sadder than anyone else, sweetheart. Incidentally, when was the last time you attended a school event or meeting?* Mainly, though, we're grateful grade five is going well so far. Jonah's first-term report card showed improvement from last year in French. In a new subject, social studies, the teacher's comment was: "Jonah makes a positive contribution to classroom activities." This remark, incidentally, represents years of ABA therapy: first getting him to raise his hand at all; then getting him to raise it at the appropriate time; finally, getting him to raise it only when he believes he knows the answer. In subjects that are harder for him—like reading comprehension and math problems—he's struggling, but the teachers are encouraging. They recommend tutors, extra homework, doing the best we can. Most of all, we're just glad we've made it to November, especially since it didn't look like we would at the beginning of the school year.

Late last August, Hillcrest's principal called Cynthia at five o'clock on a Friday afternoon on what was officially Jonah's final day of summer vacation. The reason was to inform us that she wouldn't be able to keep the verbal promise she'd made a few months earlier. It was the previous June that she had informed Cynthia that Jonah could have his ABA-trained shadow, that's to say Jessica, attend grade five with him. In short, we'd have to send Jonah by himself, starting, well, on that coming Monday morning. Cynthia got off the phone, pale and trembling. I asked what was wrong; I tried to get her to tell me, but she insisted on waiting until Jonah's grandparents had picked him up for the evening before she told me who had called and what about.

"It's not good," she said, slumping into my arms, finally providing an explanation to match the look on her face. She was on the verge of tears, but she didn't cry. Instead, she breathed deeply a few times and clung to me. I massaged her neck and told her everything was going to work out, but my heart wasn't in the promise. Frankly, my heart is never in such a promise any more. This is another fact of life with autism. There's always some new occasion you are expected to rise to, some new challenge you are not sure you will be able to meet. These days, whenever I come upstairs from the basement, after spending a few hours at work on the memoir I am supposed to be writing, I have the same feeling—that I am about to walk in on some crisis, actual or emotional, looming or already in progress.

Still, we'd faced this particular crisis before—annually—a fact I reminded Cynthia of. This was my uncharacteristic attempt at perspective. Maybe everything would work out this time because it had before. Ever since kindergarten Jonah was allowed to have an ABA shadow, hired, trained, and paid by us, accompany him to his classes. Still, we were continually advised that this unique accommodation was just that—unique. It couldn't be expected to last. Hillcrest's administrators as well as some teachers weren't particularly fond of the idea of parents hiring their own shadows, shadows the school had no influence over and frequently regarded as spies. What was there to prevent one of them from reporting every little thing that happened in the classroom to their employers, the children's parents? After all, parents like us were, from the school's point of view, overprotective and hypersensitive, prone to either over- or underestimate our children. We were helicopter types, that awful, dismissive term, and we were a safe bet to demand *special* services for our *special* children.

At the end of every month Jonah comes home with a newsletter from the principal calling our attention to upcoming events and pedagogical or ped-days, the days teachers routinely take off to do who-knows-what. There are reminders, as well, of our parental responsibilities. The information is useful, though often condescending. We are lectured about everything from suitable footwear for our children to proper nutrition. These newsletters invariably end with an inspirational quote or poem about the importance of teamwork and trust between home and school. In "Whose Child Is This?" an unknown author penned this paean to the happy consequences of parent–teacher cooperation:

"Whose child is this?" I ask once more
Just as the little one entered the door
"Ours," said the parent and teacher as they smiled
And each took the hand of the little child
"Ours to love and train together
Ours this blessed task forever."

Who, I always wonder, is asking this question? Who wants to know?

Another month, another anonymous poem—it's about two sculptors, a teacher and parent, joining forces to mould a child's mind out of clay—even creepier this time. The tools the teacher uses are books, music, art, while the parent uses "a guiding hand and a gentle loving heart." What, we don't read? Speaking of which, why are these inspiring little ditties always anonymous? I think I can guess: who would want to sign them? Still, I confess I wait for the next poem with a perverse kind of anticipation. I want to see just how clueless they will be and how annoyed I will become. By now, Cynthia dismisses my monthly complaints with a simple joke. "Hormones," she says. Everyone in this house is, by necessity, a comedian.

The truth is that the relationship between school and home, particularly in the case of a special-needs child, is often adversarial. We'd heard a story, perhaps apocryphal, of a grade-six teacher at another school who verbally abused a boy on the spectrum—rumour had it the word *retard* was used, as in "you fucking retard"—and the boy's shadow, a private ABA shadow, relayed the details to the boy's parents, one of whom, it so happened, was a lawyer. We heard about the school and the school board being threatened with a civil suit if proper disciplinary action wasn't taken. At the very least, the teacher would have to take sensitivity classes and apologize to everyone involved. All of which seemed to be a reason why a school like Hillcrest, with its high proportion of students on the spectrum and otherwise coded kids, was looking for an excuse to be free of shadows like ours. We were, as far as they were concerned, a lawsuit waiting to happen. So it wasn't a surprise that they'd eventually come up with some excuse to get rid of Jonah's private shadow. The only surprise was that they'd come up with this excuse the day before our son was going to start grade five.

"But what's the reason? What are they saying?" I asked Cynthia, who shrugged. She'd already decided to spare me the details for my sake and her own.

"You don't want to know," she said and retreated to her office, to go online, gather her resources, most of all, gather herself. I followed her there and found her hunched over her desk, breathing deeply. "All right, I'll tell you, but ..."

"But what?"

"Don't freak out. The principal said something about a two-tier system—how they couldn't have a two-tier system. She apologized, sort of, but she said it wasn't her decision. It was the school board's."

"Was it her decision to wait until the last minute to tell us? And what the hell does that mean—a two-tier system?"

"I don't know exactly. I think it means if some other kids can't afford to have their own private shadows it's not fair for Jonah to have one."

"Let me get this straight. Because we're trying to help our son become more independent, more integrated, we're undermining a system that doesn't work? God forbid, they should train their shadows so they could deal with kids with autism. The lowest common denominator—that's their pedagogical philosophy, is it? That's how they spend their ped-days—coming up with this ... this ... Does any of this make any sense to you?"

"It doesn't, and don't shout at me." Cynthia's head was in her hands now.

"This is bullshit. And I'm not shouting at you."

"You're shouting next to me."

"I'm sorry." I was sorry. But all I could think of was the scene with Al Pacino from the cloying movie *Scent of a Woman* where he's blind and he gets up in a room full of snooty prep school administrators and gives his Oscar-winning flame-thrower speech. "Remember, he says, 'I ought to ...'"

"I don't have time now."

"'... Take a flame thrower to this place.' That's how I feel. Where are you going?" Again, Cynthia was on the move. I lost track of her for a moment and then heard her purposeful, deep breathing coming from our bedroom. I was still ranting when she held up her hand. She was on the telephone, a fact I was ignoring.

"Remember what they used to teach us in school about how to spell principle and principal? The principal is your pal. Ha! I'm going to write about this, you know. I swear. It's going right into the ... I mean, they can't get away with this, can they?"

"That's what we have to find out," Cynthia replied. "They didn't give us notice. We have that going for us at least. I also have the email the principal sent me last June, at the end of grade four, saying we could use our own shadow for this academic year. And, please, don't you see I'm talking here?"

"Who to?"

"My brother."

Cynthia's brother is a lawyer. As it turned out, so was the father of another child in the school on the spectrum and in the same situation as Jonah. Promises had been made to him and his family, too, and also broken at the last minute. So we had a case or a cause. We presented it, via email, to the school board and waited. Jonah stayed home for the first few days of the year, but eventually we got the reply we were hoping for. We bought him one more year, this year, grade five, with his shadow. In the end, we chalked it up to one more close call and then proceeded to not think about it any more. Cynthia and I have happily resigned ourselves to doing what we do as a matter of course now: worry about next term next term, next year next year. Cynthia works hard at staying hopeful while I plot my revenge—on our pal the principal, for instance. *You can always put it in your book, sweetheart. Just don't use anyone's name. Jonah still has one more year to go in that place.*

LEAVING ASIDE *The Book of Job*'s phony fairy-tale ending, disappointment is what the story is about. It's what gnaws at Job, even worse than the tragic events of his life, worse than God's silence, worse than those festering boils. Disappointment is the itch he can't scratch. There's no question God screws with him, but Job finally has to take some responsibility for all his whining. He has to move forward to stage five—acceptance. Life goes on, even on the ash heap.

Anyway, my advice: if you're going to read *The Book of Job*, read it on a warm summer evening. Take it out into your garden, if you're lucky enough to have one, just as the light is fading. That's what I should have done. I shouldn't have waited. I should have been rereading it a decade ago. On one of those evenings when my infant son was asleep on my chest, our breath rising and falling together, in sync; and when Cynthia was at the kitchen table, scribbling on a notepad, planning our collective future. "Plans you shouldn't worry your pretty little head about," Cynthia liked to say back then and still says sometimes. Vacations, real estate, Jonah's bar mitzvah, his first car, his college fund, his wedding. The sky was the limit. Grand, long-term plans that would have scared me silly, it's true, if I'd ever been asked to listen to them. What, I wonder, was I doing instead? It only occurs to me now that *The Book of Job* is not merely about disappointment or suffering or injustice; it's also about counting your blessings. That is its true literary achievement. To make sure we're grateful for every little thing we have, every camel, every goat, each and every patch of unblemished skin. Gratitude is the takeaway. Only don't leave it too late. Don't wait for trouble to come.

SIX

Variable Weather

Last summer, Jonah learned to ride his bicycle in the cul-de-sac, a small circle really, behind his grandmother's house. There's hardly any traffic there, so that when cars do appear they do so with what we hoped, fingers crossed, would be sufficient warning. We were depending on the fact that the driver would have plenty of time to see Jonah or, worst-case scenario, time for him to be guided to safety. Jonah's grandmother volunteered to teach him once his training wheels were off, and we took her up on the offer and removed them. Actually, Cynthia did, after I complained about rusty bolts and improper tools. "This isn't as easy as it looks," I muttered under my breath, loud enough for Cynthia to hear, adding, "Nothing ever is." For her part, Cynthia looked at me with her standard mix of amusement and quiet restraint. *You always say that, sweetheart.* In the end, she borrowed some WD-40 and an adjustable wrench from a neighbour and, with some persistence and surprising, embarrassing ease, removed the damn things.

More difficult than removing the training wheels was making the decision to remove them. Jonah wasn't lobbying one way or another. Most kids his age would be clamouring for this first taste of independence, but when we asked Jonah to choose—training wheels: yes or no?—he was indifferent. In the end, Cynthia and I disagreed about how to proceed. On my part, it wasn't just about being a klutz with a wrench. I wondered if we might be rushing things. I thought we might want to wait until Jonah was more confident steering, braking, wearing a helmet, and understanding the rules of the road. A distracted and tentative pedestrian, he is never left alone crossing the street, but I constantly worry about the day he will be. Given that, I couldn't imagine him being ready to ride a two-wheeler. That was my side of the debate. Cynthia, however, had had an urgent look in her eyes. She didn't have to say anything. She just had to think it: *Most kids Jonah's age are already riding a bicycle.* Meanwhile, I was thinking: *Didn't you get the memo? Jonah is not most kids his age.*

The first few times I dropped Jonah and his two-wheeler off at his grandmother's I didn't stick around. I left as soon as I could. I didn't want to distract either of them—that was my excuse—and I promised to be back in an hour. Even so, as I was getting back into the car, I kept the door open to eavesdrop. I heard Jonah giggling at his grandmother's warnings, at her insistence that he keep his helmet on. One time, I also heard a tiny crash. Jonah, who will cry for reasons it can sometimes take us days, considerable paperwork, and a costly meeting of a team of ABA therapists and our consultant to unravel, doesn't cry when you expect him to—scraping his knee, say, or bumping his head. So he'd be silent after what I assumed was a fall and I listened as his grandmother praised him, telling him he was doing fabulous, telling him not to worry, and that he wasn't going to fall again. She wouldn't let him. Then I'd hear her shouting, "Pedal, Jonah. You have to pedal to go." I sat in the car for a moment, marvelling at her patience, but not just hers. I marvel at everyone who manages to be patient with my son, even for a little while: therapists, teachers, classmates, neighbours, store clerks. I should have watched her, maybe learned something. Instead, I drove away.

The real reason I wouldn't stay to watch was because I couldn't. I have a lousy imagination, remember, and I couldn't imagine how this was going to end well.

WHENEVER JONAH AND I are out walking, I try my best to leave him to his own devices at intersections and crosswalks. I view it as a kind of training run for the future. Still, I make sure he's wearing a hooded sweater, even in warm weather, so I can keep a firm but largely undetected grip on him. Too often, I've had to yank him back to the curb, an action which is usually followed by an angry lecture about the importance of paying attention to the traffic. You can't be drifting off into La La Land, I told him once and immediately realized my mistake. He found the phrase La La Land irresistibly funny. This is not a joke, I told him. This is serious. By then, I was shouting and he was scared, just not as scared as he should have been, as I wanted him to be. Instead, his shock was tiny and temporary like the kind you'd receive after scuffing your shoes across a carpeted floor. The spark was quickly gone and I uneasily watched his expression shift—from fear to a small, gradual, unconcealed smirk. He repeated what I said—"This is not a joke"—then repeated it again. I knew I needed to be more patient, react properly, according to the rules of ABA, information I should have had at my fingertips by then. I was, I also knew, giving undue attention to his inappropriate behaviour. But the pulse in my neck was throbbing. I was scared and the fear was not dissipating. Human variables, that's the problem with intersections. There was no foolproof way to test or trust my son's knowledge or lack of it when it came to something as simple and crucial as crossing a busy street.

The other day, after another one of these incidents, I dragged Jonah back to a nearby bench and sat him down so I could go over the rules of the road with him yet again. I lectured him about traffic lights and stop signs, about the importance of looking both ways. "You're almost eleven," I said, waiting again until he stopped giggling. "You have to know these things. Don't you ever want to go out on your own or with friends? Don't you want to drive a car one day?" But, once again, the lecture wasn't sticking. So I thought, out of the blue, what would a yak do? Or a cow? Or a camel? I thought of *More Bad Animals,* that book we hadn't started yet, and the chapter we could devote to traffic safety and autism. We could write it down later, but for now we could talk it out and take some notes when we were back home—before bed, maybe. The kind of thing you always do when you're procrastinating and looking for a way around a bad case of writer's block.

"So, listen Jonah, this is a story about how Deedee, remember Deedee the cow, from your book, from *Bad Animals,* well this is a new story about how she ..."

"What's La La Land?"

"Never mind that, Jonah, listen ... you have to listen.... So Deedee is crossing the street one day in La La Land and along comes ... who? Help me out."

"Rooney, the camel."

"And Rooney is?"

"Driving really fast, in a convert-a-bull."

"I get it. Convertible ... Converti-bull, right?"

"Right."

"So his humps stick out, right?"

"Right," Jonah says.

"Great." Now, we're clicking. "Where was I? Right, Rooney is about to run Deedee over because she's not, not what, Jonah?"

"Not looking."

"Right. And Moe, the yak, grabs Deedee's cow tail and pulls her back so she's off the road just as Rooney whizzes by. And Moe is ... what is he, Jonah?"

"Mad."

"How mad?"

"Really mad."

"Yes and you know why Moe is mad? It's because he's scared, so so scared. Do you know why? It's because Moe can't hold on to his friend's tail forever."

MY JOB AT THE cul-de-sac last summer was exactly as easy as it looked. I was to drive towards Jonah, make sure he noticed me, and then under no circumstances run the kid over. That was it. After just a few lessons with his grandmother, Jonah was not only riding his bicycle unassisted and without training wheels, he was riding it exuberantly, recklessly, the way any kid would. True, he had only the most rudimentary grasp of what his brakes were for, but we weren't focusing on that. Anyway, it was clear he had no intention of stopping, so who needed brakes? It turned out this was wonderful to watch, and I regretted that I hadn't stuck around all the other times so I could see how he had progressed to this point. How he had gone from being indifferent to pedalling, simply pedalling, to this—this combination, rare in Jonah, of purpose and delight.

"Look at him," his grandmother said. "He loves it." Then she added: "We have one problem, though. You see."

I did. I saw that Jonah insisted on riding in the middle of the road and he couldn't be convinced to do otherwise. Put another way, I couldn't run out to the middle of the cul-de-sac and take hold of Jonah's hood. There was simply no way of knowing what he would do if and when a car approached. My initial thought was to stand guard at the entrance to the tiny circle. Stop each car as it appeared and run a background check on each driver before making it clear to them that they were to watch out for the kid with autism.

Do you even know what autism is? No. Well, here's some reading material you might want to take a look at. There'll be a quiz later. No, I don't care how many times you've seen Rain Man. *Yes, Hoffman deserved the Oscar. All right, let's start with the spectrum.*

A real plan, however, eluded me until I realized I could simply drive my own car around the cul-de-sac and head slowly, very slowly, towards my son. I felt like Pavlov. I'd devised my own experiment.

On the first try, Jonah didn't notice me until I was right in front of him, the car securely in park, my foot firmly on the brake nevertheless.

Initially, I worried that I would scare him, that he would be startled and fall off his bike; then I worried he wouldn't. That he wouldn't notice me or he would and find the whole thing hilarious. Mostly, he was surprised to see it was me in the car. I waited as he zipped by. But when he returned I stepped out of the car and put my hands on the bicycle's handlebars. I told him to stop for a second and then, as calmly as I could, I explained that from now on whenever he saw a car, any car, not just mine, he needed to steer his bicycle out of the middle of the road and towards the sidewalk. The next time I drove into the cul-de-sac he rode past me again, but we kept at it. Each time I stepped out of the car and stopped him. Finally, I suspect he was so irritated at having his progress interrupted he got the message. The next time I drove towards him he pulled his bicycle over to the sidewalk, watching me all the while. I drove out of the cul-de-sac, then parked the car on a nearby street, and ran back to congratulate him for listening, for following *my* rules of the road. That's when I noticed he was exactly where I'd left him, by the sidewalk, standing beside his bicycle. His grandmother was telling him he could get on again and go. But he seemed to be waiting for an okay from me. I hugged him and told him to take off.

"One problem solved," his grandmother said.

"And another one created," I said. I repeated the experiment a few more times that afternoon and a few more afternoons after that. Each time, he pulled over as I'd taught him; each time, he got off his bike and waited for me to leave the cul-de-sac. It wasn't ideal but it was a start. Besides, I knew it was a safe bet that at some point, down the road, so to speak, the next car he would have to avoid would not be mine.

JONAH WILL BE ELEVEN in a couple of weeks. It's always around this time, around his birthday on Christmas Eve, that I find myself clinging to him being ten the way I clung to him being nine last year and on and on back to the year he was about to turn four and we first received a diagnosis of autism. It's curious how the feeling hasn't changed, how even then it seemed like we were running short on time. Age matters for Jonah in a way it doesn't for neurotypical kids. We are way beyond *What-to-Expect* milestones now; we are into a serious countdown. The clock is ticking on Jonah's potential as well as his limitations.

At our December ABA meeting The Consultant and Jessica, now his only remaining full-time therapist, brought him presents. He quickly unwrapped and mostly ignored the puzzle and the book he received and was keen, instead, to return to swinging on his exercise bar. Meanwhile, Cynthia and I held hands and waited as The Consultant prepared to read us the highlights from her end-of-first-term visit to Jonah's school. Her report was generally positive, she said by way of introduction. Jonah was doing his schoolwork with a minimum of assistance from Jessica. He listened to his teachers, often better than other kids in his class. It's all that behaviour modification kicking in, she boasted, and Jessica nervously cheered. Swinging, Jonah disappeared behind the door jamb and then reappeared. I was close enough to hear him mangling some lyrics, "'You could be better than a car. You could be living in a jar.'" Cynthia nudged me as The Consultant continued to say that while Jonah wasn't interacting much with his peers in the classroom or during recess or lunch, his behaviours, by which she meant inappropriate behaviours, had diminished, and that's what counted. That was encouraging. He was not shouting out as he'd done in the past or raising his hand when he didn't know the answer to a question or laughing for no apparent reason. All very good, she concluded. I took Cynthia's pen out of her hand and wrote her a note: "What about you know what?"

UNFORTUNATELY, NOTHING IN The Consultant's report explained why, if everything was going so well in her opinion, Jonah was waking up most weekday mornings bitterly complaining about his own behaviour. That includes this morning. Jonah is in the middle of what feels like a pre-emptive strike, anticipating a day of warding off inappropriate behaviours. When I turn on the light in his room, he piles his *Madagascar* comforter on top of his small body like his very own ash heap and burrows under it. He's not hiding from me so much, I'm guessing, as from the prospect of another trying day at school.

"I'm not great, Daddy. Not great." He says this so sincerely I can't help smiling. Jonah often sounds and looks younger than he is. (His pediatrician, who missed Jonah's autism completely, once referred to him as immature. Jonah was barely three at the time.)

"You're great, kiddo," I hear myself say and realize I could be more convincing. I need coffee. I need sleep.

"I'm bad, Daddy, what should I do?" His voice is high-pitched and babyish now, and I'm guessing it would break my heart every time if I didn't know it so well, if I wasn't so accustomed to its nuances by now. It is part heart-wrenching anxiety, part performance art.

"Speak properly, Jonah, you know how to speak properly." He is quiet for a moment, long enough for me to wonder if I did something right. Then he grimaces. The good news is he's no longer mad at himself; the bad news, he's mad at me.

Jonah still has tantrums but they're less frequent and don't last as long as they used to. And while this is something to be grateful for, it also means that when the tantrums come they're harder to predict or prepare for. It means you've allowed yourself to forget. You've allowed yourself to be lulled into a false sense of normalcy.

"I didn't do well on my French test," Jonah goes on. He is trying hard to modulate his voice, to speak properly; however, I know his statement isn't true and say so.

"Bogus, Jonesy. You made seven out of eight. Mommy saw your French teacher the other day at the parent–teacher's meeting and Madame Melanie said you were her best French speller," I remind him. He hasn't been bad either. How could he be? He isn't even out of bed yet.

This is my first task of the day: to get my complaining, occasionally inconsolable son dressed and still remain unaffected by whatever he may say or do, no matter how odd or unsettling it might be. As I've learned over the years, a great deal will depend on me—on modifying my behaviour. This can sometimes feel like I'm walking on a balance beam. Even if I don't fall, the possibility of falling is always in my mind. This is why it's essential to keep all those negative feelings— self-pity, doubt, disappointment, resentment, just the exasperation that I normally harbour on mornings like this—from showing up on my too-easy-to-read face. Likewise the tone of my voice, so often transparent to my son, has to be controlled. Keep it upbeat if possible, neutral at least. If it's not, things will get worse. If you don't believe me, we have compiled evidence, empirical evidence, as proof.

Cynthia keeps a large binder full of behaviour sheets, which we use in Jonah's ABA program to keep track of what might have set him off on a crying jag or a downward spiral of disparagement, or both, as is the case this morning. Whatever it might be, the binder has the data and the data holds the answer and the answer invariably is: we aren't reinforcing enough. Or I should say I'm not. That's why when I finally pull Jonah's comforter off him with a little too much force I know I've messed up. And when I tell him to hurry up or there won't be time for a proper breakfast, in a tone that's a little too desperate, too needy, I've really messed up.

"I'm not happy we won't have time for a *proper* breakfast. Why won't we have time for a *proper* breakfast?" Jonah says. I will have to regroup. And do another thing I didn't want to do this morning: ask Cynthia for help.

"Remember the ABCs," she says, her voice sleepy and barely audible. She's in bed and I'm standing in the doorway of our bedroom, wondering how she and I could be so different. How, for instance, she can sleep through all this. In the next room Jonah is whining and slamming his door repeatedly. If I didn't know what was worrying him before, I can make an educated guess now. He is going to be too late to have breakfast, or, more to the point, he thinks he is. This is the worry I planted in his head. This is plainly on me. The only good news is that Cynthia was sound asleep when I managed to make things worse. It's a mistake I won't have to own up to, not right now anyway.

One of the early deals Cynthia and I struck in raising Jonah is that I do most morning duties and she does most everything else. She'll deny this. She's always telling me I take on too much as it is. But behavioural psychology, which is at the core of Jonah's ABA therapy, has a way of infecting a whole family. Having learned to use positive reinforcement on my son, I also have my suspicions about when it's being used on me. "We're in this together, remember that," Cynthia mumbles as she attempts to fall back to sleep.

In more than a decade of marriage, I've come to a conclusion: All marriages are mixed in the end. It's not just that you're a morning person and she's not or she's a vegetarian and you're not, it's that every-thing is contested. These days, everyone calls their spouse their partner, but I don't get that. In its constant push and pull, its ongoing tally of ups and downs, marriage is more competition than joint venture. This realization becomes unavoidable when you add a special-needs child to the mix. You're constantly keeping score. Who slept in? Who lost their temper? Who capitulated and asked for help? *There's nothing wrong with asking for help, sweetheart.* Who just can't take it any more? Who needs a break? Well, take a guess.

"WE LIVE BY ONE ANOTHER'S variable weather," Peter De Vries says in *The Blood of the Lamb*, and he's turned out to be right when it comes to Cynthia and me. I want her to feel what I'm feeling. Hopeless. I am slouched in the doorway, waiting as she sits up in bed and reaches for her glasses. She does it calmly. Calmly, too, she takes note of my poor posture and offers advice. "Listen, get a behaviour sheet from my office and take the data. It is going to help, really. Do the ABCs."

"Fuck the ABCs and fuck the data," I say under my breath as I walk away, which is, incidentally, the way I say most things these days: to myself, and in a position of retreat. Someone once said that a woman only falls in love with a man when she has a higher opinion of him than he deserves and I'm starting to wonder if this fact has, of late, occurred to my wife. Or if it's occurring to her now as I have to wake her up again to ask where the damn binder with the damn behaviour sheets is hiding.

ABC, I should explain, stands for "antecedent, behaviour, consequence," and it is one of the guiding principles in ABA therapy. The theory is if you know what caused your child's behaviour then you can understand what the behaviour is and you can figure out what the most suitable consequence would be. For example, if he's seeking attention, you ignore the behaviour, though not the child. If he's avoiding a task, then you make sure he completes it. We were taught this when we hired The Consultant seven years ago now. Everything Jonah does, she told us, can be analyzed if we rigorously, consistently record the ABCs. The implication has been clear from the beginning—our son is not a mystery, he is a puzzle. I'm not convinced. In his essay "Open Secrets," *New Yorker* writer Malcolm Gladwell argues for the essential distinction between the two. With a puzzle, if you uncover the crucial missing piece of information then the problem is solved. But with a mystery, there is no missing piece. In fact, the more things you learn about a mystery, according to Gladwell, the more unsolvable it's likely to become.

"The binder is not in the office. Do you want to tell me why we can never find anything around here?"

"Not right now, I don't. Look in the therapy room then."

Lately, I've watched Jonah get into shouting matches with inanimate objects and it's strangely encouraging. After all, it is a kind of conversation. It is also funny. If he's having trouble hanging up his jacket, for example, he will tell off the recalcitrant garment, give it a final warning. "You better stay on the hanger." Sometimes he'll shake his fist at it: like John Cleese, at the end of his rope, in *Fawlty Towers*. When I find the binder, I also plan to give it a piece of my mind: *You bastard, how dare you disappear when I need you? How dare you make an idiot of me? I can do that myself.*

"Where exactly in the therapy room am I supposed to look?"

"I don't know … wherever." We are weary people. Fatigue is our default position. It could, if we wanted, explain everything. But to Cynthia's credit, she doesn't take the easy way out. I could hardly blame her now if she pulled the covers over her head, if she threw a pillow at me, if she screamed, but she doesn't. "Sweetheart," she says with a forced patience and a tone I recognize. I know what's coming: *the pep talk.* "You can do this. You can. And once you write things down you can start to, you know, properly analyze the problem." The truth is I don't need behaviour sheets or a binder to be B.F. Skinner or Ivan Pavlov, to know that the problem with Jonah this morning—the antecedent—could be anything. It's like proofreading a manuscript— you go over it again and again and somehow you still know there's something you missed. Jonah might have woken up with a stomach ache; he might have had a bad dream. Then again, this morning's tantrum might be attributable to something that happened at school yesterday or last week or last year. Or it might be everything. It might all be accumulating, all the hours at school and hours of therapy, all our badgering and desperation. With the positive reports we have received from The Consultant and from Jonah's teachers, we forget sometimes the toll, the incalculable toll, that behaving appropriately takes on him and us.

WHEN HE WAS LEARNING to speak Jonah routinely confused his pronouns, saying "you" when he meant "I." At first, we thought this was cute. Later, we learned there was a term for this—"pronominal reversal"—and that it's common among children with autism. It's sort of like neurological crossed wires; it causes children on the spectrum to echo what is being said. But I'm not sure crossed wires are all that's going on. If there's no distinction for Jonah between "you" and "I," then there's no distinction either between everything being done by him and everything being done to him. In the last few years we've taught him his pronouns the way we've taught him everything else, methodically, step by step, according to the ABA rule book. But he still slips up sometimes, particularly when he's upset or anxious or just inattentive. In his vulnerable, open heart and his curious, exceptional brain, Jonah still can't help thinking the world is against him. And, for this reason, he so often seems at its mercy.

Autism can be defined by the ways in which a child separates himself from everyday interactions. But there are ways in which Jonah can never be separate enough. I'm guessing that's why he will sometimes become angry at me when I get a song lyric wrong or accidentally mispronounce a word. It's as if "he" was "you"—as if both he and you were the ones making the mistake. Lately, he's also become obsessed with the weather. If he looks out the window in the morning and spots so much as a dark cloud he will run to the TV and turn on the weather channel. If it does happen to rain, he will become angry, personally offended. "I'm going to be mad in my room until it stops raining," I heard him say the other day. He was sitting on the floor, his knees up, his hands balled into fists and covering his ears. He is practising a kind of reverse magical thinking and he won't be talked out of it. Still, I wish I could convince him sometimes to take credit for a sunny day. But my son is, autism notwithstanding, a natural-born pessimist. When he launches into these elaborate complaints there's often no way for Cynthia or me to respond without laughing and without realizing, at the same time, that while this is undeniably funny, it's not funny for him. If you are convinced the world revolves around you, that means any time anything goes wrong in that world it's logical to assume that it is somehow your fault.

In an essay in *Harper's* entitled "On Spectrum," Sallie Tisdale, the mother of a twenty-six-year-old woman with autism, writes about how hard it can be to distinguish between behaviour that is autistic and behaviour that is simply quirky. Researchers, Tisdale adds, are starting to speculate that the so-called spectrum is, indeed, all-inclusive—a kind of sliding scale of normal. If her point is that we are all a little autistic, I can vouch for that. I'm reminded daily of the ways in which Jonah is like me or, perhaps, I'm like him. We are both victims of subjectivity. Thinking everything is your fault can be described as a spectrum disorder, but you could also call it vanity, self-absorption, creative non-fiction, first-person narrative.

The ABA binder, incidentally, is where Cynthia said it was—in Jonah's therapy room. Which is why, just for the hell of it, I decide that this morning, this difficult though hardly unusual morning, to stick with the program, to give neutrality, consistency, careful analysis, a fair chance.

Jonah is dressed and having his Cheerios but still carrying on a spirited debate with himself when I take out a behaviour sheet, sit down next to him at the kitchen table, and fill in the box provided for the date, time, and my initials. Someone has to be accountable; another way of saying someone has to be blamed, if you ask me. Still, I squeeze my notes into the three other boxes on the sheet. These are for describing what happened immediately before this morning's behaviour (antecedent: he woke up), what he did and how often (behaviour: he complained and stimmed, verbal stims mostly, saying the same things, asking the same questions over and over), and what happened immediately after the behaviour (the consequence or how I reacted? N/A for not applicable. We're not there yet). The problem with these little boxes, of course, is that they are such little boxes.

All the years I've spent as a book reviewer have made me fond of the voice on the page, the intimacy of a conversation between writer and reader. Forget what they say in creative writing classes about showing not telling. I want to be told. I want a lecture. Go ahead, feel free, talk my ear off. Give me a glimpse inside your head, your world, and don't think for a second that I care how unpleasant, how petty it looks. That's what I want. In *Out of Sheer Rage*, Geoff Dyer, a British travel writer and novelist, rants about everything, from the sinister influence of IKEA in his life to his unwillingness to start the biography of D.H. Lawrence he is supposed to be writing and the rest of us are supposed to be reading. Incidentally, if he needs an alternate title, I have one for him: *Let's Talk About Procrastination*. Dyer's inner life is an open book. That includes his internal meltdown when he learns that the luxury doughnut he desires from his local deli is unavailable. He imagines explaining his terrible state and the reason for it to the deli staff:

> What you have to understand is that I am allergic to disappointment. I have had so much disappointment in my life that the tiniest amount of it is now enough to drive me to despair. I am so brimful of disappointment that even one more tiny drop will send me spilling over the edge.

I suppose I am drawn to writers who feel the need to write a theme into a corner in order to understand it. Writers who appear to have no clue what they are going to say, let alone do next. I believe in variables, and complications, the absolutely reliable fallibility of human behaviour. That is what literature provides and what behavioural science won't, can't. If a character in a novel or a memoir does A, then proceeds logically to B, then on to C, he can be dismissed, in literary terms, as not credible or, worse still, dull. So, even as I'm filling in these little boxes, I want to believe neither my son nor I can be so easily reduced to data, to ABCs.

By now, Jonah is so angry at himself he occasionally hits himself in the head. Usually, it's a tap but sometimes it's more like a clunk— the sound dismaying, even to him. He looks at his hand like it's someone else's, like it had no right to do that. Unfortunately, I can't witness this with anything resembling neutrality or objectivity. He sees the disapproval on my face and probably sees more—despair, worry, disappointment. By the time he's down to his last spoonful of Cheerios, he might as well be reading my mind: *Jonah, eat properly. Jonah, sit properly. Jonah, behave properly.*

In addition, he's spilled some milk on the kitchen table and the floor, and that's given him some new mishap to focus on, to blame himself for. He's riffing on his failings now with an impressive dexterity, like a jazz musician improvising on a standard—John Coltrane doing "My Favourite Things."

"Of course, my very angry father will be mad at me because I didn't do well. I spilled my milk," Jonah says, his voice relentlessly sing-songy now. He appears to be interrogating himself. "I am not excellent, not an excellent boy. I have a problem. How do you solve your problem? By being excellent and Jonah is not excellent."

This is untrue, too. He is often excellent. But to explain what I mean by this I'd have to resort to even more exposition. I'd have to explain, in particular, everything he's up against: how autism affects his brain; how it makes it so much harder for him to learn, to play, to make friends, to just have a simple conversation, and how, despite this, he goes to a regular school with regular kids; how good he is at speaking French to his grandfather and spelling words like *hippopotamus* or *irrelevant;* how, despite the stereotypical view of autism, he is, much of the time, a charmer. I'd have to explain, in other words, things for which there are not enough little boxes, things I don't really understand myself, even after all this time. I'd have to explain how he is constantly one thing *and* another.

By the time we arrive at school, Jonah has calmed himself down.

It's as if nothing ever happened. The key to dealing with Jonah, The Consultant has told us, is to let things go. Don't dwell on the difficulties of the past hour or two or, for that matter, the past day or week or month or year. Look, instead, for some way to be reinforcing, positive, in the moment. The key for me, in other words, is to be a completely different person than I am. Just before the school bell rings, I hug Jonah and straighten his backpack. Then he tells me his old joke about the elkaholic and I pretend I've never heard it before. Perseveration or the endless repetition of a word or phrase is common in autism. Think of it as perseverance, only run amok. Sometimes, when I am trying hard to be analytical, I think Jonah's fondness for a running gag goes back to those final trimester lectures of mine: the knock-knock jokes and Abbott and Costello routines I shared with Cynthia's belly. Of course, there it is: your antecedent. I point to some of Jonah's classmates in the schoolyard and encourage him to go up to them and tell them this joke I know too well. "Just say it once, though, Jonah, just once," I advise him. Then I put my arm over his shoulder and half-hug him. A different ten-and-nine-tenths-year-old would resist. He would find this unnecessary show of affection embarrassing. But Jonah puts up with it. He puts up with my apology for this morning, too, for my part in making things worse before they got a little better. He looks at me as if to say we're even. We both drive each other crazy. I'm about to tell him how much I love him, about to take a stab at it anyway, when he interrupts.

"Daddy," he says and I wait for the setup yet again. *What do you call an animal with antlers* ... But instead he says, "I don't like that word."

"What word, Jonah?"

"Properly." His criticism is a welcome surprise. When it comes to telling me off, he's long overdue. After all, he's heard it—that word—far too many times, especially from me.

"All right, Jonesy, from now on, I'll say something else. After school, we can think of other words I can say instead, okay?"

"We'll do it ... nicely," he says. I watch him until he disappears into a crowd of kids, all around his age and size, all looking, in their bulky winter coats and hats, vaguely similar.

SEVEN

Mr. Potato Head

Every second Friday our ABA team meetings are held in what used to be our dining room. Now, there's just us—Cynthia, Jonah, and me—as well as The Consultant and Jessica sitting in a semi-circle, discussing what we will be focusing on in the next couple of weeks. But in the past, with as many as four therapists doing three-hour shifts seven days a week, the room could get crowded.

Once Jonah was diagnosed and his therapy was about to begin, Cynthia and I returned the dining room table and chairs we'd bought with money from our wedding reception. We replaced the set with a room full of functional white plastic furniture. All that remains of our former dining room in its brief, wannabe grownup glory is an ornate chandelier we also received as a wedding gift. The chandelier no longer suits the room or its reappointed purpose; instead it serves a new purpose as a reminder of a time when we thought we had real problems. Like what we were going to do with a chandelier. We also filled our reconfigured dining room with IKEA bookshelves and stocked them with empty binders, now with years of data, as well as a serious and seriously expensive collection of new educational toys and games. The special-needs market is a seller's market. They see you coming, as my father would have put it. There is no better motivation to spend money than hopeless desperation. In the beginning, throwing money at the problem, even money we didn't have, felt good; it felt like we were doing something. We bought everything The Consultant recommended, anything she even mentioned in passing.

One of the first deficits noticeable in a child with autism is an inability to play appropriately, which is to say the way neurotypical children play. In addition to parallel play, repetitive play is an early indication of a problem. Jonah's response to a package of animal figurines or toy soldiers or a set of blocks we bought for him was always the same—he lined them up. He was, at this activity, impressively focused. So much as nudge a piece out of line a half an inch and he'd spot it, even if you distracted him and did it when he wasn't looking. That half-inch was enough to induce him to line up his animal figurines all over again. He did this without complaint or resentment. It was his job, that's all, a job I obviously couldn't understand.

Before we knew Jonah's diagnosis, his preference for order over imaginative play appeared to be just that, a preference, albeit an unusual one. It was as if all that information on ordinary early childhood development you find in the *What to Expect* books were beneath him somehow; as if he, a self-assured toddler, had better things to do with his time than to bother making things up. "A chip off the old block," I joked to Cynthia. "Real life is strange enough for him." *I'll explain it to him one day*, I thought—the quote from Philip Roth that's always pinned to the bulletin board in my office, part credo, part admonition: "If only I could invent as presumptuously as life."

However, after Jonah's diagnosis, I realized that a genetic predilection for memoir was not the issue. Jonah didn't know how to play. Yes, we had to teach him that, too. It was one of the many moments at the beginning of all this when a new or at least renewed understanding of exactly what I was dealing with hit me so hard it left me winded, practically gasping for air.

Turn-taking games, for instance, are crucial in a child's development and are learned by imitation and instinct. We couldn't rely on either. Instead, we had to show Jonah what he had to do step by step and then show him again. Everything we did we did in increments; likewise, every success was measured in components so small sometimes you couldn't help wondering if this really could be called success. Still, we experimented, then waited to see if the new information would stick: "Now it's your move, Jonah; now it's Mommy's." We watched to see if he took his turn and then waited his turn. First, we'd use a physical and verbal prompt together; then a physical prompt; then fade the prompt; then there's no prompt at all; then in another game or circumstance we'd see if he'd generalized that tiny but essential bit of information. Everything had to be broken down—jigsaw puzzles, Legos, Hot Wheels, board games—hand over hand, step by step. It would take days to finish a game of Candyland. Nothing could be taken for granted; everything had to be reviewed. Later on, his therapy sessions included a script for him so he could play cops and robbers or doctor and patient. He memorized his part quickly, but never altered his lines, as he was eventually expected to, as a neurotypical child soon would. When this issue came up at one of our Friday meetings, I could see a shadow of concern cross The Consultant's characteristically confident face.

But the simplest tasks, even broken down, sometimes proved impossible. In early books on autism, like Clara Claiborne Park's *The Siege* and Barry Neil Kaufmann's *Son-Rise*, the extraordinary patience required to instruct a child with autism in even the simplest task is described in painstaking detail. It can make for dreary or, if you find yourself in a similar situation, terrifying reading. Park even warns her readers about what they're in for. Her account of teaching her daughter Elly to speak is accurately titled: "Towards Speech: A Long, Slow Chapter." It's as if she's saying, "You might want to skip this one."

Jonah revealed himself early on to be an impressively stubborn child. The Battle of Mr. Potato Head, as we eventually dubbed it, became the first major struggle Jonah's therapists would lose to him.

They tried for weeks, months in the end, to get him to put Mr. Potato Head's body parts in the appropriate slots, but Jonah steadfastly refused. "As if" is the way Park describes her daughter Elly's behaviour in *The Siege*—"as if she could but wouldn't." "As if" she had her reasons for deciding not to learn, not to connect. In Jonah's case, it was "as if" there were some as yet unannounced principle behind his obstinacy, "as if" he fancied himself a kind of abstract sculptor following his own aesthetic credo. "Every child is an artist," Pablo Picasso said. "The problem is how to remain an artist once we grow up." No problem, Pablo. Jonah happily put the nose where Mr. Potato Head's mouth should be. He jammed the bright red lips over the eye holes like a unibrow. His matter-of-fact resistance was met with a disproportionate urgency by his therapists. They ramped up their efforts "as if" they were invested in making sure the toy tuber looked the way it was supposed to. And when their efforts failed repeatedly the feeling of disappointment shared by everyone involved, except Jonah, seemed palpable and out of all proportion. "We'll have to shelve it for a while," The Consultant finally concluded, stolidly giving us the bad news at the end of a meeting. Cynthia was depressed for days, while all I could think was: *Mr. Potato Head?*

If those early setbacks began to feel ominous, the good news was that there wasn't a lot of time to dwell on them. New toys replaced old or rejected ones; old and rejected toys were eventually stored in the basement next to the office where I work. Back then, our weekends were given over to garage sales. We'd be up early to cruise the neighbourhood, searching for the perfect deal on the perfect toy. Usually, I'd wait in the car with Jonah. I quickly had my limit of rummaging through other people's junk. I'd get in the backseat with him and we'd belt out "That's Life" along with Frank Sinatra. We learned the P-part together—the paupers and pirates and poets. Not to mention those appealing opposites: riding high one month, shot down the next. Meanwhile, Cynthia pursued her own obsession. "I'm going a little crazy," she'd confess once the weekend was over. "It's just that you have a child and he can't play and you think there's something, some toy or game or book that will make a difference. So you buy everything. You fill up the attic, the closets, the basement."

I still pass the remnants of our consumer craziness every morning on my way to my computer and my manuscript, so-called, where I spend my time, weeks, months, years now, moving fragments around, trying to fit the right words into the right slots. My own Mr. Potato Head. We don't go to garage sales much any more, but the pile of ineffectual, discarded stuff still seems to grow higher and more chaotic each day. As if it's reproducing. The pile overshadows what now seems like the mere handful of things we bought for Jonah before we knew his diagnosis. It's hard to remember now that there was a time before outsiders took over the job of telling us what toys our child should be playing with. I can still spot my purchases, though—my little corner of clichéd expectations. So predictable: a tiny, plastic Montreal Expos baseball glove—the city still had a team then and I still daydreamed a few years ahead to taking Jonah to a pennant-clinching game—a foam basketball; a poster of the Marx Brothers; an illustrated, abridged version of *The Three Musketeers* I bought months before Jonah was born. There's the honking red clown nose I bought at a dollar store across the street from the hospital the day after Jonah was born. "In case he's colicky. You know to cheer him up," I explained to an indifferent clerk. Every now and then the pile of junk—that's what all of it is now, junk—shifts and Mr. Potato Head rears his asymmetrical plastic dome. His ears are where his eyes should be, but they seem to be judging me nonetheless.

We are less wistful about our old dining room. If we had some plan to have impromptu, banter-filled dinner parties every weekend, the casual kind they always seemed to be having on *thirtysomething*, for instance, it was never a real plan. We have gone to dinner parties where our hosts have the menu for the evening printed on a tiny chalkboard. We've sat down to a real dining room table set with real dishes and an array of forks, with cloth napkins and crystal ware. *How ridiculous*, I remember thinking, *how wonderful!*

The fact is we became, after Jonah was born, isolated and self-sufficient. We were a content, busy little island. Permanent population: three. We all got used to each other fast and, at the same time, kept surprising each other. Cynthia and I hadn't been together very long after all, and that made it easy to let go of our short-lived coupledom and carry on living our lives as a trio. *The Three Musketeers*: one for all and all for one. Jonah didn't change our family dynamic; he provided our family with its dynamic. The situation suited us fine for long stretches. My sisters were in and out, videotaping, bringing new clothes. Cynthia's parents also visited regularly. Other relatives and friends would show up now and then. Otherwise, they waited for an invitation that we simply forgot to extend. Whenever the phone or doorbell rang we jumped like we'd received a small shock. My initial reaction to visitors, however welcome or needed, never changed. *What do they want now?*

This may explain why I still can't get used to our regular Friday meetings, not even after all this time. The meetings can be hard on everyone—on our consultant, who feels pressured to show that, even in the last two weeks, there has been some small but identifiable progress; on the team of therapists, who are likely to be criticized if things aren't going well; on Cynthia and me, who can't win either way. We are not usually criticized directly by the team or directly critical of it, but we are keenly aware of how most meetings will encompass both possibilities, switching, without much warning, from our feeling blamed to our feeling like blaming someone else. We are always aware that while we are an essential part of the team, we are apart from it, too.

The meetings are also hard on Jonah. He doesn't deal well with the expectations of others, no matter how modest those expectations might be. Often, it's my job to distract him at those times during a meeting when it might be better if he didn't hear what's being said about him. Mostly, though, he needs to be around, so the therapists can practise new programs and strategies on him and so The Consultant can observe and take notes. Of course, hypersensitivity is a characteristic of autism, but—who am I kidding?—it's also a family trait. What, then, is the determining factor in Jonah's personality? Would he be hypersensitive even if he didn't have autism?

This is one of the controversies stirring around autism now, one of the debates you'll find addressed in websites like Neurodiversity.com or "Demystifying Autism from the Inside Out" at williamstillman.com. William Stillman is the quintessential insider. His website identifies him as "The Autism Whisperer." He has Asperger's syndrome himself and advocates for others on the spectrum. He's a fierce opponent of treatments like ABA and encourages parents to accept their children for who they are. His books—like *The Soul of Autism, The Autism Prophecies,* and *Autism and the God Connection*—go way beyond acceptance as a matter of fact. They identify autism as a kind of supernatural gift. Stillman believes autism can imbue in people psychic and spiritual powers. "What if it has a purpose?" he asks. "What if there is a plan?"

These are not questions I've ever asked myself. Still, I wonder sometimes, as most parents of a child with autism do, what is the dividing line between an autistic personality and simply personality? Autism, like so many other things these days, has become politicized, an issue of equal rights and advocacy for some, including some very high-functioning and highly motivated adults on the spectrum. More and more, these are individuals who, as they grow older, refuse to be defined by their disorder or even view autism as a disorder or disability at all. For them, it's hardly more than a difference, a variation on our infinitely various human nature. No different from skin colour, say, or sexual orientation. They also insist that if a vaccine were created or a magic pill introduced that would cure autism and make them neurotypical overnight, they would not take it. They wouldn't even consider it. Take away their autism and you take away a fundamental part of who they are and what they have achieved. Not to mention what they might one day be capable of achieving.

TIM PAGE, A Pulitzer Prize–winning music critic for the *Washington Post*, was diagnosed with Asperger's syndrome as an adult. He wrote about this discovery in *The New Yorker* and then later in his memoir, *Parallel Play: Growing Up with Undiagnosed Asperger's*. His discovery that he was on the autism spectrum, even the highest-functioning end of it, helped him to identify what he calls "my lifelong unease." What also became clear to him was that much of his success as a music critic happened "not despite but because of Asperger's." He seems both unable and unwilling to separate the disadvantages from the advantages of autism. Being on the spectrum meant a lonely childhood as well as a lifelong capacity to see the world around him from a unique and uniquely insightful perspective. This proved to be a useful skill set for a critic and a journalist.

Then there's the increasingly celebrated case of Temple Grandin. Grandin has a Ph.D. in animal science and teaches at the University of Colorado. Her ideas and inventions, dedicated to improving the lives and particularly the deaths of livestock, are used in more than half the animal-handling facilities in North America. She acts as a consultant to multinational corporations like McDonald's and Burger King. She also has autism; in fact, she is arguably the most famous autistic individual in the world, perhaps even more so than Dustin Hoffman's fictional character, Raymond Babbitt, in *Rain Man*. Oliver Sacks brought her story to public attention in his 1996 bestseller *Anthropologist on Mars: Seven Paradoxical Tales*. (The title paradoxical tale is about Grandin, a reference to the way she defines herself and her interaction with the rest of the neurotypical planet.) In recent years, she has lectured widely about autism. She's also written about the subject, most notably in her memoirs *Emergence: Labeled Autistic* (co-written with Margaret M. Scariano) and *Thinking in Pictures: And Other Reports from My Life with Autism*. Both books were the basis of a 2010 Emmy Award–winning HBO movie with Clare Danes playing the part of Grandin.

Neurodiversity is a new term that further stretches the already elastic nature of the autism spectrum. It is a kinder, less stigmatizing label. Simon Baron-Cohen, the British psychologist and autism expert, has gone so far as to say that in the future "it is going to be increasingly controversial whether autism is something that needs to be cured or not. Perhaps it is more a personality type."

It helps, too, when there are talented writers around like Page, Grandin, and Kamran Nazeer to tell their stories from the inside out. Though, in some ways, their ability to articulate their experience alters it to the point where it is no longer purely autistic. At the end of *Send in the Idiots*, Nazeer gives some credence to the neurodiversity argument, but he concludes that while there may be something distinctive about the autistic mind, even advantages to it, "at least some of that autism has to be removed, or eased, before autistic people can communicate meaningfully, even with one another, and set their minds upon the world."

Grandin no longer thinks of herself as autistic in the classic sense. But she recognizes she's not indistinguishable either. She figures if she were evaluated today the diagnosis would likely be Asperger's. In her books, Grandin is straightforward, almost matter-of-fact about her disorder—about the deficits she has because of it and also some obvious advantages it has afforded her. (The advantages, not surprisingly, are emphasized in the HBO movie.) Like most people with autism, Grandin is a visual thinker; in her case, this has made her an expert at empathizing with animals. "If I could snap my fingers and be nonautistic, I would not," Grandin told Sacks. "Autism is part of what I am."

Neurodiversity has its selling points for parents, too. It can be a convenient way to dodge the big question, the one that will invariably come up for every parent of a child with special needs or, for that matter, special problems. Would I take away the autism now, knowing what I do about my child, knowing him or her the way I do? Would I flick a switch and have it vanish, understanding that this would fundamentally change my child's personality, change who he or she is? I can't deny it would in Jonah's case. How could it not change the funny, unusual, mostly happy boy I love so deeply and am so deeply frustrated by? So, would I do it? Perhaps the more significant question is: do I have to think about whether I would? No. If it were up to me, I'd do it in a heartbeat, one guilty heartbeat.

"HE'S SO CUTE," The Consultant says during every Friday meeting. In fact, she says it so often it begins to sound like *her* verbal stim. She hasn't always been an easy person to work with or to have as such an important part of our lives. This has been especially true for Cynthia: the two are always butting heads. I'm convinced now, after seven years, that's the way The Consultant wants it. Parents are an occupational hazard in ABA therapy, just one more variable that has to be managed, manipulated, modified. They are too emotionally involved and, as a consequence, prone to inconsistency. As an added consequence, they can't always be expected to know what's best for their child. No one ever comes out and says this of course; it only feels as if they have. But if our relationship with The Consultant has had its inevitable ups and downs, her dedication to Jonah is genuine. It's true, too, that he listens to her and behaves well for her in ways he seldom does for us. There's a reason for this—she's unflappable. She has no buttons to push. Whereas I sometimes think I am nothing but buttons: big flashing, beeping, unconcealed buttons. The Consultant's ability to keep Jonah in line is another source of frustration for Cynthia and me. *Why can't we do what she's doing?*

"Just be his parents, just act like his parents," she told us at a meeting a few years into Jonah's ABA therapy. It was delivered like a pronouncement. It was received like a head-smacking revelation. *Why didn't we think of that?* By then, though, it was no longer so simple. By then, we had spent too much time studying him, analyzing him.

Besides, he *is* cute. Still, there are times when The Consultant's impulsive, almost compulsive comment about Jonah's appearance can't help sounding like a euphemism. Like a default position. As if, after all this time and all this therapy, that has remained the best thing she can say about him.

"He's so interesting. Don't you find him interesting?" she asked Cynthia in the course of one particularly stressful meeting about two years into ABA therapy. When Cynthia didn't answer, she repeated the question. Then she turned to me. I didn't answer either. Instead, I bit my lip so hard I could taste a tiny drop of blood. This new question came at a time when Jonah's therapy was going poorly for reasons no one could seem to figure out. The Consultant was insisting there was an antecedent for his behaviour; according to her there always was. So, yes, in that regard, the mystery of his misbehaviour was interesting. However, the misbehaviour itself was driving us crazy. Jonah had stopped complying with the simplest requests. He wasn't doing well in his sessions with his therapists. It felt as if we were starting over again. As if we were back in those early days, when his sessions were torture for everyone involved.

There were times when he would cry through the entire three hours of therapy. Times when his protests would become so vehement, so painful to hear, Cynthia and I retreated to our bedroom, closed the door, and put pillows over our heads to shut out what was being inflicted on our son, what we were, by proxy, inflicting on him. Often, I had to physically restrain Cynthia from leaving the room and putting a stop to what was going on at the other end of our house. Often, she did the same for me.

Things weren't much better in daily life. Tantrums had become routine—for Jonah and me. He'd cry and rage and I'd explode. I can't count the number of times I was exiled to the basement. "If you have to brood, brood there," Cynthia would say. During one particularly bad patch, I stayed with my sister for three weeks. I'd come down with a flu, which persisted and developed into pneumonia. Cynthia was at the end of her rope. "I can't take care of both of you," she said. I know there were people close to us who couldn't understand what was going on. I couldn't either. That's what I said anyway whenever my sisters or a friend tiptoed around the question of whether this was some kind of trial separation. But I knew why I had to leave. It's because the worse Jonah behaved the worse I behaved. Or perhaps, it was the other way around. There was no way of telling. It was entirely possible that I was the antecedent. I talked to Cynthia on the telephone every night, and our conversations became increasingly strained. Things were fine, she'd say, a hard response to interpret. Did that mean she was managing? Or that she was managing better? Once I was feeling better, I visited Jonah a few evenings a week, which provided a glimpse of what it might be like to be a part-time father, to be one of those men who leave. It had never occurred to me before that I could do that. Simply go. I could dispense with responsibility, obligation, loyalty, the way you dispense with old clothes that don't suit you any more. I could be one of those guys—a selfish jerk, an oblivious asshole.

There was something to be said for being an asshole, for leaving. I learned that while I was away. It required a kind of boldness I began to believe I might be capable of. A person could get used to the anxiety of coming and the relief of going, even used to the guilt attached to both. A person could pretend he was free to meet other people, to start over. A person could see how that might be feasible, might even make him happy again.

Anyway, it was during this period that The Consultant began to mention the possibility that Jonah might be shutting down. This is a persistent worry in ABA therapy: that a child will regress, find his treatment program aversive, and lose all the skills he has been so painstakingly taught. It's not always clear why this happens. Often, it can be as simple as thinking a child is capable of doing something he's not capable of. This explains the decision to shelve Mr. Potato Head. The consequences of a simple mistake or miscalculation can be devastating. It can mean starting all over again, returning to a time when Jonah had to practically be dragged, kicking and screaming, to his table for a session. Compliance is an essential starting point in ABA therapy, and when he first began ABA, Jonah had learned it slowly and also grudgingly. Still, once it was mastered I assumed it was mastered. Didn't Pavlov's dog respond to the ringing bell forever after? Wasn't that the whole point of behaviour modification? That the new behaviour, once established, stuck? Money in the bank: bell, salivate, bell, salivate. Except Jonah was taking a stand; he was no longer doing what the science, the data, expected of him.

There were reasons for this—extinction burst was one. We heard the term used often as a way to explain why Jonah sometimes seemed to be regressing when, in fact, he was not. It was just a jargony way of saying things were likely to get worse before they got better. This time, though, they just got worse. Jonah's tantrums became more frequent, more intense. That's what The Consultant found interesting enough to comment on repeatedly that day at the meeting—our son's unexpected, unexplained turnabout, our son as the exception to the ABA rule. Clearly, this was a turn of events she could learn from, if not for Jonah's sake, then for the sake of future clients. This is, clearly, the advantage of being the person who is running the lab experiment as opposed to the people being run through it.

During the remainder of the three-hour meeting, The Consultant returned frequently to some variation of the isn't-he-interesting question. For this meeting, anyway, it had replaced her usual running commentary on Jonah's cuteness. I even began to develop a conditioned response to when she was going to ask it. After an outburst by Jonah, followed by a particularly uncomfortable silence in the room, I'd flinch and then there it would be—that question. Cynthia sensed when it was coming too because she got up and left the room just in time and did so more than once. The entire session was beginning to feel like a kind of enhanced interrogation, as though we, Jonah, Cynthia, and I, were being pressed to divulge some secret. The assumption was we knew more than we were letting on. We were like spies: we knew the antecedent, but we'd trained ourselves not to reveal it. The Consultant assumed that something must have happened or changed at home, some inconsistency, some slip-up that had set all this off, that served as the missing piece in the puzzle. The other therapists squirmed on our behalf and tried, without success, to change the subject. Meanwhile, Jonah became less compliant, even aggressive. He bit his arm and then tried, half-heartedly, to bite one of his therapists. We'd never seen that combination of behaviour before. He was not an aggressive child. The level and frequency of his stimming, particularly his verbal stimming, escalated, too. He babbled non-stop and incoherently.

I did my best to convey a look to The Consultant that would indicate we'd had enough, all of us. And that if she really wanted to see an extinction burst, I was about to give her one to remember. How about the flame-thrower scene? Like Pacino, like Jonah, I had had my limit; I was regressing too. I'd have to be retrained. But, to her credit, The Consultant was not concerned with me. *I would have to say something*, I thought, *but what?* All I could think of was a simple unmistakable request for her to shut up. *Shut the fuck up.*

It also occurred to me, at one point, that maybe this torture wasn't deliberate on her part. Maybe, she wasn't trying to put us on the spot. It might have just been a habit she'd fallen into, her own kind of perseveration, a sort of nervous tic. She also didn't have children herself so maybe she was curious. She wanted to know what we thought of him as his parents. Maybe she just wanted a simple ABC answer to a complicated question. I realized awfully late that I could, in fact, give her one. I could let her know that her question—*Isn't he interesting?*—wasn't rhetorical after all.

"No," I finally said, "we don't find our son interesting."

JONAH STARTS EACH DAY in the schoolyard alone. I try to stay focused on him until the morning bell rings, but I usually find my attention divided. I find myself observing other kids, instead—kids who should be his friends. I watch as they shout and bounce off each other. I'm like an anthropologist, making assumptions, drawing conclusions, which I hope I can then apply to my main subject, my son. How, for instance, do creatures typically survive in this environment? By forming cliques and coteries is the conclusion I've come to. Boys push and punch one another. Girls tease each other and giggle at the boys. Some boys chase some girls; some girls allow themselves to be caught. Some girls do the chasing. Others look on and gossip. The noise, incidentally, is as loud as jungle chatter, punctuated by high-pitched squeals and stunningly elaborate curses. Incidentally, Jonah said *it* the other day; he said the word "fuck," and started laughing. It was oddly reassuring to know he'd learned the word the same way everyone does—in the schoolyard, though not only the schoolyard.

Once he's out of school for the day, it's like he was never there. He only talks about it when he's pressed and only then to volunteer the minimum amount of information. "I did math," he will say. Or "I worked hard." Occasionally, he will reveal that some other kid was punished for pulling a classmate's hair or saying a bad word. He finds the misconduct of others endlessly fascinating. The important, real details about Jonah's day—how *he* behaved, how *he* coped—we invariably learn from Jessica. She writes long, detailed reports about what happened in all that time that Jonah has been out of my sight and sometimes, I confess, out of my thoughts. I can usually tell how things went by Jessica's body language or tone of voice. A slight shrug and a feeble "pretty good" delivered like a plea, a plea to leave it at that, for instance, means there isn't much that's encouraging to report. An unequivocal, enthusiastic "great" means he managed to master some small thing; he raised his hand, asked a peer for help.

Occasionally, we'll hear from one of Jonah's teachers. Their casual remarks are generally upbeat as are their report cards, but then they don't have the same level of expectations for our son that we have. The fact is: they have few expectations. He is coded, as far as they are concerned: ASD, on the spectrum. The word autism isn't used much. He tries very hard, his teachers usually tell us. Compared with other kids, he is a treat to have in class, mostly well-behaved, mostly happy. Sweet is the word we keep hearing. On the days I pick him up, I like to tell myself his solitariness, his strangeness are visible only to me. If I'm standing next to another parent, I will glance over at them to see if they are paying attention to Jonah. Usually, they aren't. Mostly, I leave it at a glance. If I'm not exactly rude, I'm in the vicinity. Mostly, I'm trying to avoid eye contact; in particular, that "So which one is yours?" look I used to relish before all this, when boasting about my son was second nature.

According to the information we gather from Jessica and Jonah's teachers, Jonah is well liked. It just takes too much effort, too much attention, too much empathy for the other kids to befriend him. So far, though, they have been remarkably kind to him, even protective. Still, I routinely see other kids walk away from what looks like a conversation with Jonah, shaking their heads and rolling their eyes. But if this is noticeable to me, it isn't to Jonah. He is not indifferent to friendship, but he's not motivated by the possibility of making friends either. Friends are, for him, just more people who are likely to become an unnecessary distraction, who will ask him questions he doesn't understand and demand responses he is unprepared to give. In this respect, potential friends aren't significantly different from therapists or teachers. Or us. This is not to say he doesn't like the company of other kids; he just hasn't learned yet to see the point of it, to grasp its pragmatic importance. He is immune to peer pressure, which is both admirable and worrisome. He is impervious to embarrassment.

Sometimes, I imagine Jonah as an anti-hero in an existential novel, a character capable of existing outside convention. I imagine him taking secret pride in his outsider status. Contemporary literature is replete with this type—loners and misfits, from Stephen Dedalus to Holden Caulfield to Bridget Jones. In fact, one of the reasons I became a writer was because that's how I wanted to see myself. I honestly believed that I didn't care what anyone else thought of me. It wasn't until I became the parent of a child with autism that I stopped thinking that way.

Jonah ends each day in the schoolyard alone. After the final bell rings I have to concentrate to find him in the outpouring of kids. When I do spot him he's usually singing to himself. Sometimes, he's spinning—gleeful but solitary. Sometimes, he's tracking his fingers through space like he's trying to break free of everything else— complicated equations, French pronunciations—he is forced to do during the long school day. There are six hours of confusing instructions five days a week to contend with. There are inane rules, indecipherable warnings, stressed-out teachers to steer clear of. I imagine him, as he exits those doors at two-seventeen every afternoon, welcoming back his authentic self. *His autistic self?*

Second Term

Fail better.

—SAMUEL BECKETT, FROM *WORSTWARD HO*

The animals wanted to know what's a limit?

Moe the Yak and Rooney the Camel didn't know. The Worst-Monkey-Ever didn't know. No one knew. The Worst-Daddy-Ever said he knew but he wouldn't tell anyone. That would be a limit, he said.

—JONAH, AGED 11, WITH DADDY FROM *MORE BAD ANIMALS: THE SEQUEL*

EIGHT
Harriet

Our new shrink has a manuscript. It's her Ph.D. thesis, which she completed years ago, though she's reluctant to say how many years. Her subject is narrative therapy. Loosely defined, that's the practice of employing storytelling techniques to achieve therapeutic objectives. In recent years, she's talked to a couple of publishers about turning her thesis into a book. But she's not sure what her next step should be: an outline and sample chapters? An agent? She has some questions for me. Are academic publishers worth looking into? Or should she think about making her manuscript more accessible to a mainstream audience? She knows my name from the newspaper—book reviews, right? She heard me interviewed on the CBC, too—and any advice I might offer would be appreciated. But some other time is what she means, of course, not now, not during our session. She apologizes, but I tell her not to worry about it and I mean it. I know something about unfinished manuscripts. In fact, at the moment, I'm an expert on the subject.

Harriet is a friendly, tireless woman, and the one character trait sometimes infringes on the other. She has a sympathetic manner; she's also hard to set up an appointment with. Harriet has numerous children—I don't ask, but my guess is five—and is a practising Orthodox Jew, which makes her already unimaginably full week fuller, with no time to catch up on her work Friday afternoons or Saturdays. She also writes a regular column for *Exceptional Family*, a Montreal-based special-needs magazine. She has two practices, one in the city and one in the suburbs. She teaches a junior college and a university course on early development. And she recently opened a third office, which she is in the process of turning into a centre dedicated to treatment based on neuroplasticity.

For anyone interested in the field of cognitive psychology, neuroplasticity figures to be the next big thing. The brain, it turns out, still holds surprises for researchers who were, until only a couple of decades ago, inclined to think of it as a complex but mainly inflexible instrument. Now, it's beginning to look as if a damaged brain can be self-correcting in a variety of circumstances. For instance, there are more and more case studies of remarkable, inexplicable recoveries by stroke victims. The new hope is that the brain can be trained to self-correct—to form new neural connections throughout a lifetime. This is exciting, cutting-edge stuff, which has obvious implications for injuries—severe concussions, for example—as well as other diseases and disorders, such as Alzheimer's and Parkinson's. So far the promise neuroplasticity holds when it comes to autism is the notion that early intervention, or EI, while important, is not as essential as parents of children with autism are routinely told. EI was all we heard about when Jonah was diagnosed. As a result, there has always been the gnawing worry that we were somehow too late. Everything Cynthia was reading at the time held out the same number, five, his fifth birthday, as a benchmark or, more ominously, a deadline. If we didn't see significant progress by then, we were out of luck. Good luck, that is. In fact, with the emphasis on early intervention, our bad luck had suddenly compounded: not only was Jonah one in the one hundred and fifty or so children on the spectrum, he was one of those on the spectrum diagnosed late. Jonah didn't begin his therapy until he was almost four, and the worry even then was that his brain was already fixed, hard-wired. Which raised the question: what had we been waiting for? A clue, I suppose. But were there clues? Should we have known? Should the daycare or our pediatrician have picked up on signs when he was three, even two? Would that have made a difference? Neuroplasticity doesn't make these questions moot, but it mitigates them. What's reassuring about all this new research is the possibility that the brain is not only adaptable but that it never stops adapting—even long after we turn five. This is another subject I'd be glad to discuss with Harriet.

But we're not in her office to talk about publishing contracts or the latest neurological advances. We are, supposedly, here because I am, supposedly, not happy. Well, not happy enough. This isn't a conclusion I have reached, by the way, it's a family consensus. *All for one, indeed.* How happy I am supposed to be is open for discussion.

"So how can I help you?" Harriet asks.

"Well, our son has autism," I begin and then abruptly stop. It's as if that single fact explains everything. As if, having said it, I'm done. We can all go home now. Better yet, we can go back to talking about publishing our respective long-shot manuscripts, hers and mine. Maybe even collaborate, write a book together called: *Let's Talk About Changing the Subject.* I don't know about anyone else's brain, but these days mine seems pretty inflexible.

"Jonah, that's our son, he's why we're here. That and our relationship with him, mine and Joel's," Cynthia says, continuing on my behalf. Even though we both agreed that it would be a good idea to speak to a therapist together again—we didn't give Jeff, our last therapist, much of a chance—we both developed cold feet in the car on the way here. As I pulled into the parking lot outside Harriet's office, I wondered out loud how much notice we would have to give to cancel our session and not pay for it. Cynthia, a professional, suggested it would probably have to be more than two minutes.

"Jonah's older now. He turned eleven two months ago," Cynthia goes on to tell Harriet. "He's started his second term in grade five. I know it's still winter, but that means there's what, less than two years until high school. He's going to be a teenager soon and we know that's going to raise other problems. So while there's always been a lot to worry about, to consider, now there seems to be so much more. And ..." Cynthia pauses and glances at me.

"It's all right," Harriet says, "take your time."

"And I think because of all that, because things are going to get tougher, not easier, we need to be, as his parents and, as a couple, on the same team. If we're going to help him we have to be working together, and sometimes it feels like we're not. I feel like we're pulling in different directions."

Harriet's yellow legal pad is out on her desk, but she asks first if we mind if she takes notes. I shrug. *Somebody should.*

"He thinks I overestimate Jonah," Cynthia tells Harriet.

I stare at Harriet's poised pen. I am waiting, I suppose, for Harriet, who knows nothing about me as a father, as a person, to come up with a reason to disagree. But Harriet is just smiling benignly at me. I assume it's my turn. I assume that this is how it works. Everyone gets their chance to say something they'd rather not say. So I speak, finally.

"And she thinks I underestimate him."

I'VE BEEN TO FOUR shrinks in the last eighteen months; two on my own and two—including Harriet—as part of a couple. Cynthia has the advantage of being in the therapy business, so she knows how this process works better than I do. She understands, for instance, that there is no such thing as an advantage—therapy is not about keeping score. My advantage is that this is all relatively new to me: new and, even now, unexpectedly exciting. The real surprise for me so far is how much I have, even now, enjoyed my brief encounters with therapists. Not because I have any illusions about them helping me. There have been no breakthroughs as yet; in fact, I can't even begin to imagine what a breakthrough would look like. Besides, as more than one therapist has already implied, self-awareness may not be my biggest problem. (A fellow writer once called me "malignantly self-absorbed," and meant it as a compliment.) No, what I like about therapy is that it is a performance, first and foremost. It is, for all its supposed probing and promised emotional upheaval, good clean fun. Go figure. For fifty minutes every week or two, you are centre stage, in a spotlight in which self-absorption and uninhibited confessions are not frowned upon but encouraged. It is a memoirist's paradise. And you only have to pay one hundred bucks or so for the privilege. This is, if you ask me, a steal.

I've also discovered I have a knack for charming shrinks. Maybe because I've spent so much of my time turning the events of my life into stories. I have a narrative sense of what to put in and what to leave out. Maybe it's just practice. In any case, "the charm issue," as Cynthia calls it, is one reason we quit Jeff. Cynthia was convinced he liked me more than her and, therefore, couldn't be counted on to be objective. And while it's true Jeff seemed to keep taking my side—he was surprisingly tolerant of my self-pity—my point was that would change once he got to know me better. This was what we were paying him to do, after all. Cynthia wasn't so sure. She suspected the more he got to know me the more likely we were to find out about the manuscript he had tucked away in a drawer.

"You know what it is, don't you?" Cynthia said as we sat in Harriet's parking lot, deciding whether to stay or go. "You care more about being liked than being honest. Try that for a change. Say what you think, really think. It doesn't make sense to be doing this otherwise."

"Yeah, right!"

HARRIET IS EXCEPTIONALLY GOOD—perceptive and sensible and, most important, caring. She's succeeded, in a very short time, in charming me and Cynthia, too. It helps that we know, going in, something of her back story, her personal narrative, you could call it. We learned from a friend of a colleague of hers that she is the mother of a daughter, an adult now, with special needs. All parents understand worry, how sometimes it's reasonable, sometimes not. Unreasonable worry, however, is a luxury you can no longer afford once that label, special needs, is attached to you and your family. Now when you worry it's never merely theoretical. You're not just daydreaming about some possible occurrence somewhere down the road; now there's always something immediate and coming straight at you. Worry becomes like a hobby that has gotten out of hand. It takes up more and more space in your life, in your head, especially your head; it consumes more and more energy. It leaves you exhausted, either incapable of or just not very good at doing anything else. The good news is we don't have to waste time explaining this to Harriet. She knows. She gets it.

HARRIET PUTS AWAY HER cellphone and apologizes several times for taking a call in the middle of our session. She has no excuse, she says, except she's been waiting to hear from her teenage son. He wasn't feeling well this morning. If she sometimes seems overwhelmed by her unimaginably busy life, she also seems more generous because of it. She is the type of person for whom the more there is to accomplish the more she is capable of accomplishing. She volunteers, for instance, to help us with Jonah's school, to act as an intermediary, an advocate if necessary. She has some experience in that area, both as a psychologist and a mother. This offer is unsolicited. So is her offer to put our fee on a sliding scale should we decide to continue. All of which is more reason to like her and listen to her advice; even if I'm not sure I'm going to like that advice; even if Harriet, glancing down at her legal pad, is starting to get specific.

"Now where were we? Yes, Cynthia, you were saying that you feel like the two of you are not in sync? As a couple? Is that what I'm hearing? Can you give me an example?"

"Yes, well, there's this book I asked him to read a while ago. Months ago, right?" Cynthia glances at me. I didn't realize we could complain about each other—we didn't agree to this in the parking lot. Did this mean all bets were off? What was next? Were we going to stop pretending that there was nothing wrong between us that a miracle of neuroplasticity—on my part if not Jonah's—wouldn't cure?

"Months, really?" I say. In fact, it's been longer. *The RDI Book*, by psychologist Steven Gutstein, the founder of RDI or Relationship Development Intervention, is on my night table, at the bottom of a stack of other books I haven't started. For instance, Rupert Isaacson's uplifting memoir *The Horse Boy: A Father's Quest to Heal His Son*. From what I gather from the dust jacket, Isaacson, a travel writer and something of an adventurer, takes his son Rowan, who has autism, to Mongolia to ride horses and meet with shamans. The uplift, incidentally, is right there in Isaacson's subtitle. It tells you everything you need to know. Whoever heard of a quest ending in failure?

"I hate having to nag him about this, about reading a book. I mean it's what he does anyway. Isn't it?" Cynthia asks Harriet, who treats the question like it's rhetorical, and it might as well be. All three of us know Cynthia is right: she shouldn't have to nag me. I should have read the book by now. I should have read every book on my night table by now.

"The thing is this Gutstein book, it could change our lives," Cynthia says, taking a Kleenex from the box on the corner of Harriet's desk. There are ways in which the RDI method of treating autism complements ABA, the treatment we've used from the beginning. It does this by adding the relationship variable to what is a more detached, scientific approach. In other ways, RDI and ABA are contradictory. Where ABA can provide a child with the tools he needs to control his behaviour and succeed at school and at basic tasks, as it has with Jonah, RDI focuses on interpersonal relationships. In ABA, parents are trained, but grudgingly. The parents, in our experience of

ABA, are often assumed to be an irritating obstacle, at best, a kind of perpetual fly in the ointment; in RDI parents are required to be part of the solution. It's the parents and parents alone who can provide the missing connection in the autistic brain, a connection that comes naturally to neurotypical children and their parents. Of course, even if it made sense to combine the two treatments, you'd be discouraged to do so by the RDI and ABA experts, who seem to be engaged in their own power struggle. At the moment, proponents of each are as suspicious of each other as corporate rivals: like Coke and Pepsi. *You're exaggerating a little, sweetheart; maybe you could just read the book.* As a parent, you are expected to choose one or the other. When it comes to autism therapies, you are either all in or all out.

"Can you explain why you haven't read the book?" Harriet asks. Her cell rings again. She glances at it and, this time, ignores it. *My luck.*

"I've been busy. I have a lot to read. It's kind of my job."

Cynthia doesn't roll her eyes, though she'd be well within her rights to. She knows this isn't true. She knows that I have just about given up on so-called serious literature. Instead, I spend most of my time watching mindless sitcoms and old movies on TV after Jonah has gone to bed. I am a couch potato by choice, not accident. By now, Cynthia is no longer sure if I'm joking when I say I'm done with books, that I've read enough of them.

"Is there, maybe, some other reason why you haven't gotten around to this book?" Harriet asks again.

"Nothing occurs to me." But there is a reason and you'd think this would be the ideal place to reveal it, here in Harriet's functional office, in Harriet's empathetic, reasonably expensive company. But I don't want to hear myself say out loud what I am thinking. *ABA was also supposed to change our lives.*

CYNTHIA AND I ARE IN Harriet's office for another reason—because of what we have come to call our crack-ups. It would probably be more accurate to describe these outbursts of ours as just that, outbursts, tantrums for grownups—temporary and banal. But I prefer the more romantic term F. Scott Fitzgerald coined in his famous essay. Published in 1936 in *Esquire* magazine, "The Crack-Up" reads, in retrospect, like a tour de force of self-indulgence, a gut-wrenching, personal account of decline, of how "an exceptionally optimistic young man experienced a crack-up of all values, a crack-up that he scarcely knew of until long after it occurred." Writing about a failing that personal was the kind of thing people didn't routinely do back then, certainly not in non-fiction and not anyone as famously literary as Fitzgerald. But he didn't just chronicle his emotional deterioration and his subsequent recovery, he updated it, wrote a sequel and then another. In doing so, he acknowledged that he hadn't recovered at all. He wrote unflinchingly about his weaknesses, complained about his friends and lovers, the people he could no longer tolerate, about "the blow that comes from within—that you don't feel until it's too late to do anything about it, until you realize with finality that in some regard you will never be as good a man again." He was criticized by fans of his novels for revealing too much, for embarrassing himself, even embarrassing literature. He acknowledged this was true, but he didn't care. He couldn't stand himself and he took some pleasure and pride in letting everyone know.

There is a kind of pleasure, usually unspoken, in pitching a fit, blowing off steam, cracking up. It's like a high fever. You're better off succumbing than resisting. When Jonah becomes frustrated, he's been instructed to punch his pillow, but it seldom works for him, and I wonder if it's because he's being asked to punch his pillow for a specific purpose. Perhaps he prefers, as I do, ineffectual, impromptu rage. So, on occasion, I will bang my fist against the wall, slam a door, or overturn a chair. More often, though, I'll just rant, invariably in Cynthia's direction. My crack-up speech always begins with the same phrase: "I can't take this any more." What follows is a soliloquy, often of such unremitting hopelessness, such disdain for everything we are trying to do or will ever try to do to make Jonah better, to make him fit in, to make sure he has friends, achievements, a future, that I wonder how I will ever take these words back. How I will be permitted to, I mean. But I am, and this is, as far as I'm concerned, a testament to marriage, to mine anyway. At some point, I will want Harriet to know this.

Cynthia's crack-ups are quieter and, as a consequence, scarier. She expresses anger and discouragement in the same way, by sleeping more and speaking less, hardly speaking at all when I'm around. She is a person who tends to choose her words carefully anyway, so it can take me a while to realize that something is wrong. But eventually I notice her silence is somehow different, more deliberate and ominous. So while she knows exactly what I'm thinking once I start in on my "I-can't-take-it-any-more" speech, I haven't a clue what might be going on in her head on those occasions when she may also be fresh out of hope and patience. I only know what it will lead to: a determination on her part to make things better.

This is what I resent about Cynthia's crack-ups; she uses them productively. She convinces herself that people are capable of change. I can provide her with quotes to prove the opposite point. I've collected them. "People do not change, especially seen from up close; they just grow more elaborate" (Russell Banks). Or: "People make momentous shifts, but not the changes they imagine" (Alice Munro). "People don't change. They only stand more revealed" (Charles Olson). Clearly, though, I'm not about to change Cynthia's mind. She has a quote of her own: "Most women will tell you you're a fool to think you can change a man, but those women are quitters" (Marge Simpson). Cynthia's no quitter either. Because if she doesn't believe she can change me, how can she believe she can change our son? All of which may explain why it can be hard at times for us to work together the way we know we should. Maybe that's what we're looking for here in

Harriet's office, some kind of consensus. Maybe it's time for all of us to agree that something is going to have to be different. My concern is that something, according to the consensus, will be me.

"We alternate," Cynthia explains to Harriet. "Between crack-ups, I mean. Like shift workers. I have one. He stays calm. Then he has one and all of a sudden I'm calm again. It never fails."

"That is a kind of teamwork, isn't it?" Harriet says.

"Exactly." I smile at Harriet, appreciative of her efforts to put a positive spin on this.

"He has more … more of them." See what I said about marriage? Someone is always keeping score.

"Why do you think that is?" Harriet asks me.

I shrug, again, and can see, out of the corner of my eye, Cynthia glancing at Harriet and Harriet glancing back. A sight like that will make even a self-assured man shudder. Two women, who clearly know too much about you, sharing a secret—about you.

"Tell her about *other* kids," Cynthia says.

There is a silence then that Harriet permits. As a journalist, I've done enough interviews to know the trick. Silence is a trap. You set it and wait for your interviewee to take the bait, to fill the uncomfortable, eventually unbearable void. He will, if he is like most people, say something, anything. Often, it will be precisely the thing he was determined not to say and, at least for the purpose of the profile you are writing, he will give more of himself away than he ever intended. When I can't bear the silence any longer I end up caught in my own trap. Once again, I say what I don't want to.

"I hate other kids."

NINE

Okapis

Jonah is three months younger than his first cousin, Cynthia's brother's son. Even before Jonah was born there was the assumption that the two boys would grow up together and be close if not best friends. But that was unlikely from the start. The more everyone pushed the two together the more they seemed to be a bad match. As toddlers, they tolerated each other but hardly more than that. Jonah was the happier and more outgoing of the two, and, as a result, more of a fuss was made about him and not just by us. He was a smiley, good-natured kid. He didn't talk much, but he sang all the time, a kind of human jukebox with the lyrics serving as a substitute for ordinary, basic communication. On weekends, he'd sing "Jolly Holiday"; at meal time, "Apples and Bananas." It was undeniably odd, but also undeniably winning. His tastes, for a toddler, were eclectic—running from Raffi to Frank Sinatra. Most of all, he was happy, especially compared to his cousin, who brooded more. I suspected some instinctive baby-style jealousy was at the core of their relationship. After all, Jonah had come along like a little brother might, only sooner. This was an arrogant thought on my part and I did my best to keep it to myself. Still, I couldn't help noticing how routinely the two resisted each other whenever they were forced together. "They don't have anything in common," I finally told Cynthia. "Don't be ridiculous," she said, "they're two years old. They have everything in common." It was around the time Jonah's cousin turned three that I began to notice he and I were engaging in small talk. He seemed curious to hear what I had to say on subjects like stuffed animals and apple sauce. He listened and looked for clues in my body language, tone of voice, expression. Jonah talked, but at you more than to you. He usually used words or phrases he'd heard somewhere else and then inserted them, like song lyrics, into a conversation. He developed catch-all phrases he could use whenever he was asked a question. "Too mad, too sad," was his response to a simple request about how he was feeling. In retrospect, we may have judged this remark to be more profound than it was. I remember once, out of the blue, Jonah saying, "The hippopotamus is an incredibly territorial animal." This was, for a two-year-old, an impressive feat. I knew he'd heard the line on TV and knew, too, he had no idea what it meant. Still, it was a mouthful. "Territorial is, what, five syllables?" I said to Cynthia. So I beamed and encouraged Jonah to say it again and again. No encouragement was necessary.

His cousin's vocabulary was more rudimentary. But he could play Candyland without lining up all the pieces. He could throw and catch a ball without wandering off. He would answer you when you asked him a simple question and then ask you a simple question in return. There was back and forth, give and take—the elements necessary to an ordinary conversation. He wanted things from you, too, wanted them fiercely: toys, attention, approval, success. Jonah wanted nothing. He was, we told ourselves, self-reliant, easygoing, a free spirit.

I MISS EASY THINGS. I miss taking things for granted. Like a trip to the supermarket or the park. Like me, pushing my newborn son in his stroller, all the while quoting from *Henry V* or explaining some odd ruling in last night's baseball game. I miss elderly women stopping me in the street to say Jonah should be wearing a hat or that his stroller strap isn't tight enough. I would nod and accept this unsolicited advice or at least pretend to. I acted as if I was grateful to strangers for keeping me informed about my parental incompetence. Secretly, though, I was like the latest John Grisham novel, impervious to criticism. Thinking: *Do you know who you're talking to? I'm the kid's father. I'll teach him what he needs to know. I'll teach him stuff you never dreamed of—about Shakespeare and Sinatra. I'll teach him spit takes and fist bumps.* I was like a goalie standing on his head, a three-point shooter who can't miss. I was in the Daddy Zone. Like an athlete who knows he can do no wrong, I was all intuition. I didn't have to think twice or even once; I was unconscious.

Ever since Jonah was diagnosed, there's been nothing but advice—all of which I feel compelled to listen to. I have learned to watch my step. Everything is a test—something you grit your teeth and accept or go out of your way to avoid. I find myself constantly wishing for quiet destinations. I plan even the most mundane outing so as to avoid long lines at the store or crowds at the playground. And I am done in daily by unavoidable miscalculations and overwhelming envy; by the briefest glimpse of a father and son chatting matter-of-factly about the day's events. I'll also find myself eavesdropping on parents and children only to be reminded of how much you can take these little things—a simple conversation, a game of catch—for granted. There comes a time, I've been told, when you adjust, when you don't even think about such comparisons. But that time hasn't come for me yet. I still worry constantly about how others will judge Jonah's behaviour and judge me for it. Wherever I go I find myself wishing I could hand everyone within shouting distance a five-page, single-spaced, footnoted explanation, a cheat sheet, of why my child behaves the way he does. *Let's Talk About Autism*, I'd call it. And then, just to be on the safe side, I'd have them sign an affidavit acknowledging that none of this is my fault. When, I want to know, did this become so important to me—not being embarrassed?

EVERY PASSOVER WE attend the first Seder at my in-laws. Passover is the Jewish equivalent of Thanksgiving. People you haven't seen for a year reappear and you catch up on one another's lives before losing touch with them again for the next eleven months. When Jonah was younger it was the ideal time to show him off to Cynthia's extended family. Dressed in the preppy clothes my sisters bought him—those argyle vests—and with more product in his hair than was seemly for a toddler, we arrived at holiday dinners with what can only be described as a swagger. *Here we are,* we might as well have announced, *let the fawning begin.* And it did. Jonah was something to behold. I taught him "Dayenu," a Hebrew song which traditionally comes after the telling of the story of Exodus in the Seder service. Jonah belted it out, ending every chorus with an inappropriate but amusing Cossack-style "hey." This was a crowd-pleaser and so was Jonah.

Dayenu is Hebrew for suffice as in "It would have sufficed." The song itself couldn't be more obsequious: a previously oppressed people sucking up to the capricious, spiteful God who had deigned to free them after he'd orchestrated their enslavement in the first place. But, hold on, you're not quite ready for freedom. First, there would have to be a forty-year layover in the desert. Imagine it, the dusty, incredulous crowd gathered around Moses when he broke the news. *And now,* they must have thought, *we're supposed to be grateful?* "If he had brought us out of Egypt. *Dayenu,*" the first verse of the Passover song goes. "If he had executed justice upon the Egyptians, *Dayenu.* If he had executed justice upon their gods. *Dayenu.* If he had slain their first born. If he had …" Well, you get the idea.

Now, when I show up for my in-laws' Passover Seder I'm holding my breath and I have my fingers crossed. I come with a prepared list of excuses. Jonah is tired. He had a rough day at school. He's been chatty or grumpy or hyper for hours. You should have seen him at my sister's on the weekend, he was an angel.

Jonah isn't good at drawn-out events. He isn't likely to sit still, eat the unusual holiday food, engage with the adults, or play with his cousin. As for me, I always seem to be perfectly positioned to watch some distant relative or friend of Cynthia's family we see only once a year staring at Jonah. When he shouts or answers their simple questions with a strange non sequitur about zebras or yaks or an out-of-the-blue knock-knock joke, I will watch them react either with frustration or confusion. I can practically read their minds. I can see them thinking: *What's this about?*

In other words, if Jonah can get through the evening without saying something inappropriate, something wildly inappropriate; if he can avoid a tantrum; if he can avoid a prolonged tantrum; if we can get home in a couple of hours, tops, well, that, *Dayenu*, will have to suffice.

WHEN I WAS JONAH'S age there was a boy on our street with whom I shared a birth date. He'd remind me of this fact every time we bumped into each other. This was our only connection, but it was one too many for me. Our common birthday gave him an excuse to go on at length about the weather. He was the street's self-appointed meteorologist, a job he took seriously. He behaved as if the rest of us could not have made it through the day without his forecasts. I tried my best to avoid him on the street as well as at the elementary school we both attended. When I couldn't bear his company any more, I joined the other kids in making fun of him. I tried not to do it to his face, but I can't say I always tried hard enough or worried enough about succeeding. Still, the teasing didn't seem to bother him, at least that's what I told myself. I can see now that he was quite likely on the spectrum, quite likely Asperger's, before anyone ever heard of either label. On our street, we had our own names; likely, strange and slow were the least offensive.

In his memoir *Not Even Wrong: Adventures in Autism*, Paul Collins, a contributor to *McSweeney's* and a historian, alternates the story of discovering that his two-year-old son Morgan has autism with stories of famous undiagnosed "autists." He begins with Peter the Wild Boy, who first came to public attention late in the seventeenth century. He was twelve when he emerged from Germany's Black Forest, naked and foraging for food on all fours. He didn't talk or look anyone in the eye. He was, in the parlance of his day, a freak. But he was a mystery, too, and lucky enough to be befriended by another special boy—the prince and heir to the British throne, the future king of England, George I. Brought to the royal court with George, Peter became a fixture, a kind of mascot to the monarchy. "The simple boy from the Black Forest had landed squarely in what was, for all purposes, the centre of his era's intellectual universe," Collins writes. Jonathan Swift likely based the feral Yahoos in *Gulliver's Travels* on Peter. The Wild Boy also became the prototype for Jean-Jacques Rousseau's romantic vision of man in "the state of nature" in his most famous book, *Confessions*. Peter the Wild Boy was also plainly on the spectrum.

The narrative in *Not Even Wrong* is constructed around Collins's dogged, often desperate effort to understand his two-year-old son Morgan's world through researching and retelling the story of Peter as well as other overlooked or misjudged historical figures. It makes for a fascinating investigation into how elusive autism has always been and, to a great extent, remains. *Not Even Wrong* is also about how easy it is to misjudge and misunderstand people once a label has been affixed to them. It is, finally, a book full of sympathy for a group of people who are consistently misunderstood in a multitude of small and big ways. "Autists are ultimate square pegs," Collins writes, "and the problem with pounding a square peg into a round hole is not that the hammering is hard work. It's that you are destroying the peg." In the end, he decides he'd rather his boy be happy than forced to become something he isn't, something he can never be. It's a tricky argument, made trickier by the severity of Morgan's condition. What's wrong, for instance, with trying to smooth out the square peg just a bit before you start hammering it into the round hole? Collins's argument is also one made under pressure, the pressure of the author's own unresolved, open-ended narrative. Resolution is always going to be the problem, the nut to crack, in any honest story about autism. Your choices are limited and arbitrary. You can opt for acceptance or hold out for a miracle. But the trouble is that the one often seems as unlikely as the other.

Morgan makes progress in *Not Even Wrong*, but Collins doesn't put as much emphasis on that as he does on learning to celebrate his son's uniqueness. By the end of the book, Collins has admirably researched and written a community into existence for and around his son. He's succeeded at putting Morgan into historical context as if he were one more unrecognized, unsung hero in a long, ongoing narrative. Collins chooses acceptance, in other words, or as close as he can come to it. In the book's final scene, Morgan is having a meltdown in the neigh-bourhood supermarket and Collins's achievement lies in his ability to endure it, to ignore the stares of the strangers around him. "It's not what they think," he tells himself. "It's not a tragedy, it's not a sad story, it's not the movie of the week. It's my family."

It's a lovely scene, just not one that resonates with me. Perhaps because I'm not there yet, not able to ignore the stares of strangers, not by a long shot. Instead, there's another scene near the end of *Not Even Wrong* I can't get out of my head. Here, Collins is in a crowded café observing a man making a nuisance of himself, asking inappropriate questions in an odd voice to a table full of college students, who are, in turn, making fun of him. The man seems oblivious to their teasing, much of it casually cruel. Then the man turns to Collins, sensing a sympathetic presence perhaps, and goes right on babbling. Collins is polite and tries to engage him in conversation, but it's pointless—the man is incoherent. Collins quickly leaves the café and, moments later, is sitting on the steps of a nearby church, crying. He's not religious, he writes, it's just that people are less likely to bother you if you cry on the steps of a church than on someone's front lawn. Eventually, he explains why he's crying: "I can't bear the thought that someday, somehow, someone will be cruel to my child. Or pretend that he is not even there."

ON CYNTHIA'S RECOMMENDATION, I've finally finished one of those books from the pile loitering on my night table. Cynthia read Mark Haddon's bestseller, *The Curious Incident of the Dog in the Night-Time*, months ago and insisted that I read it. I resisted at first because I have been contemplating writing a novel of my own on the subject of autism. The idea was born out of desperation late one afternoon while I was facing my unfinished manuscript in my basement office. I was making no progress telling our family story, so I thought, why not fictionalize it? The character of the father could be a little more open to change, for instance; the character of the son a little more communicative. There'd be a breakthrough at the end, obviously: nothing dramatic or uplifting, but moving and profound. Then again, why not dramatic? I assumed I could do in a novel what was proving so hard to do in this so-called memoir of mine. I could dream up a satisfactory resolution. What if, for instance, Jonah or Jacob, let's call the protagonist, reveals in the final chapters that he's imbued with superpowers only individuals with autism possess? What if he also reveals in a final moving speech that he's part of a group called the S.O.S. League or Superheroes on the Spectrum, who meet regularly and secretly to maintain order in the overly emotional and cripplingly empathetic neurotypical world. You see, the Nits, as neurotypicals are called, have a disabling flaw. They can't think straight. They are incapable of doing advanced math in their heads or reciting long poems or even living in the moment. They're always dwelling on the past and feeling sorry for themselves. They are always worrying about what other people think. Or they're making foolish plans for a future they are clueless about. The Nits also judge others by how they behave rather than what they are capable of. It's a world, in other words, turned happily upside down. Jacob and his S.O.S. friends—because that's what they would be most of all, friends—also keep track of everyone who's ever teased, misdiagnosed, dismissed, or underestimated them and then seek their revenge on teachers, classmates, therapists, parents. It's nothing drastic or violent, just some turn-about-is-fair-play resolution, done mainly by a comic character, perhaps at the low-functioning end of the spectrum, who would, at the most inappropriate moment, repeat a favourite catchphrase—"Gotcha!"—and make the Nits see what nitwits they really were. She'd also get big laughs from her S.O.S. colleagues. She'd be a girl, a love interest for Jacob, perhaps. Her superpower would lie in her ability to embarrass people who deserved to be embarrassed. Jacob's particular power would be that he could see into the future and thereby reassure his beleaguered but otherwise well-intentioned and unusually tall and handsome father that every-thing was going to be fine. The father would finally learn to trust his son's powers. Then, I don't know, they'd all have pizza and ice cream. The End. It's probably obvious by now why I gave up on the novel. Still, it was fun to contemplate.

There's no such silliness in *The Curious Incident of the Dog in the Night-Time*. Haddon's novel ends much the way you'd expect a work of literary fiction about autism to end—with its teenaged hero and narrator, Christopher Boone, making significant progress but staying true to his essential high-functioning Asperger self. He is going to be all right, he assures us, perhaps better than all right. We learn that he's passed his exams and done so impressively. In order to commu-nicate his feelings, he draws a happy-face emoticon. He vows to attend university, live on his own, and become a scientist. "I know I can do this," he says, "because … I was brave and I wrote a book and that means I can do anything." This feel-good conclusion aside, Haddon's hero is, throughout the novel, painstakingly believable. It's this realistic portrait of Christopher Boone that Cynthia found worth recommending. She's right. Christopher is a significant improvement over the stereotypical view of the individual with autism, which, until not very long ago, began and ended with Dustin Hoffman's hammy "idiot savant" in *Rain Man*.

In Haddon's story, Christopher is nothing if not focused. He assigns himself the task of investigating and solving the mystery of who killed his neighbour's dog. This whodunit subplot is barely even that. It's obvious, after just a few chapters, that the reader is going to know who killed the dog and why long before Christopher does, if Christopher ever does. What we are privy to is the way in which Christopher interacts with the world. That's the novel's strength—we see everything as Christopher sees it, through his eyes, and as a unique challenge. We also begin to realize that every detail, even something like the colour of a subway ticket, is open to misinterpretation. Every decision, even the simplest one, is filled with peril. It's not that Christopher gets things wrong; it's that *he* gets them the way *he* gets them. He is not, as most reviewers tend to describe him, an unreliable narrator. If anything, he's the opposite. He is absolutely reliable, for someone with autism, that is. Dramatic irony is the novel's governing literary device but it's also more than that—it's a metaphor for the gap between the brain and the brain on autism. Christopher and the reader will always reach different conclusions. It's inevitable.

Still, empathy is literature's trump card; it's what literary fiction does better than any other art form, and *The Curious Incident of the Dog in the Night-Time*, as a reviewer in *The New Yorker* wrote, is "a triumph of empathy." Reviews have invariably focused on the ability of the author to get inside the head of his idiosyncratic hero. Good old negative capability. There are some clues as to how Haddon did this. His bio reveals that he worked with kids with autism at one point, and that serves as a kind of stamp of approval to his own idiosyncratic stylistic choices. Haddon uses diagrams, for instance, and graphs and math problems to illustrate the strange (to the reader) and perfectly sensible (to Haddon's hero) way in which Christopher thinks.

Haddon also hits all the predictable talking points; it's kind of autism-by-numbers. Christopher's facility for math, his obsession with order, his trouble reading other people's emotions, his unwillingness to be touched or held, his confusion at jokes, all of it rings textbook true. Haddon's thoroughness is commendable, as are his good literary intentions. In Christopher, Haddon creates a character, not a caricature. But here's an argument I never expected to make, one a person who reads and writes for a living should never make: where does Haddon get off? Why doesn't he find his own problem to write about? Until then, he has no business pretending or even imagining he can understand someone like Jonah ... I mean Christopher, of course. Here it comes, incidentally, my ineffectual rage, my latest crack-up. Write a letter, Harriet recommended to us recently, and then don't send it. It's the kind of thing she says she does in narrative therapy; it also seems like sensible advice:

> Dear Mr. Haddon,
> Research is overrated. So you had some part-time job
> working with kids with autism. Good for you. Seriously,
> I'm glad someone got a bestseller out of this disorder.
> But don't you think I wouldn't love to do what you've
> done? Fictionalize my relationship with my son. Pretend
> I understand him as easily as I understand the protago-
> nist in your quirky little novel. You think if I could have
> figured out some way to make Jonah, that's my son, less
> mystifying I wouldn't have done it by now. P.S. My wife
> loved the book.

The other problem I had with *The Curious Incident of the Dog in the Night-Time* was the father. Who do you think turns out to be the villain in the end? "Not the father," Cynthia says when I finally hand the novel back to her. She is surprised I finished it. We're both in bed reading. Actually, she's flipping through *The RDI Book*, which she's already read and is now littering with Post-it notes on my behalf, I'm guessing. Evidently, she has new-found hope that I am finally ready to take her recommendations.

And she's right about the father—labelling him the villain is a stretch. Still, he does, throughout the novel, do everything wrong. That includes forcing, albeit unintentionally, Christopher to run away, keeping Christopher estranged from his mother—he does that deliberately—and, oh yes, killing the damn dog.

"The book is not about the father, sweetheart. It's about Christopher," Cynthia says. "Did you see my note? The one right near the end?" *Wait, who's the reviewer here?*

"It must have fallen out," I say, but I'm lying. I routinely skip other people's highlighted passages or ignore Post-it notes in the same way I don't read other reviews of a book I'm supposed to be reviewing. I don't want to be influenced. I don't believe in much, but I believe in my own screwy opinions.

"I think I know where the passage is," Cynthia says as she flips through the novel, finally coming to the part she was looking for. It's a part where Christopher envisions a world devastated by a mysterious super-powerful computer virus. The result of this technological meltdown is that there are only people like Christopher—i.e., people on the spectrum—left in the world. As a consequence, these so-called "special people" are no longer a minority and no longer special. They're the typical ones now, the accepted norm, even though, Christopher says, "they like being on their own and I hardly ever see them because they are like okapi in the jungle in the Congo."

Cynthia reads the passage to me. She isn't crying, but there is an audible tremble in her voice. Then she stops and puts the book down. "Do you ever wonder what kind of teenager he will be?"

"I don't know. I can't…. So what is an okapi anyway?"

If Jonah were awake I could ask him. Instead Cynthia blows her nose and reads aloud from Haddon's novel before she puts it back on her night table: "'The Okapi is a kind of antelope ... very shy and rare.'"

CYNTHIA IS IN CHARGE of arranging play dates for Jonah. She does this in concert with Jessica, who will sometimes let us know about a classmate who has gone out of his way to approach Jonah. Cynthia then tracks the child down, talks to his parents, and offers to take him and Jonah to the park or invites him to our house to play our newly purchased Nintendo Wii game, which we bought at The Consultant's urging. The idea is to get Jonah interested in the kind of game kids his age are playing so he has some common ground with them, something he can talk to them about in the event, mostly unlikely, that an ordinary, unforced conversation occurs. Jonah is uninterested in Wii, but the game has proven to be a significant draw for potential playmates. There's Jonah's cousin, for instance. Cynthia thinks of it as an investment; I think of it as four hundred dollars down the drain. *Potatoes, patatoes.*

Each year Cynthia invites a few of Jonah's classmates to his birthday party. She also organizes an end-of-the-school-year lunch. She takes every opportunity to introduce Jonah to whatever kids they happen to meet in the park. She is like an old-world matchmaker, constantly on the lookout for a promising connection. I am a consistent no-show at Jonah's play dates. If I have to I will go so far as to fake a headache or pretend I have to get back to work on my so-called memoir. I will hide, literally hide, in the basement, sometimes listening at the top of the stairs to make sure the coast is clear before I emerge. Cynthia is so used to my habit of disappearing by now she will often give me a heads-up so I can devise a less transparent, less embarrassing excuse. As for the events I can't avoid, like Jonah's birthday parties, I keep my expectations low and go into these organized activities with my eye on my watch. *What's the minimum amount of time I am required to keep up this cheerful demeanour?*

Most of my encounters with Jonah and other kids are of the unplanned variety, usually occurring when he and I are running an errand. The experience has taught me that even though it's hard for Jonah to make friends in the conventional sense, he does seem to have a knack for accumulating acquaintances. When he and I are out together we're always running into kids he knows or who know him. Some are from school, others from camp or the theatre group or swimming classes he used to attend. Some he hasn't seen in years. I generally have no idea how he knows them or even if he really does. Jonah finds the idea of seeing someone in a place they aren't supposed to be thrilling. He'll shout out their name—Aja! Adewale!—and beam. Sometimes, he'll ask them their name, even if he knows it. Often, that's the extent of the exchange. The conversation tends to be stilted on both sides, which is to say the other kid can't think of anything to say to Jonah either. Even so, there's something sweet about these meetings, something encouraging. Walking around the neighbourhood with my son is a little like being out with a celebrity. The encounters are brief, a bit awkward, generally good-willed, and acknowledged to be limited. The other kid may not know what to say to Jonah but he seems happy to have run into him like this—without warning or expectations.

There are so many things to worry about, I try not to worry about my son's future prospects for making friends. Like much of what he's learned to do—dress himself, make his own breakfast, use the computer—it's one of those things that will eventually take care of itself, whether we worry about it or not. The list of things he's accomplished so far that I never expected him to accomplish is long, so there is some justification in holding out hope for him having a real friend one day. But that doesn't keep me from speculating about what that friendship will be like. There is no getting around the fact that whatever relationship Jonah may have in the future will require not only enormous effort on my son's part but, quite likely, an equal or greater effort on the part of the other person. This is, I realize, a lot to ask of any kid. *You're underestimating him again, sweetheart. Aren't there enough people doing that?* I know because it's a lot to ask of anyone.

TEN

Old Sperm

What is love? What is autism?

These two questions were ranked one and two a few years ago on Google's top-ten list of the most frequently searched for "what" questions. *Google knows everything*, I remember thinking. But how? How could Google possibly know you have to answer the first question before you can even attempt the second? That they are inextricably linked? More to the point, how does Google know Jonah and me?

Obviously, the two Google questions aren't linked. That they ended up combined in this online survey is random. For most people, for instance, the neurotypical and the parents of the neurotypical, one question will have no conceivable connection to the other. The first states the obvious: everyone is bewildered by love. The second question is pure percentages: it's an indication that autism—and the public concern about it—has become ubiquitous. The second also explains why personal writing on the topic of autism has boomed in the last decade. It's simple: autism is booming. Statistics are all over the map, it's true, but when Leo Kanner first identified the disorder in 1943, he reported a rate of incidence at 1 in 10,000 children; now the Centers for Disease Control (CDC) in Atlanta report a rate of 1 in 110 (just a few months ago it was 1 in 150). The numbers for boys are even more alarming, as high as 1 in 70. The reasons for this increase are open to debate. Is it an epidemic or is it just more likely to be diagnosed today? Is it environmental or genetic? A curse or fluke?

In his book *Unstrange Mind: Remapping the World of Autism*, Roy Richard Grinker, a professor of anthropology at George Washington University, makes a case for over-diagnosis. "The incidence of autism has not increased," he says flatly in his introduction. "We are defining it differently and counting it differently than in the past." For Cynthia and me, the count goes on in classrooms, playgrounds, shopping malls, restaurants. Something we were never aware of before is now impossible to miss. It's like when you fall in love and all you hear on the radio are love songs. Wherever we are, Cynthia and I will catch each other's eye once we've identified another member of the special-needs tribe—our tribe now. What did I do before this became a part of my life? I was oblivious, of course. Either that or I looked away.

Still, with the reason for the increase in autism anybody's guess, literature has done what it invariably does in the absence of scientific certainty or credibility—filled the vacuum with stories. There are countless websites and blogs; there are documentaries and memoirs on the subject, all more determined than ever to locate the meaning at the core of this elusive disorder. Most of these are the work of parents of children with autism or organizations begun by these parents. Grinker is an example. He wrote his memoir because of his daughter Isabel. She was two and a half when she was diagnosed in 1994, and Grinker admits he didn't know anything about autism then; neither did anyone he knew. His book, published thirteen years later, is part anthropological study—he focuses on how different cultures view autism—and part tribute to his daughter's brave struggle. He also talks about his own struggles: "I am not a religious person," Grinker writes, "but there is something profoundly meaningful, if not spiritual, about being the father of a child with autism that has pushed me to consider lofty, abstract principles of life like truth, beauty, and goodness."

What's hinted at here is the central theme in what has become a new kind of autism narrative: one dramatically at odds with what has been, in autism's brief history, a narrative that has invariably blamed parents for their children's behaviour. "The view of the parent as sinner," Kamran Nazeer writes in *Send in the Idiots*, "is even present in the scientific literature on autism." The earliest scientific literature, he means. Leo Kanner lectured, "often aggressively, on the cause of autism, which he summarized using the term 'refrigerator parents.'" Kanner would apologize twenty-five years later for this label—"Herewith, I especially acquit you people as parents," he told a gathering of parents of children with autism—but by then the damage was done, repeatedly by Kanner's successors; in particular, the charismatic author and talk-show guest Bruno Bettelheim. When Bettelheim, an Austrian-born psychologist and self-proclaimed disciple of Freud, published *The Empty Fortress: Infantile Autism and the Birth of the Self* in 1967, it instantly became *the* book about autism. It also became *the* book for blaming parents, specifically mothers. Bettelheim popularized the term "refrigerator mothers." (The role of fathers, I'm guessing, was deemed too inconsequential to matter.)

Today, though, the typical autism story is more likely to feature super parents—mothers, of course, but more and more fathers who are willing, happy even, to do everything in their power on behalf of an afflicted child. Books like Catherine Maurice's *Let Me Hear Your Voice*, Clara Claiborne Park's *The Siege: A Family's Journey into the World of an Autistic Child*, and Barry Neil Kaufman's *Son-Rise* are early dispatches from a frightening frontier. They bear witness to parental perseverance. Their aim is to inform, but also comfort and inspire. These memoirs follow a common narrative path. First comes the realization, as Maurice writes early in *Let Me Hear Your Voice*, that "'the experts' I was consulting didn't know a whole lot more than I did.... Worse, they could delude themselves, with their degrees and their windy verbosity, that they were 'helping.' I could afford no such pretensions." In *Son-Rise*, Kaufman reaches a similar conclusion: "The professionals offered no real hope or help, but in our love for our son and his beauty we had found a determination to persist."

This leads to the battle plan; namely, the decision to take matters into your own hands—"The Siege" of Park's title. Of her strategy to reach her daughter Elly, who dwells in "a solitary citadel," Park writes, "We must intrude, attack, invade.... We would use every stratagem we could invent to assail her fortress, entice, seduce her into the human condition."

In other words, it's the kind of narrative that puts most books about autism at odds with the books I've spent most of my life reading, reviewing, caring about. If literature has taught me anything, it's that believing you can understand the human condition is a mistake. Worse, it's hubris. The human condition, like the human brain, will always confound and defeat you. Or as Chekhov said: "It's about time that everyone who writes—especially genuine literary artists—admitted that in this world you can't figure anything out." But while this kind of uncertainty may have worked fine for Chekhov, most people dealing with the incomprehensibility of autism nowadays are more likely to be drawn to the somewhat less eloquent prose of model/actress and now autism activist Jenny McCarthy. McCarthy keeps it simple. In *Mother Warriors: A Nation of Parents Healing Autism against All Odds*, McCarthy recalls appearing on *Oprah* to talk about her son Evan for the first time. She was terrified, she admits, but she focused on her only reason for being there: "to offer hope, faith, recovery."

This promise of recovery probably explains why I'm inclined to avoid books like McCarthy's or why I approach them gingerly. I read them only when I absolutely have to and only then for bits and pieces, fragments of information. I also don't want to put myself in the position of criticizing another parent's good intentions on literary grounds. What kind of person would do that? All right, a professional critic; it's an occupational hazard.

So if I started Rupert Isaacson's *The Horse Boy*, as an example, but didn't finish, it was because I didn't like *my* reaction. I didn't like how irritated I became when Isaacson compared autism to the experience of being an immigrant to the United States, "living with one foot in (your) home language and culture, the other in the West, walking in two worlds. It's a rich place to be." *Rich?* There's more to it, though. I also didn't want to be reminded of something I already knew—how hard it was going to be to measure up to what is attempted and achieved in books like McCarthy's and Isaacson's and Park's and Kaufman's. I didn't want to know how much superhuman effort was going to be required of me.

In *The Horse Boy*, Isaacson demonstrates that he's the kind of father, not to mention writer, for whom nothing is out of the question. Quite simply, he will do anything, go anywhere, to reach and rescue his six-year-old son Rowan from the devastating isolation of autism. If this means an arduous, seemingly foolhardy trip to Mongolia so Rowan can ride horses and be analyzed by shamans, so be it. When do we leave? Isaacson reportedly received a million-dollar advance for his book proposal. A documentary was made to coincide with the release of the book, and there are plans for a feature film for which Isaacson is writing the screenplay. The book's dust jacket says it's a "dramatic and heart-warming story of ... impossible adventure ... of a family willing to go to the ends of the earth to help their son." The blurb on the front cover, from Temple Grandin, says: "This is a story everyone needs to hear." Isaacson's publisher told the *New York Times* something similar: "I felt this was a story entirely driven by the chances you'll take for love ... who's not going to want to read [it]?" So the question clearly is: what's wrong with me?

I suspect the problem I have with memoirs like *The Horse Boy* is the same as the problem I have with the memoir I've been trying to write for the last seven years: I have trouble believing it. Read enough contemporary fiction and you can't help thinking every narrator is unreliable, that everyone is leaving out something crucial. What is Isaacson leaving out? What am I?

The uninspiring everydayness of living with autism, its routine weirdness, its unbearable bearableness, its incremental ups and downs, is what so often goes unstated. Memoirs skip this part. So, for that matter, do news reports and documentaries. They don't have much to say about the frustrations of doing homework with your child or coaxing him out of bed in the morning; no conferences on teaching him to swing on monkey bars; no PowerPoint presentations on the effort required to have a conversation, a simple, ordinary conversation with your child rather than spending your day speculating on what that might be like. What's more, there is no behavioural therapy, no gluten-free diets for what autism takes out of you as a parent, the flaws it reveals in your character on a daily basis. All of that has proven to be either not worth conveying or, more likely, impossible to convey.

Whenever I try to tell someone about my life with Jonah it always sounds either far harder or far easier than it actually is. If the person I'm talking to looks overly sympathetic, I try my best to make it clear that Jonah is doing fine, all things considered. If the same person then complains to me about the difficulty their child is having getting along with his best friend, I wait, impatiently, for my chance to point out that Jonah doesn't have a best friend or any friends, really. The same problem arises when I try to write about autism. How do you make it clear to readers that you are coping and not coping at the same time? How can both things be true?

Of course, I know what my criticism of Isaacson's memoir sounds like—pettiness and professional jealousy. So I'm not blaming him or any of the other writers I've read or tried to read for just doing what writers are supposed to: make something incomprehensible comprehensible. So what if someone has to appear preposterously, incredulously heroic along the way? That is the tyranny of the happy ending, the perhaps unintended consequence of the ends-of-the-earth narrative, the epic quest. So what if I don't believe these stories or believe them enough to cancel out my own day-to-day experience, or the perpetual worry that maybe there are sacrifices I can't make? Chances I won't take for love? There are no anthropological studies for me to immerse myself in, no shamans on horseback for me and Jonah to ride alongside. Oprah is not waiting patiently to hear my tale unfold.

Or maybe it's just that I don't understand how anyone else does it. Gets through the day, I mean. Or manages to explain to other people—readers included—the tightrope you walk every day between despair and hope, embarrassment and persistence.

MY SISTERS WOULD RATHER not know about the time I'm spending in the basement writing a book they hope I will never finish. When the subject comes up, they counter with the latest childhood catastrophe they've spotted in the newspaper or on TV, a story about a child abducted or wasting away or set on fire by bullies. They collect these cautionary tales for me, a reminder of how things could always be worse. *Put that in your book,* I imagine them saying. My sisters love Jonah unconditionally and will always defend him, especially against me. I understand this. I appreciate it too. Even so, I've never been good at putting things in perspective. In my experience, autism is uniquely cruel, uniquely elusive. It's like nothing else. As a consequence, comparisons don't apply. But if autism makes a lousy metaphor, it works well as a Rorschach test. It's often an accurate definer of character, and I don't mean my son's, I mean other people's.

On hearing the initial news about Jonah, a close friend said, "What happens in twenty years?" My guess is that the question just slipped out and that it was mainly rhetorical in any case. There was no answer. There still isn't. My guess is my friend, a lawyer, a compassionate but also a practical man, was just doing what we weren't prepared to yet, what I confess I am, after all this time, still unprepared to do—face facts, plan ahead. Cynthia insisted, when I told her what he had said, that he didn't mean it the way it sounded. This was undoubtedly true; still, it didn't change how it sounded to me. Like Jonah was being written off from the start. Either that, or accepted from the start. To be honest, I've seen too much of both—too many people who have given up on my son and too many who have accepted him too easily—and my problem is I don't seem to know which is worse. *You have to let this go, sweetheart.* So, all right, I will. I'll cut everyone some slack. That includes the husband of one of Cynthia's friends, who always looks, when he asks how Jonah is, as if his dog just died. Or the colleague of mine, a father of four girls, who, when I told him about Jonah, said: "Oh yeah, autism. We know lots of kids with that. It's no big deal; they grow out of it." And while I'm prepared to admit that when we first found out about Jonah, no one could say anything right, it's also true no one seemed to come close.

This is not unusual. I'm guessing every parent of a child with autism remembers the top five or, for that matter, top fifty unintentionally dumb or hurtful things said to them. In *Let Me Hear Your Voice,* Catherine Maurice recalls the doctor who joked about how the lack of factual evidence about autism had provided a wealth of business for psychologists and psychiatrists. In *The Siege,* Clara Claiborne Park remembers a pediatrician who tried to reassure her by saying of her daughter, "I don't think you got a lemon."

In our case, there was a neighbour with a son Jonah's age who wondered out loud if maybe we'd spent too much time when Jonah was younger encouraging our son's more offbeat gifts. Cynthia had sought out this neighbour to confide in her because the neighbour had done some volunteer work years earlier at a school for children with developmental delays. This made her, at the time, the closest thing we could find to an expert. An appointment at a clinic was weeks off for Jonah, maybe months. We also hadn't told anyone anything yet. We thought we were alone. We didn't know then how many other people, parents of children with autism, there would be to consult with, in person, online, in books. In the meantime, our neighbour listened to Cynthia's concerns patiently, sympathetically. Then she said: "It could be you pushed him too hard." She went on to repeat a theory she'd heard discussed at the school where she volunteered. It was about parents who sometimes unwittingly encourage counter-productive traits, stims—it was the first time I heard that word—in their children, children who might be predisposed to this type of issue. She'd seen it, she said, at this place where she volunteered. Well, she'd heard about it anyway from some of the staff there—child care workers and psychologists.

This was all nonsense, of course, and tactless. But later when Cynthia, in tears, repeated it to me, I couldn't keep from wondering if our neighbour might have a point. After that, I couldn't help reviewing what *I* might have done to make this happen. For instance, should I have taught Jonah the St. Crispin's Day speech from *Henry V* when he wasn't much more than two? I remember I taped the Kenneth Branagh movie version and played it repeatedly for him. He loved learning it, or so I thought. (I certainly loved teaching it to him.) In any case, I could probably find Jonah reciting the lines on one of those tapes my sister transferred to DVD, the DVDs she reluctantly gave me on Jonah's eleventh birthday, with a note that said, "You should look at this, really!?!" Then I could watch him exclaiming:

> This story shall the good man teach his son;
> And Crispin Crispian shall ne'er go by,
> From this day to the ending of the world,
> But we in it shall be remembered;
> We few, we happy few, we band of brothers ...

Jonah had and still has an extraordinary head for arcane facts. When he was two and a half he memorized a deck of playing cards, featuring the names of fifty-two breeds of horses. Words like Lipizzanner and Clydesdale rolled off his tongue as Cynthia held up a card and quizzed him. He never seemed to grow tired of the game. I can see now how this all must have seemed to other people, like party tricks— *Henry V*, for heaven's sake—or hubris. At the same time, who didn't find it endearing? Who didn't get a tremendous kick out of Jonah's precociousness and our preposterous pride? I couldn't leave a family get-together or a visit to a neighbour's without Jonah showing off, without me coaxing him to do one of our routines. Our fist bumps, our running gags, all our shtick.

> Me: See you later ...
> Jonah: Alligator.
> Me: In a while ...
> Jonah: Crocodile.
> Me: Stay loose ...
> Jonah: Mongoose.
> Me: Don't be late ...
> Jonah: You primate.
> Me: Tamarra ...
> Jonah: Cabybara.

We could have gone on; often we did. We boasted about Jonah's love of books, a genetic predisposition, no doubt, and his obsession with the alphabet. He knew it backwards and forwards almost before he could walk. But now here was our neighbour, with perfect hindsight, pointing out to Cynthia what we were too crazy in love with Jonah to see, that there was something wrong. "You know what she's really saying," Cynthia said. "She's saying we did this to him."

WHAT WENT WRONG? It's a question you're forever asking when you have a child with autism. Perhaps, as a consequence, other people are drawn to the question, too, even if they aren't tactless enough to come right out and ask it. In the last few years, we've received emails and phone calls with a heads-up about everything from the dangers of vaccinations to the merits of green tea. Television and video games and computers, anything with a screen, have recently taken a share of the blame. Some studies link an infant's exposure to flashing images with an increased inability to process information. A Facebook friend recommended a blog that suggested giving marijuana to your child with autism. Another acquaintance Cynthia occasionally runs into never fails to request a sample of Jonah's pee. The urine is supposedly some kind of crystal ball, an indicator of procedures to avoid and those to pursue. There are also studies showing a higher incidence of autism in the children of older parents, forty and up, or of parents with graduate degrees. Did we know that? *I did,* I felt like saying, *and if I could give back my useless M.A. now I would.* Why didn't someone tell me this at the time: that there was a price to pay for being an unemployable book nerd? I would have gladly skipped my graduate courses on Old English and library science. I could have lived without Chaucer and the correct way to format a bibliography. Some studies suggest that parents who may have exhibited mild autistic traits of their own when they were younger are more likely to have a child on the spectrum. *Is that us?* We've been informed, by friends and acquaintances both, about the latest link between old sperm and autism. That would be *my* old sperm they're talking about. There's the missing gene theory and the testosterone theory, which suggests that boys with autism tend to be extreme boys. They have too much of the male hormone, and too much of it is distributed in the wrong places in the brain. I thought that just led to more offensive linemen, but what do I know? So, yes, we're used to all of this theorizing and guesswork by now; we've learned to take it in stride. We even learned something from our neighbour and our first experience with generalized, uninformed, and unsolicited blame; we learned that what went wrong is beside the point. No good can come of asking the question. Not now and not for us.

IN *THE EMPTY FORTRESS,* Bruno Bettelheim draws an analogy between his experience in Nazi concentration camps and the experience of children with autism. He explains that for these damaged children a cold, uncaring mother was the equivalent of an S.S. prison guard. In his personal writing, Bettelheim demonstrated the memoir's dark potential. You could write about your terrible experience and make it worse. You could turn lemons into poison.

Bettelheim's theories were largely discredited by the mid-1970s, though the after-effects linger. The notion that parents must somehow be doing something wrong has remained a convenient way of explaining an inconveniently mysterious disorder. So while it's true that parents no longer have to take the rap for making their children autistic as they once did, they are often blamed or feel blamed for not knowing the best way to make their children better. Maybe they haven't read the right book, or sought out an effective treatment. Or maybe they have, and failed to carry it out rigorously, consistently enough. You should have been more vigilant. You should be collecting the kid's pee and testing it. Or maybe you should have sewn a red ribbon into every stitch of underwear you owned the day your son was born and never ever removed it.

ELEVEN

Welcome to Autismland

"My son Ben's original diagnosis was 'severely impaired with infantile autism.' He carries a secondary diagnosis of profound mental retardation. But he's a lot more than his diagnosis. He's eighteen now and has made far more progress than anyone ever suggested. He currently functions at what's called a moderate level," Susan F. Rzucidlo says. "I would rather this not be what my son lived with because my fear is what happens when I'm not here to care for him. Still, so much good has come from the people I've met and the friends I've made and the people who stand beside you and the work I've done, I can tell you that has been a blessing."

Rzucidlo is on the phone from her home in suburban Delaware. I found her on Facebook, but I learned about her before that because of an essay she wrote called "Welcome to Beirut." It is, in the world of parents of children with autism, a subversive tract, cherished mainly for its honest, angry prose. For Rzucidlo, though, it was a one-off. She doesn't consider herself a writer. Instead, her way of dealing with her son's situation has been to become a community activist. Rzucidlo has been working at instituting what she calls a "premise alert system," first in her hometown for her son, then elsewhere for others like him. Her idea is simple, so simple you wonder why no one ever thought of it before. Rzucidlo's goal is to educate first responders, such as police or paramedics or firefighters, about special-needs individuals in the community. If there is a call involving Ben, for example, the first responder will ideally arrive at Rzucidlo's house knowing that he's dealing with an individual with autism and knowing that that individual's language and communication skills may be limited and that he may not answer when called. The system caught on in her community, and Rzucidlo has pushed, with some success, to have it adopted throughout the state and some day, she hopes, even wider. This is, she tells me, one of the positive things to come out of her son's condition.

"Of course, in the end, I'd still knock over my grandmother or anyone else's to get to a cure if there were one," Rzucidlo says. We've been on the phone for about an hour, though I know that what I'll find out when I sit down to transcribe the interview is that I've talked much more than she has. I've gone on endlessly about the book I'm trying to write for starters, about how my wife hasn't read it yet and how I worry about what she's going to think. I talk about Jonah, too, and it becomes clear from her response that she thinks I'm lucky, that Jonah is more high-functioning than her son. I'm tempted to try to make up for this randomness—Whose kid is doing better?—by pointing out how much more high-functioning she is than me. But I don't know how to say that and make it come out right either. So, finally, I shut up.

"I don't know that I'll ever accept this," she goes on. "It's a chronic pain and it comes like the wind. Sometimes you go along and you really barely feel it and other times, it knocks you to the ground. Milestones especially do that—like when Ben turned sixteen and I thought he should be driving now and, you know, he will never drive. For the most part, though, you walk around with the wind ever-present but also not all that noticeable. You get used to it: the abnormality of it." She has, she added, mellowed since she compared the experience of finding out her son has autism to that of being kidnapped by terrorists:

One day someone comes up from behind you and throws a black bag over your head. They start kicking you in the stomach…. You are terrified, kicking and screaming you struggle to get away but there are too many of them, they overpower you and stuff you into a trunk of a car. Bruised and dazed, you don't know where you are. What's going to happen to you? Will you live through this? This is the day you get the diagnosis. Your child has autism.

Rzucidlo wrote "Welcome to Beirut" as a response to "Welcome to Holland," Emily Perl Kingsley's inspirational essay, which is ubiquitous in the special-needs community. It's available online, and for years it was regularly reprinted in the "Dear Abby" newspaper column, anthologized in books like *Chicken Soup for the Mother's Soul*, and set to music as a choral piece. Like us, Rzucidlo received her first copy soon after her son was diagnosed. "As a matter of fact, in that first week I remember seven different people giving me a copy of 'Welcome to Holland.' I almost lost my mind," Rzucidlo says. "So I just sat down and wrote my version in one sitting. It just poured out of me. I'd love to go back and edit it, but I also think I should just leave it rough because this *is* rough. This is a hard path."

In the beginning, Rzucidlo's path consisted of dealing with a clueless bureaucracy. This was in the early 1990s, and she was routinely denied services. "The woman in our community who was in charge of Ben's case when he was first diagnosed was dead-set against any child having autism. She wasn't going to permit it in her county."

At the same time, she was dealing with psychologists who were recommending she put her son in an institution, who told her he would never be able to eat with a spoon, never tie his shoes, never talk, and never know she was his mother. When she refused to listen and walked out of one psychologist's office, the psychologist sent Rzucidlo an unsolicited report—about her. "It said that I was in deep denial about the severity of my son's disability and that I needed therapy. Well, you know, I may very well need therapy, but it's not because of that."

You are dropped into the middle of a war zone, Rzucidlo writes in "Welcome to Beirut": "You don't know the language and you don't know what's going on. Bombs are dropping—'Lifelong diagnosis' and 'Neurologically impaired.' Bullets whiz by—'refrigerator mothers,' 'a good smack is all he needs to straighten up.' Your adrenaline races as the clock ticks away your child's chances for 'recovery.' You sure as heck didn't sign up for this and want out now! God has overestimated your abilities."

DURING THE WEEK-LONG March break, Jonah's therapy continues at home. Jessica comes for a couple of hours, but that still leaves a lot of free time, so Cynthia has been taking Jonah to the park every day. This is Montreal, and there is still a lot of snow and slush on the ground. It has also been unseasonably cold, but the two of them dress in layers, take snacks and blankets, and are gone for hours. Things are easier for all of us when Jonah has some physical exercise, and Cynthia says they just need to get out of the house for a while. This is hard to argue with; I am not good company. Even when I'm holed up in the basement, my general gloom somehow seeps upwards. *My So-Called Memoir* is now, in lieu of anything better to call it, the unofficial title of the book I am writing, and it's not going well. I've sent proposal letters to a few literary agents in Toronto, and so far only one has gotten back to me requesting an outline. *Outline? If I could come up with an outline I wouldn't need a book.* I find myself giving up on the manuscript daily. There's too much to say and nowhere to start. So I try to break the process down. I know what I have to do—just write a sample chapter, one chapter I'm happy with, and that will be enough. But it's not. I find myself giving up on the sample chapter daily.

The same goes for *More Bad Animals*. The characters are not exactly coming to life. The problem is: they're less sympathetic in the sequel. The delight Jonah took in their misbehaviour is missing. While we've had some time to work on it during this break, even when I can coax him into sitting with me for a few minutes, it feels too much like homework and he bolts. So I've taken the liberty of turning his characters into whiners and complainers, passive-aggressive, self-pitying, insufficiently evolved cows, yaks, and camels. The two monkeys I've introduced to the story, son and father, are even worse. They have forsaken swinging through trees and eating bananas for sniping. Which is another problem: there's not enough action in the story. Maybe all the bad animals should go on a road trip or something—head out for the moon or Mongolia. Cynthia was right: sequels don't work.

"So what are you two doing in the park?" I ask Cynthia when she returns late one afternoon.

"I can't tell. It's a surprise."

"Come on. I'm terribly bored with myself."

"You?"

"Surprise me."

"All right, I wanted you to see it in person. I was going to drag you to the park tomorrow, but here." She sits me down on the couch and hands me her phone. Then she calls Jonah and calls him again. He comes running in and slides to a kind of abrupt, tilting Charlie Chaplin stop. He gives us each a look, somewhere between desperation and frustration. It's unfamiliar and worrisome. *What now?* He just wants to get back to the YouTube video he's watching—Katy Perry singing "Hot n Cold"—and is frustrated because we're bothering him. I realize now why I didn't recognize the look—it's his pre-teenage scowl. He hasn't perfected it yet, but it's reassuring to know that he's working on it. If there was a book called *What to Expect from Your Eleven-Year-Old*, I'm sure this look, what it means, what it portends, how to deal with it, would all be covered in an early chapter.

"We're going to show Daddy what you've been doing in the park," Cynthia says, "and then you can go back to Katy Perry." We all huddle close so we can watch the small screen on her phone together. "I hope it's clear enough. I'll put it on the computer later, but look. Jonah, tell Daddy who that is and where."

"That's Jonah, in the park," he says, still distracted. His mother gives him a look and he says, "That's me in the park." I hear him, on the video, singing—"You could be better than a jar"—before I can make out what he's doing. Then I see him on the move, swinging from one bar to the next. There must be a dozen on this particular jungle gym. He's not smooth but he keeps going, slowly, deliberately. He's wearing winter clothes and gloves, which are probably making the task harder. Still, if he feels the strain, he's not showing it. He's certainly not hurrying. His arms are strong from all the practice he's done at home. Cynthia zooms in for a close-up, and that's when I see another unfamiliar expression on my son's face—absolute determination.

Then I watch as two boys, a little bigger than Jonah, come up behind him on the bars. Even after the fact, I can feel a knot of worry settle in my chest as if I am there with him, right now. He's not going fast enough. I almost shout out at him to hurry. But the other boys are watching him closely. They're also humming a tune I can't quite make out. When Jonah finally makes it to the last bar and drops to the ground, the other two boys fall along with him and pat him on the back.

"This is the first time he made it all the way around on all the bars. Right, Jonah?" Cynthia says.

"Right."

"And who are those guys?" I ask.

"Jonah, tell Daddy who they are." Cynthia smiles at me and gives me a nudge with her shoulder.

"My friends from the park."

Okay, then, I want their names, their telephone numbers, land line and cell, their email addresses, Twitter accounts, all their particulars. Cynthia takes my hand and squeezes it. But before I can ask Jonah anything else, he's gone, back to the computer, like none of this is a big deal.

FOUR YEARS AGO, Cynthia and I met Allison when she moved to Montreal from a small town out west. She had a daughter, Emily, eleven, and a son, Matthew, five, two years younger than Jonah was then. Matthew also had autism, but his was more apparent, more distinguishable than Jonah's. He grunted rather than talked. His hands flapped constantly. He seldom made eye contact or acknowledged your presence. When we finally met, though, I avoided eye contact more than Matthew did, and not just with him, with his mother too. I was afraid she would see what I was feeling, what I couldn't help feeling. Perhaps because I had so often been forced to compare Jonah with other kids, neurotypical kids, and so often forced to see how much catching up he had to do, it was an unspoken relief to be able to take note of the differences between our two sons. I was ashamed of myself then for feeling this; I'm ashamed, now, admitting it. Still, the truth was that in Matthew's company I could finally see Jonah and my family in a different light: as fortunate.

There was more to Allison's story. She was getting a divorce. "Can you believe it? Her husband walked out on her. What an asshole!" Cynthia said when she first told me about Allison's circumstances. I nodded because I can only nod at times like this. It's too risky to say anything else. I try to avoid being put in the position of justifying the community of asshole fathers, whom I understand better than Cynthia and better than I care to admit.

"You're one in a million," Cynthia likes to joke, and while that's not quite true, the statistics we've heard from sources like Harriet are disturbing enough. The debate continues on the internet, but the number you always see is that eighty percent of fathers of children with autism walk out on their marriages. So while I may not be one in a million, I am, arguably, one in five.

Allison, newly single, had come to Montreal determined to leave her old life behind, at least that part of it she could. She had begun a correspondence with a Montreal man online, and even though that no longer looked promising, she was staying. She had found a good school for her son, her main reason for coming to Montreal, and she was devoting what little extra time she had to making her daughter feel comfortable here. She was looking for friends, a job, a house. She was learning French; she was going it alone. Both Cynthia and I were in awe.

"She has pluck," I told Cynthia. "What I mean to say is that next to her I can't help feeling, I don't know ..."

"Pluckless?"

"You too?"

I was tempted whenever I saw Allison to come right out and ask her how she did it, how she managed everything on her own—in particular, how she did it all without complaint. At least, I never heard her complain. She was British by birth, and so, at first, I assumed she came by this stiff-upper-lip quality naturally. But it was probably something simpler—something like strength of character. *How do you get that?* I found myself wanting to ask her. But I never quite figured out how to bring the subject up. Until one day she seemed to bring it up on my behalf. As we supervised a predictably unsuccessful play date for our kids, as Jonah sat in the corner flipping through an animal alphabet book, and Matthew started, stopped, and replayed the same opening scene from a barely viewable *Thomas the Train* video, the two of them happily lost in Autismland, she anticipated the question I couldn't bring myself to ask.

"I know that I was chosen for this," she said.

"By this you mean ... well ..." I couldn't imagine what she meant. After all this time, I was still trying to figure out exactly what "this" was. I glanced over at Matthew, who was covering his ears and shrieking now that Jonah was done with his book and eyeing the VCR remote. Jonah, meanwhile, was oblivious. He was telling himself a knock-knock joke and laughing. Play date, indeed.

"*This*. Making sure Matthew has the best life he can. Whatever that is or might turn out to be. That's what gives my life meaning," she went on, shrugging, a little embarrassed perhaps by the way this confession had spilled out. Or perhaps she was uneasy with the way what she was saying sounded: too noble, too cheery, too much like a rationalization, to me and maybe to her too. So she changed the subject. "Cynthia tells me you're thinking about writing about Jonah. You should, you know. You owe it to him. You owe it to yourself."

"There's a problem. I don't seem to know where to start."

"Just start."

EVEN AS I'M ON the phone with Emily Perl Kingsley, going on, more or less unsolicited, about *My So-Called Memoir*, remembering occasionally to ask her about that little essay she wrote some thirty years ago, I know what I should be telling her: how I reacted when we received our copy of "Welcome to Holland." At some point during this interview with Kingsley, I'll have to come clean and tell her I freaked out.

But I also know why I'm hesitating. It's because even though I've never found Kingsley's essay inspiring, the same is not true for the woman herself. She is precisely that, in fact. She couldn't be nicer either. As an example: when I tell her about *Bad Animals*, the book Jonah wrote in school, she says she'd love to read it some time. Then she gives me her New York address and insists I send it. She tells me about the long Emmy Award–winning career she's had as a writer on *Sesame Street*. She joined the show in 1970, just a year after it first went on the air, and continues to work there. After her son Jason was born with Down syndrome in 1974, she was instrumental in advocating for children with disabilities to be featured on the program. Getting these kids, kids like hers, like mine, in the public eye has become her crusade much like Susan Rzucidlo has crusaded for a premise alert system. "There's been progress, but it's so slow," Kingsley says. "People with disabilities are the country's largest minority—by far, far, far—more than African-Americans, three times Hispanics, six times Asians. And that's not counting people like you and me who are not disabled but who care about them. If you added those people in, it would be, well, almost everybody. Still, we can't get representation. It's appalling."

Another reason I'm having a hard time getting around to my confession is that I'm trying not to choke up as Kingsley tells me the story of what happened when her son was born. "We were given the worst possible scenario. We were told he would never walk or talk or read or write. We were told we should send him away and tell people that he had died in childbirth. It was a nightmare."

But Kingsley and her husband took Jason home anyway. "That's when we found he was really kind of bright and delightful and that he was learning like crazy and that everything we had been told was completely crazy. We made a promise to ourselves that nobody else should have to go through what we did."

It was during a counselling session with a mother of a newborn baby with Down syndrome that the idea for "Welcome to Holland" occurred to her. "I was sitting at the bedside of this new mom and this little analogy just came out of my mouth," she said. "When I got home I thought, you know, that wasn't so bad. I ought to write it down. I found myself repeating it to more and more people. It sort of took on a life of its own. It's been translated into dozens of languages and I probably still have three to five requests a week to reprint it. People carry it in their wallets, put it on their refrigerators. It really is the largest thing I have ever done. I'm just grateful it's helped so many people."

"Have you gotten any negative responses?" I ask, and I realize I'm holding my breath. This is my opening. What about people like Susan

Rzucidlo and her essay? Or Laura Krueger Crawford, whose version, "Holland Schmolland," is also easy to find online and was written, Crawford told me, because "I'm just not one of those people who have to put a happy face on things ... who have to try to find the silver lining." What about the people "Welcome to Holland" has driven crazy with its uplifting analogy? People like me.

"The people who have been angriest with me are the autism people. I guess because I haven't made it bad enough. Well, come on, give me a break," Kingsley says.

"We can be a pain in the neck, I know."

"First of all, I was writing about Down syndrome. It never occurred to me that every disability under the sun would come along and claim 'Welcome to Holland' as their own. That's not my fault, you know."

"No, it's not," I say and then just blurt it out. I tell her I also had a problem with "Welcome to Holland" when I first read it. She doesn't respond. I didn't intend to ambush her like this, so I babble on about how I feel differently now, how what I've come to understand is that writing about this kind of thing is a way to deal with it. For some of us, it's the only way. So, yes, I understand why she wrote the essay. "But, to be honest, Holland," I finally add, a little breathless. "Why Holland?" I'm prepared for the next thing I hear to be a dial tone. Instead, she barely reacts. "I've heard about 'Holland Schmolland,' but not 'Welcome to Beirut,'" she says matter-of-factly. I guess you get a tough skin writing for Muppets. Besides, she tells me, she recently came up with a whole new analogy for parents like us.

"Look, Jason, my son, has done wonderfully. Have you read his book? It's called *Count Us In: Growing Up with Down Syndrome*. It's a wonderful book, I recommend it. Jason is extraordinarily high-functioning, but people who feel I am bragging about my kid because he did so well, that's ridiculous. So here's my new story, okay? We're all in this boat, the same boat, and whether you're sitting in the front or the back, it doesn't make a bit of difference. We are all in *this* boat.

If we all look down, we can see there are oars. If we all start rowing together we realize the boat is going to go farther than if we didn't. And we all get the companionship of rowing together, which is kind of fun. The wind is in our hair and we can sing a rowing song. But we are never going to catch up to that other boat. You know, the one that has twenty-four-hour margaritas and salsa dancing on the top deck. Forget it. You're not going to catch it. So if that's what's on your mind, get it out of your mind. Because we are on *this* boat and we are on it together. And just don't start measuring yourself against all the other people on this boat. You know why? Because this is *our* boat."

TWELVE

Poor Us

Can you write your way out of disappointment? Out of a corner?

In her last novel, *Unless*, published in 2003, Carol Shields is uncharacteristically angry. It's an uncomfortable stance for Shields. Even in her gloomiest novel, *The Stone Diaries*, the anger of the protagonist, Daisy Goodwill, is repressed. That's the point of the story, one readers often miss. Shields often expressed surprise that the novel she set out to write—about disappointment and regret—was routinely praised for being about resilience and redemption. Still, she was that rare literary writer who did not shy away from happy endings. I asked about this when I interviewed her once. It was, I explained, the thing that distinguished her work for me. Contemporary literature, fiction certainly, doesn't lend itself to happy endings. They invariably feel contrived. Put another way, you can't go wrong with doom and gloom. Which is why it takes a confident writer to even attempt a happy ending. Well, maybe, Shields said. With *Larry's Party*, for instance, she still wasn't sure she'd made the right decision in having her hapless title character reunite with his first wife. But, she admitted, the happy ending habit turned out to be a hard one to break. She'd wanted Larry to have something good happen to him and she had the power to make it so, so she did. As a consequence, she'd taken some flak from reviewers, and now, after the fact, she wasn't sure they were wrong. She worried that she'd indulged in a kind of wishful thinking, *her* own particular brand of wishful literary thinking.

At first glance, *Unless* also appears to end too well. It concludes with the novel's narrator, Reta Winters, herself a writer of books which feature happy endings, reunited with her emotionally fragile daughter. The daughter returns home, after months of self-imposed homelessness, safe and reasonably sound. She's fragile but apparently on the right track. She intends to return to university to study science, perhaps linguistics. In the final pages, Reta is cautiously optimistic. She also manages to finish the novel she's been struggling with. "Everything is neatly wrapped up at the end, since tidy conclusions are a convention of comic fiction, as we all know," Reta says. "I have bundled up each of the loose narrative threads, but what does such fastidiousness mean? It doesn't mean that all will be well for ever and ever, amen; it means that for five minutes a balance has been achieved at the margin of the novel's thin textual plan; make that five seconds; make that the millionth part of a nanosecond. The uncertainty principle; did anyone ever believe otherwise?"

Only this time, for Shields, the happy ending doesn't hold, not even for "the millionth part of a nanosecond." I'm not buying it anyway. I'm also not blaming Shields. She wrote *Unless* in the last stages of terminal breast cancer, and the knowledge of that, for both her and the reader, casts a shadow over the narrative. More than that, it makes the novel feel disjointed at times, almost unmoored as Shields is caught between resignation and rage and uncertainty. It's a tough book to get through, finally, because it highlights the limitations and the untidiness of literature. It reminds us how resistant our lives can be to the imposition of meaning, to the credible prospect of a happy ending.

"'THE JOY OF AUTISM'—and that's what she's going with?" Cynthia says.

"She's already gone with it. That's what she calls her weblog."

"And how's that working out?"

"She said it got her into trouble when she first started the blog five or six years ago. Back then, the name was controversial."

"I suppose so," Cynthia says.

"There were nasty comments. People writing to say she was an idiot and worse. But not so much now."

I'm recounting the highlights of a telephone interview I just completed with a woman named Estée Klar. She's a Toronto writer and art curator I learned about when I read her heartfelt essay "The Perfect Child." It's about her son Adam, who's on the spectrum. Not long after Adam was diagnosed, Klar started TAAP or The Autism Acceptance Project. TAAP's mission is "to bring about a different and positive view about autism to the public in order to create tolerance and acceptance in the community." She also started blogging about her life and about autism, which, she says on her website, is not an illness but a way of being. Even so, Klar is hardly starry-eyed. She knows first-hand how tough dealing with autism is. She also knows that if she were to accept all the gloom and doom heaped on her over the years she'd be incapable of doing anything, including what she believes is best for her son. Currently, Klar's blog reaches some two hundred and fifty thousand readers.

"*Still*," Cynthia says, which is what I'm thinking, too—*still?*

"I know, I know, joy and autism together; it's a stretch," I say. "But, you know, it felt good talking to her. She was encouraging. She wished me good luck. She's writing a memoir, too. I know: Who isn't?" Cynthia doesn't say it, but I know what she's thinking: *You aren't.*

My So-Called Memoir is a long-running topic of discussion in our house. Cynthia has supported me from the beginning in my decision to write about our family and continues to be supportive, even though I'm starting to feel her enthusiasm waning lately as she begins to suspect that this project of mine is still very much a work in progress, assuming you use the word *progress* loosely.

At the best of times, which is to say just after Jonah was born, Cynthia and I were already like the protagonist and antagonist in Dr. Seuss's *Green Eggs and Ham*. The former, Sam-I-Am, insisting that the latter, the obstinate, nameless fellow with the big floppy hat, try something he's determined not to try. The story ends well enough, with Sam-I-Am winning out, with the message of open-mindedness and self-improvement delivered and received. But it's the big-hatted guy's steadfast obstinacy I relate to. Let's face it, Sam-I-Am is a monumental pain in the ass—the more so for having been right about those green eggs all along. The story, even for Dr. Seuss, strains credulity. Think about it: Do you know anyone who, after protesting so vehemently, would be so quick to change his mind—so comfortable with admitting he was not just wrong but wrong all along?

Communication isn't that simple. It is clear, for instance, that there are things Cynthia and I can't talk about. We know this sometimes even as we're talking about them, whether we're in Harriet's office or out on one of her recommended date nights, over dinner or in bed, early in the morning, before Jonah wakes up. We are both holding back too much. The subject—Jonah's future, both immediate and long-term, from what high school we will choose to how he will manage once we're gone, from puberty to financial planning—is fraught with everything we can't bring ourselves to agree on.

We can agree on this, though: "The Joy of Autism" is a curious name for a blog. I've trudged up the stairs from my office in the basement to tell Cynthia about this as well as something else I heard during the course of my interview with Klar.

"Okay, forget about the whole joy business," I say. "That's not the main thing. Listen, I've got a new candidate. You know, for The List."

Cynthia looks up from her computer at the mention of The List: *Our* List, to be precise. Over the last seven years, I've had my ideas about comedy confirmed. The worse things get, the easier it is to be funny. "Tragedy and comedy have a common root, whose name at last I think I know. Desperation," as Peter De Vries said. And while Cynthia doesn't always see things this way, she still laughs at my jokes often enough to encourage me to repeat them. That is, incidentally, how a running gag is born.

"All right, tell me about The List. Who do we have now?" Cynthia asks.

"Mr. Joy-of-Autism."

"Do I really want to know this? Should you be telling me this?"

"Probably not. Definitely not."

"So?"

In a recent blog, Klar mentioned she was about to be divorced. She brought this up in our conversation as well. It was clearly fresh, and she filled out the story for me. She told me her husband, who came into their marriage, his second, with four children, was leaving her to go back to his first wife and presumably his first family.

"'The guy's like Job in reverse," I tell Cynthia. "Imagine Job bailing, throwing his hands up, saying, 'That's it for me. My limit on suffering. I won't be doing any more. I'm done.'"

Once Klar told me about her personal circumstances and once it sunk in, my interview with her might as well have been done, too. I couldn't think of another question to ask; I could only think of jokes: awful, inappropriate ones. *Take my new life, please.* I forgot about why I had called in the first place. I forgot about *My So-Called Memoir.* I forgot about asking her if writing a daily blog helped her cope with the trials of raising a child with autism. I also didn't get around to asking if she was planning to turn her blog into a book like so many people were doing these days, or if it had attracted any interest from agents or publishers. The truth was I couldn't focus on anything but her husband's behaviour. Like a kid bringing home an unexpectedly good report card, I couldn't wait to run upstairs and tell Cynthia.

"Back to his first wife? Are you sure?"

"That's what she said. Have you ever heard of anything like that? Who does a thing like that?"

"Who?"

"An asshole, exactly," we say together. There is, in both our voices, inexcusable glee. Where is our sympathy? Where is our empathy? It makes me think theory of mind is just that—a theory. It's a jungle out there, after all. Empathy is no one's top priority.

"So where does that situate you on The Asshole List?" Cynthia asks, getting up to hug me.

"I'd rather not boast."

"You've earned it, sweetheart." The hug is followed by an unexpectedly passionate kiss. Here we are making out, and in the middle of the day. Marriage, whatever else you say about it, has its astonishments.

The List, I should explain, is an inside joke, the kind couples share that should probably remain between them. But it's also an important source of self-vindication. It consists of the names and narratives of fathers and husbands behaving worse, frequently much worse, than me. This is, as Michael Chabon points out in his essay collection *Manhood for Amateurs*, the handy thing about being a father these days: "The historic standard is so pitifully low."

Fictional fathers count—from King Lear to Homer Simpson. So do celebrity fathers: from Joe Jackson, Michael's dad, to Leo Tolstoy. On that front, the horror stories are endless. Minor celebrities count, too. Like Richard Heene. Most people have probably forgotten Heene by now, but not me. He's my lodestar. If you don't remember the story, he was briefly famous for claiming that his six-year-old son had disappeared in a hot-air balloon the Heene family happened to keep tethered in their backyard. The story was a hoax, dreamed up to land Heene his own reality TV series. The trouble was he hadn't properly briefed his son on the secret nature of the plan. The kid, the Balloon Boy as the media immediately dubbed him, eventually spilled the beans in an interview on CNN. Heene went to jail for a short time and hasn't been heard from since.

There are also people Cynthia and I know on The List. Like a fellow I play pick-up basketball with who admitted to me at a bar after our weekly game that he'd recently done the worst thing a man can do. "I left my pregnant wife for another woman," he said with what seemed to me an admirable mix of self-contempt and bravado. *Admirable, sweetheart?* There's also Allison's husband and, now, Mr. Joy-of-Autism.

As I said, The List is the kind of thing that should remain private. I genuinely liked talking to Estée Klar. She is, in her outlook and love for her child, unquestionably brave. In her blog, she keeps calling for more upbeat stories—"positive autism," as she puts it—and I'm guessing that if she ever reads this, she'll be disappointed in me and my knee-jerk negativity. She'd be well within her rights, as a matter of fact, to put me at the top of *her* List.

Mothers of children with special needs, like Klar and Susan Rzucidlo and Emily Perl Kingsley, like Harriet, like Cynthia—have more to handle than they deserve. And what always astonishes me is how they do handle it. They don't run out; they don't give up. They do the best they can for their families. To her credit, Klar has found or maybe created a kind of acceptance—heroic or self-deluding, who knows? who cares?—I can't even imagine. In her essay "The Perfect Child," she writes about how she has changed her attitude: "We are far from the days when we viewed autism as an illness to be cured.... Adam is perfect. This is what autism has taught me. It is the world that isn't." There's a mother's love and strength for you: to blame the world for your problems and mean it is an enviable accomplishment, especially since the world couldn't care less.

Attitude aside, Klar and I have a lot in common. To date, we have both spent years trying to write a book we can't quite figure out how to write. We are both hoping to find an agent or editor or publisher who will somehow see the intrinsic value in turning our complicated lives into literature. We have similar concerns when it comes to narrative structure—for instance, how do you tell a story when you have no idea how it's going to turn out? Neither of us can even guess what is going to happen to our sons. What progress they will make. What setbacks they will have to overcome. That includes, for Klar, worrying about things I confess I haven't considered. Like the ethics of writing a book about her son, about how telling his story, perhaps getting it published, might adversely affect him at some point down the road. How it is, ultimately, an invasion of his privacy—an invasion he is not now in a position to object to. I have different worries—like how writing about Jonah might make *me* look down the road. How bad I mean. Of course, one editor I did tell about the book advised me to embrace my selfishness, my narcissism.

"You want to look bad, the worse the better," she said. "People will naturally feel sorry for you. That's not the problem. The problem is to not come across as pitiful." Write yourself a scene in a bar, she added, where you're drunk and horny and contemplating an affair with a stranger you've just met.

"I don't go to bars. I don't like strangers," I told her.

"Well, I'm sure you'll think of something awful you could do or you've already done," she said. I promised to get back to her on that. I am hopeful. As it turns out, there's more than one way to be an asshole. In the meantime, I'm also hopeful that Richard Heene will make a comeback by the time I've managed to write a decent book proposal and an outline—by then, he should be working on a memoir of his own—because it occurs to me that you could, without trying too hard, without being an incisive critic of our current culture, make a convincing argument that Heene's determination to exploit his son and my writing a book about Jonah are not all that different. Jonah might as well be my balloon boy.

THERE'S A SCENE IN Philip Roth's memoir *Patrimony* in which the author discovers his elderly father, Herman, in a bathroom, where he has, in his words, "beshat himself." With unfailing tenderness, the son cleans up the father and the mess he has made. This incident is, in Roth's obsessively detailed description, monumental. Here, Roth does for dealing with a shit-spattered bathroom what he once did, in *Portnoy's Complaint*, for masturbating into a raw piece of liver. He makes the scene epic, a profound meditation on a most common-place event. (Well, not the liver.) At one point, Roth inspects the shit, which is everywhere and on everything—from his father's discarded clothes to "the tips of the bristles of [Philip Roth's] toothbrush"—and thinks: "It's like writing a book.... I have no idea where to begin."

In the middle of the cleanup, Roth's father makes him promise not to tell anyone what happened. Roth gives his word. Then, of course, he writes about it. Here's the proof: you're reading it. True, this is years later and his father has died by the time the book appears, but I'm not sure that makes the promise any less broken. Roth knows this better than anyone. He knows he's betrayed his relationship with his father, all for a scene about his relationship with his father. But then this is what writers do. We are not to be trusted. We twist words, distort intentions, reveal secrets. We use our own story, and when that runs out of steam we use those of the people closest to us.

So far, Cynthia has established no ground rules or boundaries for me to follow in writing about Jonah or our family. But I'm expecting them. I am waiting for the other shoe to drop. I've seen her wince when I talk about *My So-Called Memoir* at dinner parties or book launches. Fellow writers tend to ask what you're working on, and while I'm usually vague, lately I've started to wing it and go into a little more detail than I should, which is to say more detail than there actually is. "It's not just going to be about autism," I explain. "It's going to be about parent-hood and marriage, too. About hope and despair and storytelling.... About all the day-to-day shit you have to deal with." Driving home,

Cynthia will eventually ask: "Day-to-day shit? And about marriage, too? What about marriage?" I shrug. I can probably get away with that kind of non-response response now because once the book is finished, if it's ever finished, Cynthia expects to be heard from. I've promised to interview her and she's holding me to that promise.

"You can have a whole chapter to yourself," I say. "Like Molly Bloom in *Ulysses*—only with punctuation. And you can say whatever you want as long as you say 'yes yes I will yes' at the end."

"Fine. But I think I'm also going to need veto power."

"Sure," I say, but neither one of us is convinced this is a promise I can keep. It may already be too late for that.

AT THE BEGINNING OF our conversation, Klar and I did speculate on why this subject of autism, of our children, was proving so difficult to write about. How, for instance, do you explain the feeling of having the ground constantly shifting beneath your feet? Or how you feel guilty every time you wish you could run away and how you, nevertheless, think about running away a lot? But where the hell, we both wondered, would we go?

There's a competition, seldom discussed, between parents of children with autism. Maybe that's because it's a disorder which remains largely mysterious, despite its growing prevalence. How you're treating your kid—what therapy you are using, even what book by what expert you're reading—becomes a kind of contest over who appears to be getting it right and who appears not to be. Is he taking vitamins? Supplements? Who's his doctor? His therapist? Will he have the flu vaccine? Did you read Jenny McCarthy? How could you read that crap? Have you purchased a hyperbaric chamber? Checked his urine? You've got to be kidding me. Do you accept him for who he is? Do you try to change him? As Chekhov, a writer as well as a doctor and himself a terminally ill patient, said: "When a lot of remedies are suggested for a disease that means it can't be cured."

With autism, there's also no way of knowing who will have a happy ending and who will not, or, for that matter, what might be responsible for either. I'm guessing the author of a blog called "The Joy of Autism" might also point out that it's impossible to say what constitutes a happy ending. "There is no other normal but the normal we create for ourselves," Klar writes in "The Perfect Child." Joy is subjective, too, and elusive. You'd better be prepared to make it up as you go along.

When I talked to Susan Rzucidlo she told me that the only good piece of advice she got from any doctor about her son Ben was from one of the first psychologists to evaluate him. "She said, 'Susan, we don't know which kids will make progress and which won't. So if any professional tells you they know what will make your child get to a certain level as an adult, that's when you should get up and walk out of the room. Because no one knows.' Those are the words I live by."

Autism is a spectrum, I keep reminding myself; it stretches from despair to acceptance. But there are a lot of stops in between. It's also true that autism refuses to hold still—to be pinned down or neatly wrapped up. As a result, it can make adversaries of people who should be allies. I've seen it happen. When we first met Allison, for instance, she was implementing a complicated gluten-free diet for her son Matthew. Not only that, she insisted Cynthia try it with Jonah, too. He was so close to normal, Allison explained, it could make a huge difference for our son, an even bigger difference for him than it probably could for Matthew. Meanwhile, Cynthia urged Allison to take up ABA again (she'd tried it years earlier). Cynthia introduced her to The Consultant. She also invited Allison to one of our team meetings. Cynthia's feeling was that ABA might help Matthew talk since he was not verbal at the time. But the suggestions, on both sides, must have felt like accusations, like judgments, and the friendship was effectively over.

We all want the best for our children, and none of us can ever really be sure what that might be. This isn't only true for parents of children with special needs or autism, though it may be truer, more urgent anyway. For all the new information and research out there, all the books and articles and TV news stories, we know we're just guessing. In the meantime, we're also trying to get through one more difficult day, hoping, with no real reason, that tomorrow might be a little easier. This can make us desperate, jealous, clueless, petty creatures. It can make us behave inappropriately, unkindly, selfishly. Like Jonah's bad animals. Poor them! Like more bad, flawed animals. Poor us!

THIRTEEN

Who's on First?

"How many days are there left of school tomorrow?" Jonah asks me at some point every Sunday. There is, in his syntax, a clue to how his mind works and how it can betray him. Although he is counting on the usual answer—and with March break over and no holidays coming up, it's a safe bet there will be five days, the last thing he wants to hear—he is also counting on being displeased with my answer. He is setting himself up for disappointment, giving himself a reason to fret. At the same time, he's also hoping for a recount. And who isn't? Who isn't counting on a freak snowstorm or an unexpected ped-day or a wildcat teacher's strike—one lousy little break? Jonah just wants to know if such a thing is possible—if that's too much to ask.

We're on the living room couch, watching the old, animated version of *Horton Hears a Who*, eating microwave popcorn, when Jonah's fretful question disrupts the good time I may have been too quick to presume we were having. I chose this video for its message. Dr. Seuss's books are like Shakespeare for kids; they encompass everything. I answer Jonah once and then ignore the question the next time, ABA style, the way I'm supposed to. I point instead to the screen and talk about what a great elephant Horton is. "He hears everything." But I know my son. He's an expert at *not* changing the subject. If we were to compile a list of Jonah's FAQs, this one, about his upcoming school week, would rank high, right behind "where are we having supper?" and slightly ahead of "can I have a bad day?"

So his question comes again and again, and eventually I do what I'm not supposed to: I try to be a responsible father and give my eleven-year-old son a reasonable, thoughtful answer. "It's still Sunday," I say. "What's the point of worrying about school now, Jonesy?" Then I quickly pass the popcorn to him, cross my fingers, and hold my breath.

Obviously, I'm the first to admit that I am on shaky ground here, that I am not the ideal person to be making the case for living in the moment, since to do that I'd actually have to believe such a thing is possible. I'm never quite sure how closely Jonah is observing me, but even if it's closer than I think, even if he can recognize the inherent hypocrisy in someone like me preaching the principle of mindfulness, I can only hope he'd be too kind to point it out.

Jonah's attention span for movies is limited. This I don't get. As a kid, I loved movies and watched them endlessly, at the expense of homework and a social life. I especially loved old Hollywood screwball comedies, anything by Billy Wilder or Preston Sturges. By now, I expected that Jonah and I would be spending our Sunday afternoons immersed in double bills: *Some Like It Hot* and *The Miracle of Morgan's Creek*. But Jonah doesn't like to be surprised, and surprises in movies, good movies especially, are hard to avoid. It's simpler than that, of course; it's just hard to get him to sit still for very long, to focus on or follow the story. In the case of *Horton Hears a Who,* I need thirty minutes of his attention. But even before the light begins to dawn on big-hearted Horton that there is more to that dust speck he's discovered than meets his elephant's eye, Jonah is squirming on the couch. The only thing keeping him briefly in place and focused on the screen is the fact that I'm in charge of doling out the popcorn and I'm doing it stingily. Still, popcorn can't last forever. A few minutes later as Horton reaches the conclusion that people are all just people, regardless of their size or appearance or behaviour or, for that matter, how their brain might work, Jonah is slouching and sliding onto the floor. He's upside down, and facing the wrong way. He's humming and plotting his escape. But I don't let him. Instead, I demand his attention. The movie has an important message to impart for all of us, but for me and Jonah in particular. Horton is heroic, after all, and not so much in his actions, though there is that, but in his philosophy of inclusiveness, in his determination to act as a responsible, patient guardian. "He's a role model for us all, Jonah," I say, turning my son right side up, which seems to shake today's predominant question loose again.

"Daddy, how many days are left of school?"

"Jonah, if you want more popcorn you're going to have to stop asking me that." *Remember, sweetheart, no bribes, no blackmailing.*

"Why?" he says.

"Do you want to know why? Huh? I'll tell you why. Because you're driving me crazy." But it's too late to protest. We're in the loop again, Jonah and me. He doesn't want to leave it and I don't know how to make him, or how to extricate myself. I lack Horton's talent to see beyond the nose on my face, to consider the big picture.

"I WAS HOPING the little guy would snap out of it." That's what one audience member who attended an early preview of *Rain Man* wrote on his comment card. The movie, which came out in 1988, won four Oscars including the award for Best Picture and Best Actor. Hoffman's portrayal of a character matter-of-factly labelled an idiot savant was, in its time and for a long time after, the most significant representation of autism in the public consciousness, largely because it was the only one.

"In the real dark night of the soul," F. Scott Fitzgerald writes in "The Crack-Up," "it is always three o'clock in the morning." And I'm guessing it was pretty close to three when I awoke last night and ended up back on the couch in the living room, channel hopping my way into an early scene between Cruise and Hoffman. Until last night, I'd deliberately avoided *Rain Man*. After Jonah's diagnosis it was a movie I vowed never to watch again. But there I was, up in the middle of the night, eating what was left of Jonah's popcorn and wondering why I never seemed to be able to stick to a plan, why I even bothered coming up with them.

"Two schmucks in a car," is how Hoffman and co-star Tom Cruise joked about what might be an appropriate, albeit unusable tag line to the movie during the making of it. Both were convinced *Rain Man* was destined to fail. They were wrong about that and about there being two schmucks in the car. There's only one. It's clear from the first time we meet Hoffman, method acting like crazy as autistic Raymond Babbitt, that we're intended to find him endearing no matter how weirdly he behaves. "Cute and hilarious," was what one reviewer said of his performance. Cruise is another matter. From the start, we are supposed to realize that he is at least as emotionally stunted as his brother, perhaps more so. Raymond has his share of head-banging tantrums, but it's Cruise who's always cracking up, who refers to his new-found brother as a "fruitcake" and an "idiot" without adding *savant*, who tells him: "You are killing me." And: "Stop acting like a fucking retard." Yet it's Cruise the audience is forced to relate to since we can't relate to Hoffman. He's too strange or too extraordinary, as the movie would eventually have us believe. As it turns out, it's Cruise who is going to have to "snap out of it" since Hoffman clearly won't or can't.

ON THE CAR RADIO the other day, the CBC announcer was reading a news story about a corrupt city official who had failed to act properly, at which point Jonah leaned forward from the backseat to interrupt. "Nicely," he said, addressing the car radio directly. I started to laugh and, glancing in the rear-view mirror, I could see Jonah's face become stern. He was gritting his teeth and muttering, "Don't laugh." I'm pretty sure he understood that the woman on the radio couldn't hear him, but he was acting on reflex and sending me a message at the same time. As far as the word *properly* was concerned, zero tolerance was now our unofficial policy, at least between Jonah and me. (Cynthia wasn't playing along.) *Properly* had become taboo, and Jonah was determined to stamp it out whenever and wherever he heard it.

Your vocabulary gets overhauled when you become the parent of a special-needs child. *Special*, for instance, no longer means what it once did; neither does *extraordinary* or *exceptional* or *challenged*. *Typical* is suddenly an unreliable word. And *normal* is fraught; you can forget about normal altogether.

At the gym recently, I ran into a friend who began to tell me about his visiting grandchild, a five-year-old boy, for whom he'd downloaded some games on his iPod. The child's grandmother objected. "But he loves it," my friend bragged. "Every time he sees me, he begs me for more. It's not so educational, I guess, but it's a good sign, right? At least it means he's normal." My friend clearly didn't realize what he was saying or to whom he was saying it. I understood immediately he hadn't meant anything by it, so I smiled weakly and went back to exercising. Every so often, though, he would glance at me from the stationary bicycle he was working out on. A few minutes later, he came up and apologized. "I said something terribly insensitive before and I feel awful...." I interrupted him, told him not to worry about it, that I hadn't even noticed, which we both knew, by then, wasn't true. But I felt worse for him than for myself. I realized he'd spent the last ten minutes beating himself up. Besides, I appreciated his apology. Not everyone would have realized what they had said or feel obliged to try, however futilely, to take it back. Nor should they. After all, *normal* was still a normal word to him.

But now, for me, all these words, labels, come out of my mouth tentatively, as if they should have invisible quotes attached to them, like the string on a yo-yo, so you can pull them back. With autism, there is the added issue of how to use the word itself. Do I refer to

Jonah as autistic or do I make the effort each time to say he has autism? Do I say it that way until it becomes second nature to me? Have I figured it out yet? Is autism something he has or something he is?

Then there's the R-word to consider. Still routinely used as an insult in movies or by comics on cable TV, for example, it's also on its way to becoming taboo. Even if you have, like me, always subscribed to the theory that sticks and stones will, indeed, break your bones but words are not worth worrying about. The smallest kid in my class, growing up, I learned to live with being called *shrimp, pipsqueak, midget, twerp*. But *retard, retarded*, sting now whenever I hear them, no matter how they're intended. There was a time, of course, when the R-word was an improvement, when it was intended to replace more hurtful, less sensitive labels like *moron, idiot, imbecile*. Even Clara Claiborne Park, writing about her daughter in *The Siege* in the mid-sixties, matter-of-factly uses the word *defective* for her own child. Still, it was inevitable for *retarded* to become ugly the way words do—because of how they are invested with our worst prejudices and fears. Every time Jonah was evaluated and assessed we were given the assurance he was not mentally retarded, definitely not. He had a developmental delay, we were told. We were intended to cling to this statement of so-called fact, of objective, diagnostic observation, and so we did, gladly. We didn't think or, later on, allow ourselves to think about what the word *retardation* means, what you'd learn about it if you just looked it up in the dictionary, or if you just thought about it for a moment.

UNTIL *RAIN MAN*, Hollywood shied away from stories about disabilities, intellectual and otherwise, for obvious reasons. How do you come up with a happy or at least satisfying ending? *The Miracle Worker*, the 1962 Hollywood version of the Helen Keller story, was an exception. But then it has, despite the heroine's multiple disabilities, a built-in uplifting conclusion. By the end of the movie, Helen Keller, played overenthusiastically by child actress Patty Duke, still can't see or hear or talk, but she can communicate. In fact, the movie ends with her communicating like crazy. She has hope, and, more to the point, we have reason to hope for her. And we, the audience, end up feeling the only way we are permitted to—profoundly satisfied. The kid snaps out of it, after all.

A Child Is Waiting, which came out a year after *The Miracle Worker*, is a braver and more compelling account of a similar story. With Stanley Kramer as the producer and Abby Mann the screenwriter (both worked on *Judgment at Nuremberg*, the venerable four-hour docudrama about the Holocaust), it had a lot going for it. Kramer also went outside the Hollywood box and chose John Cassavetes as his director. At the time, Cassavetes, a winning young actor, was also making a reputation as an avant-garde filmmaker. Together, Kramer, Mann, and Cassavetes hatched a big, ambitious plan to do something unprecedented—make a mainstream movie about mental retardation. There was certainly no imaginable upside to taking on this subject in the realistic, unsentimental manner they intended. That the movie was made at all, and by a big studio like MGM, with big-name movie stars Burt Lancaster and Judy Garland, was a testament to the good intentions of everyone involved. Cassavetes, in particular, was determined to push the envelope, to make sure the movie was as authentic and uncompromising as possible. This was just his third film and his first chance at a mainstream project with big-name leads. Even so, all the child actors he used, with the exception of the title character, were residents of a California institution for the mentally retarded. They weren't just extras in the story either; many had featured parts. "I realized truth is important," Cassavetes explained years later. "I needed to know that if I made a film about a sensitive subject like mental retardation, the people I made the film about would know I had done it to the best of my ability, with no copping out."

When the movie did come out, Brendan Gill, the film critic for *The New Yorker*, was dismissive of its casting choices. He summed up his experience watching *A Child Is Waiting* this way: "It is almost unbearable to be made to observe and admire the delicacy of the acting skill of Mr. Lancaster and Miss Garland as they move—the charming, the successful, the gifted ones—among the host of pitiful children. Despite the purity of their motives, as actors they have no business being there; simply as moviegoers, we have no business watching them."

In the end, *A Child Is Waiting* was admired but not especially successful. Or, as Gill bluntly put it, "We have no business watching them." It would be easy now to say that the failure of *A Child Is Waiting* was a sign of the times—that no one would write a review as appallingly offensive and cruel as Gill's any more. No one would use that phrase "the host of pitiful children" without losing their job and deserving to. No one would dare call attention to that gap—the one between "the charming, the successful, the gifted" and their opposites. But even so, Gill's reaction remains disturbingly and undeniably candid. The catch-22 for anyone telling this kind of story honestly is inescapable: people don't want to know about it. They never have and never will.

A few years ago I started looking for a copy of *A Child Is Waiting*. It had been years since it had been on TV and it wasn't easy to find in video stores or libraries, so I ended up watching it in segments on YouTube. I wanted to see it because I remembered it from decades ago and because it occurred to me, not long after Jonah was diagnosed, that the title character must have autism. That would likely make his portrayal the first feature film depiction of the disorder, which it is, even though the word *autism* is never used. Instead, the title character is described as "defective." But his symptoms—his solitude, his blank stare, his difficulty communicating, conversing, his tantrums, his underestimated intelligence—clearly place him on the autism spectrum.

Watching the movie proved to be a bad idea, a fact I realized once I began shouting at my computer screen. In particular, there's the scene in which the no-nonsense psychologist who runs the institution (played by Lancaster) and his staff are recovering from a regular Wednesday afternoon visiting day. Lancaster has been besieged by a variety of hapless and clueless parents, who are either undone by or in denial about their children's potential. They are portrayed, in other words, as monumental pains in the neck. Some miss their kids or feel guilty about not missing them. Others would secretly, sometimes not so secretly, like them to disappear. They all feel helpless and, as a result, prevent Lancaster from doing his job, which is to treat these children with a kind of tough but respectful love. Fair enough. But Lancaster's paternalistic tone leaves no room for argument or ambiguity. He views all the parents who pester him with their foolish questions or requests—if my child could just learn his catechism; if he could just speak—with a transparent combination of contempt and pity. Back in his office, with visiting day finally over, he comments to his secretary, "Sometimes I think we should be treating the parents and not the children." Then he shakes his head regretfully and says, "What a pageant! What a pageant!"

What a fucker! That's what I was thinking. *Fuck you and Stanley Kramer and Abby Mann and John Cassavetes. If you're all so smart, whose idea was it to make visiting day Wednesday afternoon?*

This is an insignificant detail, I know, one that probably nobody ever notices, let alone comments on. But as I watched *A Child Is Waiting*, I couldn't get it out of my head. *Wednesday afternoon.* Talk about retarded. How are ordinary working parents expected to get to the place and have any time to spend with their child? They've probably already been hectored into institutionalizing their kids; now they're supposed to quit their jobs to visit them, take their other kids out of school. Why isn't visiting day on a Saturday or Sunday? The whole system is nuts. Why doesn't anyone complain?

LAST NIGHT, I ALSO expected to be shouting, before long, at *Rain Man*, and, no doubt, waking my family. The movie has its infuriating moments. The director Barry Levinson's depiction of autism hasn't done anyone who has to cope with the disorder on a day-to-day basis any favours. Made before there was such a notion as a spectrum, the movie puts all the emphasis on the extreme end of the disorder. Hoffman's character turns out to be a whiz with numbers and ends up winning Cruise a small fortune by counting cards at blackjack on a trip to a Las Vegas casino. Ever since *Rain Man* there has been no shortage of stories on television programs like *60 Minutes* about true-life savants: piano-playing geniuses and math wizards. A couple of years ago I saw a local news story about a teenage boy with autism who finally got his chance to play for the high school basketball team and astonished everyone by demonstrating a remarkable knack for hitting three-point shots. He'd been a kind of team mascot before that appearance. Nobody even thought he knew how to play. Rumour has it that this story will be turned into a feature film.

Daniel Tammet, a British man with Asperger's, was featured on *60 Minutes*. In the press release for his memoir *Born on a Blue Day*, Tammet is described as "a real-life Rain Man." He has an extraordinary facility with numbers; he's also able to become fluent in a new language in a matter of days. His memoir concludes with his successful debut on the *Late Show with David Letterman*. "This experience showed me more than any other," Tammet says, "that I really was now able to make my way in the world.... I felt elated by the thought that all my efforts had not been in vain, but had taken me to a point beyond my wildest dreams."

Almost twenty-five years after *Rain Man*, the savant angle, with the adjective *idiot* usually dropped, continues to influence the public perception of autism. And for the same old reason: the message is ultimately uplifting. What the audience goes away with is the understanding that people with autism may not always be able to function in society, but they have been given some unique gift as a kind of counterbalance—compensation for all the ordinary, unspectacular things they're incapable of doing. This gift can rarely be accounted for except, perhaps, as an example of God or the human brain, whichever you prefer, working yet again in their own mysterious ways, making lemonade out of lemons. At a dinner party one night, the new boyfriend of an old friend pressed us to reveal what Jonah's talent was. He assumed there had to be something. He also assumed we were keeping whatever it was a secret until we could book Jonah on a late-night talk show or sign a major motion picture deal. "What does he do?" he kept asking. When we finally convinced him that our son was not secretly a genius, the inquiring man was disappointed but reassuring. He suggested we just hadn't found Jonah's special talent yet, whatever it might be.

So, yes, *Rain Man* plays fast and loose with the everyday realities of autism, and, yes, that hasn't always been helpful, but it's also a surprisingly endearing movie that succeeds where *A Child Is Waiting*, with its cinéma-verité good intentions, fails so miserably. *Rain Man* stumbles into an important truth if not about autism then about what it's like to find yourself suddenly living in the world of autism. Scene to scene, *Rain Man* is also a comedy, an extended Abbott and Costello routine. (Hoffman's character recites the "Who's on First?" bit whenever he's stressed or whenever there is a change in his routine.) Watching the movie this time around, I was struck by how closely dealing with Jonah mirrors the comical, absurd, confusing back and forth between the person (Lou Costello) being drawn unwillingly into a looping, loopy conversation about a baseball line-up and the person (Bud Abbott) already comfortably immersed in it. "Who's on first?" Costello asks repeatedly. "Naturally," Abbott answers repeatedly. Meanwhile, the frustration builds, and, after a while, you have a simple choice if you're a participant or an observer: you can laugh or scream.

The other takeaway from *Rain Man* comes late in the movie

when Cruise and the doctor responsible for Hoffman confront each other. Their meeting is being refereed by another psychiatrist, who is assessing what is, in effect, a custody battle. Cruise has, without meaning or wanting to, taken on the role of a parent or guardian to Raymond. Like a parent, he tends to be defensive and emotional. He argues that he has had more success making a human connection with Hoffman in six days than the experts have in thirty years. The first time I saw *Rain Man*, I probably viewed this scene the way the filmmakers intended it to be viewed—as a noble but quixotic gesture by Cruise, mainly constructed out of a love for his new-found sibling. Now, I know different. I know Cruise is simply right. On that six-day road trip, Hoffman learns to dance, kisses a woman, improves his taste in clothes, and becomes a part of a family. Insofar as it's possible, he is on his way to being integrated into the neurotypical world. You don't know him the way I do, Cruise protests to the patronizing psychiatrist, an updated, slightly more sensitive version of the Burt Lancaster know-it-all character. You haven't been with him twenty-four hours a day, Cruise goes on. Of course, this is what every parent of a child with autism thinks every time they're told what to do by people who haven't a clue—by the experts without expertise. If *Rain Man* didn't exactly set out to make this point, if that's just me talking—*projecting, sweetheart*, as Cynthia might say—the movie is clear on the fact that the hero of the story is not Hoffman, it's Cruise. Cruise changes. He's the schmuck who stops behaving like a schmuck, the one who learns something about his brother and himself. He gives the movie its redemptive Hollywood ending. He snaps out of it.

FOURTEEN
Zebras and Zebus

Jonah was born on Christmas Eve in Montreal's Jewish General Hospital. That wasn't how we'd planned it. Cynthia had had a midwife rather than an obstetrician for her entire pregnancy, but once she was a week past her due date, we checked into a hospital to be on the safe side. Secretly, I was relieved. Our sessions with the midwife had been a little too new-age-friendly for me. In the final days of the pregnancy, there was a lot of talk about how Cynthia might want to position herself during her contractions—whether she should be standing, crouching, walking. *Walking?* Lying down, evidently, was old-school, impractical, and vaguely misogynistic. There were birthing chairs, too, or we could opt for an ordinary stool. *Like a barstool?* How about a bathtub? *How about it?* We could always try that, complete with whirlpool attachments, our midwife went on. And, she added to me, if I wanted to I could be in the bathtub with Cynthia. *No one ever suggested that, sweetheart.* Most men also want to catch the baby, I was informed, but you have to be careful. That placenta can be slippery. *Catch?* You mean like a fastball?

As it turned out, no bathing or game-saving catches were required. Jonah was already nine days late by the time we arrived at the hospital and was either unprepared or unwilling to cooperate. He was then, as he remains, a hard kid to read. Cynthia was induced, but the procedure had little or no effect. Jonah simply refused to budge. Shades of Mr. Potato Head. So the doctors ordered an emergency C-section and Jonah's entrance into the world was quick, startling, and not really his idea.

Because Cynthia had a C-section, our stay in the hospital was extended from a day and a half, maximum, to four days, minimum: hospital policy. After the four days, we were informed that we'd be staying a day or two longer. Jonah had jaundice, a common problem in newborns, but one the doctors wanted to keep an eye on. Two days later, as we were packing, Dr. K., the chief of obstetrics, entered our room and explained that there was a complication, that Jonah's jaundice wasn't resolving itself as quickly as he would have liked. He explained slowly, reassuringly what was going to happen next. Jonah would require phototherapy; basically he would be placed under a set of lamps in order to lower his bilirubin count. I still couldn't tell you what bilirubin is, but, evidently, when it's elevated, it isn't good.

Cynthia was squeezing my hand. She'd already spent most of the morning answering leading questions about her emotional state from a succession of OB/GYN residents and interns. A lactation nurse had apparently tipped off the rest of the staff when she spotted signs of what she presumed to be post-partum depression. From then on, no one bothered asking Cynthia why she might be feeling down. They assumed they knew. The answer was right there on her chart.

"We want to go home," I said, as yet another resident dropped off pamphlets explaining how post-partum depression was nothing to be ashamed of. "You won't let us go home," I added as the young woman smiled at me and exited. "Seriously," I said, sinking to my knees and pleading with the slowly closing door, "can't you just let us out of here?"

"My stitches. Don't make me laugh," Cynthia said.

"Where are they now? They should see you now." I ran to the door and shouted down the empty hall, "Come see her now. She's hysterical."

"Sweetheart ... the stitches."

But once Dr. K. arrived we weren't laughing any more. Phototherapy was simple and safe, he explained, but it required a few precautions. Namely, someone had to stay up with Jonah until he fell asleep.

"He'll be wearing a mask to protect his eyes and we wouldn't want that displaced at any time. It could damage his vision somewhere down the road," Dr. K. added matter-of-factly. Then he looked me up and down as if he were measuring me. "This is a job for the father, obviously."

I spent that night in the nursery while Jonah squirmed and scratched at his face and at the paper mask covering his eyes. I talked to him, mainly, about his mother and my late parents, about my sisters, his aunts and Cynthia's parents, his grandparents. "It's a small tree, Jonah, but your tree." It was our very first one-sided conversation, though it didn't feel that way at the time. When I ran out of personal stories, I told him about fictional characters and what jerks they could be: Holden Caulfield and Molly Bloom and Jay Gatsby. Literature is one long parade of human folly, kiddo. If it teaches us anything, it teaches us that no one ever learns from their mistakes. We just make the same ones again and again. We are flawed creatures, every single one of us.

I remember a nurse glaring at me and conspicuously clearing her throat as if to say, "Is that really appropriate? Here?" I ignored her and told Jonah about Anna Karenina—"I know, I know, how could she choose Vronsky?"—and Oedipus Rex. "This one you won't believe." All the while I kept both hands on Jonah's protective mask. He squirmed, half-asleep, for hours. Then he was awake and agitated and crying in that way infants cry: with every ounce of energy and commitment they have. As if he were a competitor on *American Idol*. There wasn't much I could do to comfort him so I looked for the nurse, for instructions, but she was gone. I knew I couldn't pick him up, so I just patted his head and told him about all the things we were going to do together, about Expo games and Preston Sturges. I sang a few lines from Lou Reed's "Beginning of a Great Adventure." I quoted what I remembered from the beginning of *Ulysses*. The kid might as well know, right from the start, that his father was a pretentious clown. I was tired, and the heat from the tiny block of lamps— they were attached to each other like a miniature section of lights at a ballpark—was as irritating as fibreglass on my skin. All Jonah wanted to do was scratch; for that matter, so did I. Still, whenever his crying became unbearable, his squirming unsettling, I focused on the hot-shot doctor's words "damage" and "down the road" and I kept the mask secure. It was, to that point, the hardest thing I ever had to do.

The following afternoon an intern glanced at our son's metal chart and explained that while Jonah was doing better, his boss, Dr. K., had recommended an additional round of phototherapy. "Better safe than sorry," the intern said or words to that effect. By then, we'd been in the hospital for eight days and I knew one thing: we needed to get out. If Cynthia didn't have post-partum depression by now, another day was likely to push her over the edge. I'd started reading the pamphlets—symptoms included insomnia, intense irritability and anger, overwhelming fatigue—and I was convinced I already had it.

"We're leaving today, this morning, as soon as possible."

"But Dr. K. ..."

"I don't care who said what. We're taking our baby home today."

It was frustration talking, fear, too. I couldn't bear another night with Jonah under those lamps. Mostly, though, it was conviction. In that moment, I was certain I was doing the right thing for everyone involved, for what was now my family. I was certain we'd be fine once we were home, the three of us. (We were, as it turned out. Once we got Jonah out into the sunlight, the jaundice disappeared. "That's all you had to do," our midwife told Cynthia later. "You just had to take him home and put him in the window. Like a houseplant.")

"My hero," Cynthia said as we got into the car quickly, like we were planning a getaway. Still, even with my hands gripped tightly at

ten and two on the steering wheel, I couldn't quite keep them from
shaking. I was ready, even as I turned the key in the ignition, to do a
180, take the hospital's advice, and stay another day or two, if necessary. What difference would it make? What was I trying to prove? I
was new to conviction, and I was learning that even for a new father
it is a fleeting thing.

Close calls. When you become a parent for the first time you get a
crash course in the close call. How parenthood, like most sports, is a
game of inches, of "if this, then that." True, all those novels I'd read
had taught me the world was a precarious, fragile place, but it was
likely a fact I took for granted. Now, I no longer could. Is the kid's car
seat attached securely? Did I buy winter tires? Am I a good enough
driver? You might as well be a hack Hollywood screenwriter pitching
a disaster movie for all the time you spend dreaming up worst-case
scenarios. Eventually, you relax. But the first time you notice your
baby picking up a marble and putting it in his mouth or the first
time you take your eyes off your toddler in a bookstore and he disappears, for a second, just a second, you are reminded. *Yes*, you think,
I remember that feeling—that's dread. Of course, when you learn your
child has autism, that dread not only returns, it settles in for the long
haul.

"Now what?" I finally asked Cynthia as we drove out of the hospital
parking lot. Both my hands were still stuck to the steering wheel. Her
spirits had lifted in an instant. She was smiling and unwavering, a
woman in charge. At last.

"Take us home, sweetheart."

"COME SEE," Cynthia says. "Really." She peeks her head into the
kitchen from the therapy room where she and Jonah are working on
a timeline together. This is the latest in an ongoing series of arts-and-
crafts projects Cynthia and Jonah have embarked on. They paint and
glue and colour together. They've made calendars and plaster masks

and invented a board game called *Let's Discuss Picking Your Nose and Other Adventures*. The game, Cynthia explained, is made up of useful everyday advice, social stories we can act out with Jonah. You roll the dice and learn something about "Waiting in Line" or "Using a Kleenex" or "Speaking in a Normal Voice" or Jonah's current favourite, "The Rules of Farting." (Rule #1: Don't do it in public. Rule #2: If you have to do it in public, say excuse me.)

"I got the idea from you, when you were reading those *Let's Talk About* books with Jonah for his homework; you said you should write a book called *Let's Talk About Autism*. I thought that was a good idea."

"And you did it instead?"

"You're not mad, are you?"

I'm not—does anyone really think I'm the kind of person who should be writing a self-help book? Still, it probably doesn't hurt for Cynthia to think I am a little bit pissed off. Which makes me think of another potential title for the Joy Berry catalogue: *Let's Talk About Passive-Aggression*.

"This time I think he's interested ... really." There's that word again—"really." Cynthia repeats it like she's preparing for a debate. Like it's just the gimmick she needs to win some future and inevitable argument we are likely to have. I allow myself a minimal amount of skepticism. Show me, in other words, why this is different. This is, incidentally, the way Cynthia and I always seem to end up talking about Jonah; we weigh everything. What might be good and what might not be; what can be done about what is good and what has to be done about what is not. We were helicopter parents long before either of us had ever heard that casually disparaging term. When you are the parent of a child with autism you hover. What else can you do? The dishes, I suppose, which I'm up to my elbows in now.

"Leave them," Cynthia says. "And come in here."

"I just want to finish," I say over the sound of the running water, not to mention my running internal commentary. Still, I can hear enough to eavesdrop and gauge how things are going. So far so good, it sounds like. Jonah is not stimming or giggling, not getting frustrated or angry, which are his usual options when he's not doing exactly what he wants. Instead, he seems genuinely involved in estimating how old he might have been when we drove to Toronto for a cousin's wedding. We have a photo of him, in a sports jacket and clip-on tie, holding a microphone. He wowed the crowd with a karaoke rendition of "Swinging on a Star." On his favourite line about "all the monkeys" not always being in the zoo, he jumped up and down, his arms waving, his hands scratching his sides. He was three then, but he still asks me once in a while about that line, about why it's so funny. "Because we're all monkeys," I tell him. One day, I figure I'll use it as an opening to a social story about the spectrum, about how it's really overrated. Trust me, Jonesy, I'll tell him, we're all part of it, life's rich pageantry.

"Was I a baby then? Or a toddler?" Jonah asks Cynthia. These questions are persistent, but encouraging nevertheless. They qualify, around here, as conversation starters because they are a rarity— questions Jonah doesn't insist on first knowing the answer to. They are asked spontaneously, without his usual twisted syntax. This is what's called dynamic as opposed to static conversation, and it is, according to Cynthia, what we need to start cultivating. That's because in a dynamic conversation, a person is no longer just concerned with their side of the conversation. That's also why the first time we hear Jonah say anything new or unexpected, we get a glimpse of what it might be like if he talked like this all the time, if he had a capacity for real conversation, one where no internal script is followed, no outcome predetermined by either party, where he doesn't freeze up or give rote answers like a person struggling to understand and speak a second language. It's easy to take for granted—this capacity to engage with others through conversation, to chat, shoot the breeze, schmooze, gab, make small talk. "Communicating with one another for no immediate reason has to be the most quintessentially and exclusively human of all our behaviours," author and editor Daniel Menaker writes in *A Good Talk: The Story and Skill of Conversation*. But even though Menaker is right, I still resent the way he puts it: "has to be," "quintessentially ... exclusively human." I'm guessing he's never spent an afternoon in the company of an eleven-year-old with autism.

ABA therapy is winding down in our house. Cynthia and I are talking more, instead, about Seymour Gutstein's book on RDI or Relationship Development Intervention, the book I promised her and Harriet I would read. This is where these theories about static and dynamic conversation come from. This shift in emphasis from ABA to RDI is an indication, among other things, that Jonah's progress in social interaction has not been what any of us hoped it would be by now. RDI, Cynthia points out, offers more possibilities for improvement in his ability to make friends and conversation.

In the other room, I hear Cynthia and Jonah discussing a trip we took a few years ago to Parc Safari, a drive-through wildlife park about an hour south of Montreal. Jonah seizes the opportunity to ask his mother to answer a question about the difference between zebras and zebus. Zebras, we were warned before we entered the park, were bad-tempered and untrustworthy. "Remember, Jonah," Cynthia says, "they told us not to feed them because they bite." Zebus are just fancy cattle; they have that show-offy hump, but they are gentle and yielding and predictable. "Was Jonah two or three when we went to Parc Safari?" Cynthia shouts to me from the therapy room. "Remember," she goes on, her attention back on Jonah now, "a zebra stuck his head inside the car window looking for food and slobbered all over Daddy before he could roll up the window. And Daddy freaked out. It's lucky you were there, Jonah, to tell him not to be scared. To tell him that zebras are herbivores."

"Herbivores don't eat people, they eat plants," Jonah says, sounding a little like he's on a game show.

"That zebra was still planning to take a bite out of me ... for sure,"

I pitch in, turning off the water and shouting out my recollection from the kitchen. "You know why? Because I'm sweet; that's why your mother calls me sweetheart all the time. Am I right?" I'm probably a little too anxious to be acknowledged. Neither Cynthia nor Jonah reply, though I can imagine the look that passes between them, the one that says, *There he goes again, misremembering, making stuff up, on a tangent, missing the point, making it all about him.* Frankly, I don't remember this specific incident but I have come to accept the fact that most of the reminiscing my wife and son will do for this project and undoubtedly for upcoming ones will, disproportionately and inevitably, focus on the times I may have either freaked out or was, in their opinion, on the verge of freaking out. I'm not complaining. I'm acquainted with the unreliable nature of memory; I understand the appeal of creative non-fiction. I know every story needs a fall guy. I'm not only ideal for the part, I embrace it.

"Go ask Daddy," I hear Cynthia say. I turn, and the two of them are standing by the door. Cynthia nudges Jonah.

"Daddy?"

"Jonesy?"

"When can I be a baby again?" he says.

"He wants to read animal alphabet books," Cynthia says. "But what did we decide?" I get it: this public service announcement is intended for both of us.

"I can't," Jonah says.

"Why?"

"Because I'm eleven now and you can only read animal alphabet books when you're a baby?" Like most kids, Jonah has a way of making every statement sound like a question. Like most kids, he pursues loopholes with the vigour of a rookie defence attorney in a John Grisham novel. However, unlike other kids, neurotypical kids, he's not always good at concealing this fact. He is an open book, albeit one that sometimes seems to be printed in an illegible font—wing-dings. Being a literalist is a common feature of autism. A friend told me a story once about driving along a country road in the winter with her niece, who was three at the time, and as they got to an icy patch, my friend shouted out to the backseat, "Hold on to your hat!" A moment later she glanced in the rear-view mirror and could see her niece, looking earnest and determined, clutching her winter hat with both hands. Children learn, eventually, to understand that this kind of figure of speech is not meant to be taken literally. Jonah has yet to learn this. He doesn't get sarcasm either. Sometimes, I will say something ludicrous on purpose, like we're going to eat a hippo for lunch, and he will just look at me like I'm crazy. I prompt him to say something like, "Yeah, right," and he does, but he gets the tone of this rejoinder all wrong. He says it like he means it instead of like he's challenging or mocking me. Still, I keep at it. I keep saying the dumbest things I can think of. This is a technique I picked up from keeping my promise and finally reading that RDI book. The idea is for the parent to be delib-erately obtuse, thereby giving the child the chance to think for himself and, ultimately, be the one in the know. Deliberate obtuseness—the consensus is it's another role I was born to play.

"That's right, Jonah," Cynthia says. "Only babies or maybe toddlers read those kinds of alphabet books and ..."

"And you can't go back in time," Jonah says. He's been coached on this line, and as he says it I notice Cynthia is staring at me. I shrug, part apology, part excuse. She knows what I'm thinking, the same thing Jonah is: *Why the hell not?*

"Daddy?"

"Jonesy." A slyness sneaks into the corners of his handsome mouth, a Eureka smile. He's found his technicality, his loophole.

"When," he asks, "can I be a toddler again?"

ONCE JONAH IS IN BED, Cynthia takes me on a tour of the timeline. We sit on the floor and study the long, narrow piece of brown construction paper that extends from one wall of Jonah's therapy room to the other. That makes it about eight feet long—a work in progress, according to Cynthia. The years of the decade—from just before Jonah's birth to the present, to the most recent occurrence, specifically Daddy talking nonsense in the kitchen about man-eating zebras—are written on the bottom of the paper. There are a couple of pairs of scissors and tubes of glue at the corners, keeping the unwieldy sheet from curling. We are also surrounded by photo albums, which Cynthia and Jonah were rummaging through a couple of hours earlier, looking for old pictures to place in the appropriate year. Like 1998.

"I was so big," Cynthia says. She's flipping through a series of photos of herself pregnant. "This was just before we went to the hospital. It had to be. Remember when …"

"I remember." I struggle to my feet ahead of Cynthia and then hold out my hand to help her up. We are old parents. We have become old fast. I can see it in the photos—how we've aged. I had a lot more hair a decade ago. My beard was black. I smiled easily. If I was worried back then about what the future held, I can't see it in these photographs.

"Look at me, at that belly," Cynthia says.

"You look sexy," I say as I put my arms around her from behind, nuzzling her neck.

"I look like a hippo."

"You were aglow."

"A glowing hippo. Did you see this?" Cynthia says, leaning down to retrieve two blank panels from the floor. One has the words "bar mitzvah" on it, the other "high school"; Jonah has written both in his most legible handwriting. "We're going to attach this next time. It's a way of talking about the future. It's a good sign. You know, it's normal for him to talk about what he wants to be when he grows up. Like how he wants to drive a truck. He didn't used to. Remember, just a couple of years ago if you asked him the same question, he'd say he wanted to be a giraffe. Remember, I said I was worried about how he was going to make ends meet. Oh, come on, that's funny."

"I thought we weren't talking about the future."

"You and I aren't. Jonah and I are. You and he might also. Has he asked you what 'grounded' means?"

"A few times, I'd say, a few hundred times."

"Right, I know. But it's a good thing overall. He's starting to show an interest in who he was and who he will be. How did you explain 'grounded'?"

"I told him only teenagers get grounded, so as soon as he turns thirteen he's grounded. He seemed to find that funny."

Cynthia isn't saying so but I know she has big plans for the timeline. Her idea is to go on extending it as a kind of running commentary on Jonah's life. Autism tends to blur temporal concepts like tense and time and context. This is a concrete way to highlight these distinctions for Jonah. Cynthia's goal in working on the timeline is to solidify Jonah's emerging sense of himself as a person subject to change, a person with a past and a future. The idea is also to help him understand that he is an actor in the world, but he is not the only actor—that he has a history he shares with other people. I don't say so, but the timeline worries me. I wonder if Jonah should be dwelling on the past, if it does him any good, if it does any of us any good.

"It's been nice working on this. I mean we're having a good time, the two of us," Cynthia adds. Among other things, the timeline is also Cynthia's way of setting a good example for me, yet again. *Sweetheart, the kid can be fun, really, he can. Just give him a chance.*

"What's happening with the book?" she asks. This seems like a non sequitur, but I fill her in on my plan—my outline, you could call it. First, apply for yet another grant. Second, fashion a suitable chapter from out of the collection of half-finished and almost-finished chapters I already have. Third, look for an agent. Fourth, look for a publisher. Fifth, let Cynthia read what I've written so far.

"And there's something new," I say, a little reluctantly. "I'm also considering applying to a literary journalism workshop at Banff. But that would mean being away for a month. What do you …"

"I meant the other book, the one you and Jonah are supposed to be working on—the sequel to *Bad Animals*."

As if on cue, Jonah wanders into his therapy room in his *Madagascar* pyjamas and immediately gets down on the floor with the timeline. He finds a photo of himself at a playground. He's probably two. 2000. The year the world was supposed to implode as everyone's computer crashed. The year we were all doomed, not just some of us. Funny, I don't remember feeling doomed. In the photo, Cynthia and I are both hugging Jonah, kissing opposite chubby cheeks.

"Panini," Cynthia says. "Remember. We used to squish you and say panini when you were a baby."

"Again," Jonah says as he stands. Cynthia looks at me and we squeeze Jonah between us. He likes the pressure. This is a common feature of autism. Less common is Jonah's unusually affectionate nature. Which is, again, why they call it a spectrum: you never know what you're going to get. Still, we shouldn't be indulging in this kind of extended snuggling. He's eleven; he's too old, as we keep telling him when it comes to watching *Sesame Street* or reading animal alphabet books. Then again, this is one of the advantages, "joys," I'm tempted to say, of autism. You get to hold on to the past a little longer, a little more fiercely, than other parents. The old cliché about kids growing up too fast doesn't quite apply. Jonah isn't growing up fast enough.

"Did you see this?" Cynthia asks Jonah and shows him the photo she and I were just looking at.

"What was I then? A toddler or a baby?" he asks, studying the unfamiliar image of his pregnant mother.

"You weren't even born yet," Cynthia says. "But you were getting ready to change our lives forever. We were getting ready to love you forever like in the Robert Munsch book."

"What comes after forever?" I ask Jonah.

He thinks about this for a while and then gives me the silly answer he knows I'm expecting, the one I have set him up for. Sometimes I know my son. Sometimes I know exactly what he's going to say and I know he won't disappoint.

"Five Ever."

"Very funny. Now it's time for bed," I pick up Jonah and realize immediately I shouldn't have. My lower back is on fire. How come I keep forgetting? He's getting heavier and I am getting older.

FIFTEEN
Bulletin Board

There is neurological evidence that women become measurably smarter once they've given birth. Susan Pinker, a Montreal psychologist, points this out in her book *The Sexual Paradox: Extreme Men, Gifted Women and the Real Gender Gap*. From an evolutionary point of view, this makes perfect sense. It's nature bumping up the odds on our survival, endowing the person most responsible for protecting us in our baby years with an enhanced capacity to do so. Men, on the other hand, are nine months clear of having done everything nature requires of them once a baby is born. (Unless, that is, you intend to hop into the birthing bathtub with a catcher's mitt.) We are, after conception, hanging around, pretending to be useful.

And while Pinker doesn't come right out and say men get stupider when they become fathers, it stands to reason they do. "Stud, dud, thud," is the punchline one anthropologist, quoted in *The Sexual Paradox*, uses to sum up a man's crucial but abbreviated role in the continuation of the species. My father had a running gag he would drag out whenever he was watching some old movie on television and the hero would do something that would cause his child to look at him admiringly. Like the numerous scenes in *To Kill a Mockingbird* where Scout and Jim gaze at Atticus Finch, stolidly played by Gregory Peck, with unambiguous pride. It was at moments like these that my father would blurt out: "Everybody loves their father." The joke was in what he was omitting, of course: he meant for us to add "everybody else." Often, he'd make this remark to no one in particular. He'd say it even if my sisters or I weren't in the same room with him, even if we weren't watching the same movie. It was intended, first of all, to get a laugh. But while it may be true that a cigar is sometimes just a cigar, a joke is never just a joke. My father was also fishing for compliments. He was no Atticus Finch, he knew that. But then, who is? This question was at the heart of his running gag, his ongoing plea for attention, for a little more respect. *Come on*, I imagined him saying, *cut the old man some slack*. Too often, I didn't. Too often, I was openly disappointed in him.

After my mother died, he and I argued all the time. In large part, this was because my mother was no longer around to prevent us from arguing. It wasn't until after she died that I began to understand how often she had served as a buffer between my father and my sisters and me. She'd kept us from seeing how insecure he was, how paralyzed by bitterness. My father had contracted polio when he was thirteen and had been labelled, in the parlance of his day, a cripple. For "a cripple," he accomplished a lot—he married, started his own business, bought a house in the suburbs, and raised a family, all things no one, himself included, ever expected him to do. But while he managed to overcome his physical handicap, his self-pity never diminished. It just lay dormant. The unspoken question—why me?—was always present. He always believed, like Job or Stanley Elkin, that he was owed an explanation. He knew he could have been so much more. He could have done so much more. My mother could have taken this the wrong way, but she didn't. Instead, she reassured him about his accomplishments. She was a mitigating factor in his life, and after she died, I'm guessing he expected my sisters and me to fill a similar role, to reassure him, perhaps remind him the way only my mother could, that everything was going to turn out all right, as it once had.

We were in no position to help. She had left us, too. At that particular moment, we certainly didn't believe that everything was going to be all right. If anything, I resented him for not being able to say something wise and dignified to alleviate my pain, the kind of thing you'd expect from Atticus Finch. I assumed that was a father's job: to be strong, transcendent. To rise above his own hurt for his children's sake. Because if that wasn't his job, well, then, what was? What I didn't know at the time was that my mother's death was more than he could handle. It was as simple as that. This is all guesswork and speculation now. If he were here, I could ask him: Am I getting it all wrong? Am I getting you all wrong?

Fathers are, it turns out, easy targets—fish in a barrel. I'm thinking about all the books I've read in recent years that, put together, constitute a kind of literary sub-genre—call it the disappointing dad memoir. Well-known examples include Geoffrey Wolff's *The Duke of Deception*, about his father's life as a con man; Frank McCourt's *Angela's Ashes*, about his drunken, dissolute father; and Kathryn Harrison's *The Kiss*, about her sexually abusive father. For a writer, fatherhood can be an irresistible subject, one you can't help returning to. I've written about my father repeatedly, more than I ever intended to, and each time I've tried to couch my version of his story, our story, in sentimental anecdotes. But something darker invariably creeps in, unintended, as it probably has here, something about my father's extraordinary capacity for self-pity and disappointment. I always end up blaming his chronic bad attitude on bad breaks—polio, financial struggles, the loss of my mother. But I wonder now if those are just convenient excuses for other flaws, if there was something else in his makeup at work, something in the makeup we share.

Past a certain point, fathers, alive or dead, have little or no influence on the theories their sons are bound to devise about them. I can only guess what Jonah will think of me one day. In the last couple of months, I've been spending more and more time in the basement, so it may turn out he will have this book to investigate for examples, evidence of another man who couldn't quite cut it. Every son is entitled to their disappointing-dad memoir, so I am writing this on Jonah's behalf. Which raises another question: Will this book do us more harm than good?

JONAH'S SCHOOL YEAR IS almost over. There is less and less homework, as his teachers coast through June, getting a head start on their summer vacations. Jonah brought his report card home today for us to sign. And while other kids would have had a song and dance ready to explain why they got a D in physical education—"I lost my running shoes"—Jonah is blithely indifferent to the contents. There's something admirable about this. I'm glad he somehow knows now what only growing up teaches the rest of us—that we fretted over our grades for nothing, that there will come a time when no one will care how you did in grade five or grade ten or, for that matter, grad school. Still, Cynthia and I make a point of sitting Jonah down to read him what is, all things considered, pretty good news. He's been promoted to grade six, first of all. There have been improvements in French and math; his work habits are getting better; his computational skills are great; and he's a heck of a speller, or words to that effect.

"How about that?" Cynthia and I ask him in unison.

"Where are we having supper?" he asks in return.

"No supper tonight," I say. "Your report card is much too good." Jonah and Cynthia both stare at me, at which point I whisper in Jonah's ear, "Yeah ..."

"Yeah, right!" he says, picking up his cue.

"Sarcasm 101," I say to Cynthia. "See he's getting it. You won't learn that in school."

"Don't be silly, Daddy," Cynthia says, reassuring him and shaking her head at me. "We're going to celebrate, right?"

So we do. We go out for pizza and ice cream. Of course, there are, despite the reassuringly average grades on his report card, raised flags we ignore, at least for tonight. Like Jonah's persistent problems with reading comprehension and problem-solving. I also find myself puzzled by a "general comment" tacked on to the final section by Jonah's homeroom teacher. What exactly does she mean by this: "I continue to encourage you to always demonstrate dedication and *hard effort* in your *everyday challenges*. Demonstrating this will result in a successful and *rewarding life*." The italics, incidentally, are mine.

"This doesn't sound odd to you?" I ask Cynthia after we're home and Jonah's in bed. "I mean, 'everyday challenges.'"

"Do you really think she's being sarcastic? His grade five teacher?"

"All right, tone deaf."

"You know you're over-analyzing this. Don't you think she says more or less the same thing to everyone?"

"No. This is a weird comment, trust me, I can read between the lines. It's my job."

"Sweetheart, let it go. School is over. We made it. We survived."

But I can't let it go. I read and reread the report card like it's a Michael Ondaatje novel. I'm pretty sure there's a hidden meaning waiting to be uncovered, but, for the life of me, I can't figure out what it is.

OUR REGULAR ABA TEAM MEETINGS are a thing of the past. That's because we're no longer a team. In the first few years after Jonah's diagnosis, his therapy schedule couldn't have been fuller. There were sessions after school every day as well as sessions on weekends and throughout the summer. We were always juggling timetables, double-booking, losing track of who was going to be where when. Now, there is really only The Consultant and Jessica to keep track of. The Consultant will be available to us if and when she is needed. Jessica will keep doing a couple of sessions a week with Jonah and look in on him at day camp now and then to see how he's managing. After the summer, we'll be seeing even less of them. Starting in September, we will have no one in his school to support him. Jonah will be on his own; we all will. Grade six is likely to be tough, and while this is a reality Cynthia and I have been dreading for years, we're also getting used to it. It's time to just be his parents again. And time for him to just be our kid.

"It's true, isn't it?" Cynthia says. "I almost feel like I'm on vacation."

She is standing, arms crossed, in front of our bulletin board, staring at it. "That's the trouble with these things," I say. "You have to watch them all the time." I wave my hand in front of her face, but she doesn't blink. I know that look; it means everything is up for grabs. It means a fresh start.

Cynthia has taken down Jonah's first-term report card and pinned up his new one. She got me to stop obsessing about it by pointing out that not far from the homeroom teacher's enigmatic and, I'm still convinced, secret put-down, there is a smiley-face sticker. I'm not sure what that proves; still, I wonder how I missed it.

Our bulletin board is, incidentally, out of control. It's cluttered with a school year's worth of missed appointments and lapsed opportunities: September to June. There's Jonah's now out-of-date therapy timetable. There's also the usual blizzard of scrap paper, reminders about Wednesday swimming lessons Jonah no longer takes, a Thursday play date that either did or didn't happen a month ago. It may be my imagination, but we seem to get stood up a lot. That's the bad news. The good news: I am starting to take this fact in stride. *It's not a fact, sweetheart, it's paranoia.* I don't break down or rant or suspect conspiracies on the part of his classmates and their parents the way I once did. There's also a yellowing newspaper clipping about the link between autism and aging parents pinned to the bulletin board as well as other clippings about research into autism and environmental causes, autism and art, autism and Yoko Ono (recently named autism's first global ambassador), autism and the recovered child, autism and you name it. Alongside those clippings, there's Lovaas's letter and a pseudonymous letter to the editor Cynthia wrote, criticizing our local school board for not providing parents of special-needs children with proper and promised services. She's had a few of these missives published over the years, and I can't remember if this one is recent or goes back to the beginning of this school year or another. If, in other words, it did any good or still might. Jonah's contributions to the board include a riddle—a drawing of a sleepy lion with a caption under it that reads: "What do you call a jungle beast who's tired all the time and never tells the truth? A lying, lying lion." Cynthia has also put up a recent school composition he wrote about the people who inspire him. He chose us—"My parents inspire me to go to school"—then ratted us out: "My parents also inspire me to watch TV because they watch a lot of TV." There's also the obligatory *New Yorker* cartoon, which shows a couple in bed engaged in an intimate conversation. The caption reads "How to Drive Your Man Crazy in Bed." The illustration is of a woman, up on one elbow, bombarding her sleep-deprived husband with questions. "Which is better, plasma or hi def?" and "Did you ever have this ringing in your ear?" And, of course, the inevitable: "Do you love me as much as you did when you married me?" I can't remember who's responsible for the cartoon: me or Cynthia. I had photocopies of "Welcome to Beirut" and "Holland Schmolland" up for a while, but they didn't last long. The bulletin board is no place for harsh reality. Who wants to be reminded of that every day before Cheerios?

Still, you can tell a lot about the current state of our household by keeping track of what comes and what goes. Earlier this year, for instance, you would have found lots of tips about the ABCs— ANTECEDENT, BEHAVIOUR, CONSEQUENCE—of ABA therapy. Now, there are just the words **STOP, THINK, CHOOSE** in bold block letters, on an oversized index card, which Jonah has decorated with a drawing of an eight-legged, eight-humped camel. There are directives to **CATCH HIM BEING GOOD**. And messages which require extra head-scratching on my part. Like: 80-20, which is, it comes to me eventually, a breakdown of how our daily interactions with our son should go. That's the ideal anyway. Eighty percent of the time we should be having or attempting to have a simple, ordinary conversation with him. Twenty percent of the time we are permitted to ask him direct questions and expect—in fact, insist on—direct answers.

The newest addition to the board consists of Cynthia's research into local synagogues, namely which one might be best at accommodating Jonah once he starts preparing for his bar mitzvah. She's learned enough so far to know we have left this too long. Her friends, who have already been through bar and bat mitzvahs for their kids, have a tendency to shriek, "What are you waiting for?" when she tells them Jonah is eleven and a half. There's a phone number on the board for a Hebrew tutor.

I would like to see these items removed. I had my first crack-up in a while the other day when Cynthia came down to the basement to talk to me about a synagogue visit she'd just made. She usually doesn't interrupt me in my office, especially these days, but this information couldn't wait. Evidently, Jonah wasn't getting any younger. The good news was that the rabbi she'd just spoken to was happy to meet Jonah's particular needs—his congregation had some experience with autism—at least up to a point.

"What point?"

"Well, we'll probably have to join the congregation, all of us." She was looking down at the pile of books on my desk and picked up a copy of *The Horse Boy.* "I like the picture. Is that the author?" The cover of *The Horse Boy* is, indeed, a photograph of author Rupert Isaacson, a dashing fellow, along with his six-year-old son Rowan. They are on horseback together and look as if they've joined forces to defeat Genghis Khan. Isaacson is laughing triumphantly; his son's arm is raised in the air, also triumphantly. Even the horse, grinning wildly, looks like she's on the verge of a breakthrough.

"Did you say all of us have to join the congregation? What does that mean?"

"It means we'd have to start attending Saturday services regularly, well, pretty regularly. The rabbi said a bar mitzvah is not just about having a catered party; it's about fostering a sense of community in your child. He sounded insistent, like this was a deal-breaker."

"Okay, here's what I'm insistent about," I said, as I grabbed *The Horse Boy* out of her hand. "I'm not going to synagogue. I'm not spending my Saturday morning listening to strangers praising God for no conceivably good reason. I'm just not. I draw the line there."

"And what about Jonah?"

"He doesn't need a bar mitzvah. I didn't need one. It didn't exactly make much of a Jew out of me, did it?" I pause, waiting for my wife to add: *Or a man.*

"But you had a bar mitzvah."

"How's he going to keep up? He has too much homework now as it is. Next year will be worse. You know, we don't have … we can't keep up. How's he supposed to learn Hebrew? That language is nuts. Besides, if you're telling me he's going to make friends, then … you don't know what eleven- and twelve-year-old boys in a bar mitzvah class are like. They'll eat him alive."

"There are girls, too."

"I rest my case. What makes you think this is going to be any different than anywhere else? And this is not Jonah's community. We are Jonah's community."

"I hate this. I hate it when you give up on him, on us so easily."

CYNTHIA BELIEVES IN research. She is convinced if you look hard enough for a solution to a problem you will find it. Almost twelve years ago, she prepared for our first date—a blind date—by not only reading the autobiographical novel I'd written but preparing a list of questions to ask me pertaining to it. Her most important question she saved for last. How much did I resemble my narrator? In other words, was I as clueless as he was when it came to women? I've interviewed a lot of writers over the years, a lot who've claimed that while it was true that their fiction was based on actual events, none of it was really true. I never believe them, of course, and I felt safe assuming that Cynthia wasn't going to believe a similar denial coming from me. So I confessed. My narrator was me, more or less. Less, I hastened to add, when it came to relationships. In that regard, I wasn't quite as big a knucklehead as my protagonist. What else could I say? It was our first date. You're expected to lie. Cynthia weighed my answer, and, curiously, she seemed satisfied. I think that's when I began to fall in love with her, while I watched her gradually, methodically come to the conclusion that there are limits to research, that at some point you just have to play a hunch. She did. She took a calculated risk. She believed me.

"I didn't really," she says, correcting me now, all these years later. She's holding a handful of coloured push pins. The bulletin board is almost bare. "I just thought you were cool. You'd written a book and everything. Do we still need this *New Yorker* cartoon?"

"And now?" I'm fishing, expecting to hear something I will like.

"Now, I think you should write another one," Cynthia says. "Two more, as a matter of fact—keep working on that sequel to *Bad Animals*, okay? Try, at least."

"Jonah has a bad case of writer's block. Trust me, I know what that's like."

THIS IS PROBABLY obvious by now, but with Jonah and me, new projects have a way of appearing and disappearing quickly. With his compulsive nature and my impatience, we do not always make the best team. Or maybe we're too good a team, too much alike. I worry that he is, down deep, a defeatist and a quitter like his father. I'd like to be able to teach him useful things, things he needs to know, like crossing the street safely, like understanding a story, watching a movie through to the end, things he is capable of learning, if I were just able, somehow, to figure out a way to reach him: if I had a plan, patience, follow-through.

There are lines in books that stay with you for years, not necessarily because they speak to you when you first read them but because you have a gut feeling that one day they will. It's as if they're waiting for you to catch up. I first read the South Carolina novelist Josephine Humphreys's *The Fireman's Fair* in 1991, not long after it was published. It's a lovely, funny story of an unrequited relationship, something I'd had my share of by then. As a consequence, every line in the novel resonated: none more so than the hero's declaration that "hope fails on this earth a million times a day." The first time I read this line I took it to be an eloquent commentary on the necessity of accepting defeat. It never occurred to me that Humphreys might also be making the opposite point: that the reason hope fails so often is because we have no choice but to keep trying to make it work. As it turns out, I misremembered the line. Humphreys wasn't talking about hope. She was talking about love. "When you love," Humphreys goes on to say, "you're not supposed to count the failures.... It's like tossing coins. For a given toss, the chance is even, unlinked to history."

But history, like it or not, keeps getting in the way. I've watched people give up on Jonah: doctors and teachers and therapists. If it hasn't always been apparent in their words and actions, in their general comments and formal diagnoses, I've seen it in the way he's treated. I've seen conversations ended abruptly when it was clear they weren't going anywhere. I've seen games with prospective friends suspended, rules amended, play dates cancelled. I've seen the sideways glances. I've seen him ignored and overprotected and underestimated. And the reason I know what it looks like is because I've done it myself, all of it, so many times. Sometimes it feels like a million times. I fail him every day. The difference is that I know at some point during the day or the next one or the one after that, I will have no choice but to believe he can do more and better and that so can I. It's simple really: giving up on my son is a luxury I can no longer afford.

Vacation

Be a good sport, sweetheart.

—CYNTHIA

The bad animals want a story. What kind? the Worst-
Daddy-Ever says.
They want a sad one, they said.
But with a happy ending.

—MORE BAD ANIMALS: THE SEQUEL

SIXTEEN
July

"Do you have a plan?" Cynthia asked as she left this morning for her parents' house in the country. *Her* plan was to spend the weekend there, alone, catching up on her reading, required and otherwise. Jonah was still sleeping as I watched her pack. She wasn't whistling exactly, but there was a kind of lilt in her voice, like you hear from one of those animated heroines—Cinderella or Sleeping Beauty—in the Disney sing-a-long videos Jonah loves to watch. They are perpetually rosy-cheeked and hopeful and about to burst into song. Say: "Some Day My Prince Will Come" or "It's a Whole New World." Cynthia hadn't been away from Jonah overnight for a long time, longer than either of us could remember, and she was banking on one night on her own, but if everything went all right—which is to say with Jonah and me, which is also to say if I didn't crack up—she would consider making it two. She told me this by way of advance warning. I took comfort in the fact that she was packing light—a bathing suit, a copy of *Oprah Magazine* (the summer makeover issue: "Ten Ways Oprah Changed and You Can Too"), and, her required reading, a manuscript copy of *My So-Called Memoir.*

"I was going to have it spiral-bound, or self-published, but there wasn't time."

"Can I write on this? In case I have notes."

"Okay. But, remember, it's a rough draft. It doesn't have an ending yet. As a matter of fact, I should have another look at it before you go."

"I'm leaving now."

"It will only take a couple of years."

Cynthia's parents' place is an hour's drive from Montreal, which means she's likely already there and that she'll have most of today and tomorrow to focus on what I've spent the last seven years writing and not writing. You don't have to be Rain Man to do the math. The first time I heard the word *autism* attached to my son, it was clear I was going to write about him, about us. What choice was there? I couldn't ignore this new fact of my life, our life, and I couldn't face it head-on either, so turning it into material was the remaining option. It just never occurred to me it would take so long. On occasion, however, it has occurred to me that Cynthia would have to read what I'd written and that, yes, she would have "notes."

Cynthia will not be the first person with notes. I was accepted into that literary journalism workshop at The Banff Centre after all, and I spent much of the last month there. The program consisted of eight writers, all working on personal essays or on some version of their memoirs. But the real advantage of being in Banff was not the feedback. It was being left alone for the better part of a month in a cabin in the woods to work on my stubborn story. It was a wonderful opportunity—one Cynthia wouldn't let me pass up—but even so it took me a few days to settle in. I couldn't quite get over the feeling of suddenly having no direction, no purpose. I did my laundry the second night I was there just to have something useful to do. In the cafeteria, I had to resist the urge to clear the tables. I'd plan my unencumbered days, as if any minute Cynthia was about to hand Jonah off to me for a couple of hours. I should have felt liberated; instead I felt lost. But once this feeling was gone, it was gone for good. By the end of the first week, I was beholden to no one and couldn't imagine living or writing any other way.

In Banff, my colleagues were the first to read excerpts from the bits and pieces about my life with Jonah. Their comments were mostly encouraging, but the most memorable advice I received was from a music critic and blogger, a smart, intimidating fellow in his twenties, who seemed genuinely worried that the subject might prove too daunting. "All I have to say," he added, by way of conclusion, "is don't fuck it up."

When I returned from Banff the summer was already half over, and Cynthia was anxious to cash in a month's worth of brownie points. She wasn't complaining; she was just ready to be alone for a little while. Even so, the summer had been going well for her and Jonah. He was going to day camp on his own and seemed to be enjoying himself. He'd made a friend there, too, a boy Jonah called Jumpy for reasons he never shared with us. Anyway, Jumpy was a ten-year-old, who didn't seem to mind that Jonah didn't talk much or make much sense when he did. In fact, Jumpy indulged Jonah's repeated requests for mad or sad faces and his jokes about lazy lions and drunken elks. The two also shared a love of chocolate ice cream, and, by happy coincidence, the kind you inevitably attribute to divine intervention when you're a kid, Jumpy lived a block from a Dairy Queen. I called home from Banff every evening, and though Jonah was not much of a talker on the phone I did hear a great deal, relatively speaking, about Jumpy and *his* Dairy Queen. Cynthia was succinct on the phone too. She said she and Jonah were doing fine. Things were less stressful, without school and other, well, stressful things. "It's all right," I said, "you can say it—without me."

"We miss you, sweetheart, it's not that. But ..."

"But I take up a lot of space, physically and otherwise. I know."

I also agreed during those phone calls that things would be different when I got home. I agreed, for instance, to take care of Jonah for a day or two while she took some time to herself. Even so, when I returned from Banff and Cynthia announced she was taking me up on my offer and would be going away this coming weekend, I assumed she was kidding. I hadn't spent an entire night alone with Jonah since his diagnosis. My first reaction to Cynthia's announcement that she was officially on vacation was involuntary. I said, "Yeah, right!"

"Just have a plan," Cynthia repeated as I carried her bag to the car this morning. It was heavy, even though the only significant weight in it was my manuscript.

"I do. I have a plan."

"But you're not going to tell me what it is, is that it?"

EARLY IN *The Horse Boy: A Father's Quest to Heal His Son*, Rupert Isaacson discovers a shared interest with his previously unreachable son Rowan. Both love horses. As with most parents of children with autism, Isaacson comes to this realization through a process of elimination as much as anything else. You try everything and hope something will stick, at least for a while. Isaacson grew up around horses, and so it was natural for him to introduce his son to them. And, yes, the change in Rowan when he's around a horse is immediate and dramatic. Dramatic is how it will appear to any parent of a child with autism, where even the slightest improvement in behaviour or focus can feel miraculous. Rowan stops stimming and having tantrums when he and his father are on horseback together. He's calm, present. This change in him leads father and son (as well as Rowan's somewhat reluctant mother) to make a journey across Mongolia. Why Mongolia? It seems the two ingredients Isaacson is looking for are in abundance there: horses and shamans. Indeed, Isaacson stumbles into shamans with relative ease. In Mongolia, they're a bit like big-city buses. If you miss one, wait a few minutes and another will be along— with their exotic ceremonies and their elliptical yet meaningful advice. Having eaten a reindeer more or less whole, meditated a good deal, and, along with his parents, been ritually slapped around by the aforementioned shamans, Rowan gets mysteriously better. He's not cured,

Isaacson is careful to acknowledge; he is, however, healed. This can seem, for any parent of a child with autism, like a distinction without a difference. After all, by the end of the book, Rowan is making friends; he's talking and doing well in school, often better than his neurotypical classmates. What's more, he has a career path to follow. Isaacson is informed by one shaman that Rowan has the stuff to make it in the shaman business. Like writing, not the most practical profession, perhaps, but still.

The Horse Boy reads like fiction, though not especially convincing fiction. It's too predictable for that—scenes with telepathic equines and super-wise Mongolian healers notwithstanding. It's obvious from the start that the only surprising outcome for *The Horse Boy*, for Rowan and his father, would be if this whole "quest" turned out to be a fiasco, and you know that's not about to happen. Still, there are obstacles to overcome. Rowan's mother is a tough sell. She's a psychologist by training, and while she shares some of her husband's new-age beliefs, she also feels compelled to inject a voice of reason into his plans. "Isn't it hard enough just getting through a typical day, let alone going on a crazy journey to the far end of the earth?" she asks Isaacson, who pretty much ignores the question. So after a few chapters in which Isaacson and his wife quickly quit on ABA therapy because they think it's too rigid and then dismiss a few other possible treatments, they're off on the road to Upper Mongolia. Or is that Lower? Whatever happens, Isaacson remains confident in his curious choices. "I broke all the rules. I had to," he writes.

The question I'm often asked after one of my reviews runs in the newspaper is: "How did you really feel about the book? I mean *really*?" Readers want the straight goods: thumbs up or down, two stars or four. They don't want their reviewers hedging. So let me just come right out and say, if you haven't guessed already, *The Horse Boy* bothers me, big time. There's something about Isaacson's determination, his purposefulness, and, yes, his ultimate success that I find insufferable.

Well, at least you finished it, sweetheart. At the same time, I kept asking myself what kind of person would begrudge a family like the Isaacsons their happy ending? Or Isaacson his seven-figure book deal and shot at writing a Hollywood screenplay? What kind of reader wouldn't want a spirited, charming little boy like Rowan to have his chance at a better life? And what kind of person would have to be prevented by his wife, night after night, from throwing a book as well intentioned, as uplifting, as unimpeachably heroic as *The Horse Boy* across the room?

MY SOCKS ADHERE TO the kitchen floor. The sucking sound this makes is a perfect match for the unpleasant way it feels. Still, I can't do anything, including move, until I make it clear to Jonah that he has to put on his shoes. "Right now, okay, are you listening?" If he is, it's hard to tell since he's laughing so hard. Lately, I find myself grading Jonah's behaviour as it occurs. I keep the grade to myself, of course, but it's not a bad way to stay detached. With Jonah, normal begins at around D+. Am I underestimating him again? Perhaps, but here's my thinking: when it comes to behaving well, all of us should be graded on a curve, the more generous the better. Right now, though, I'd give Jonah a B, even a B+. He's watching his father, who is up to his ankles in maple syrup and shattered glass, lose the last shreds of his temper, his patience, and his dignity. Laughing, I'll concede, is an altogether appropriate response. Under other circumstances, I'd be laughing myself.

"Jonah, go ... now, shoes! Fuck, there's glass everywhere."

"Daddy said a bad word."

The truth is I've said about a dozen. At the moment, I'm also entertaining some bad thoughts about my absent wife. Because I'm thinking none of this would have happened if we had just bought cheap maple syrup in a plastic bottle, like I wanted to and like most normal people do instead of the expensive, organic stuff that comes in decorative and, it turns out, easily breakable glass bottles. Of course, if she were here, she'd also come up with a contingency plan to clean up this mess and keep our son from ending up sticky and, in all likelihood, bleeding. What, incidentally, are the ABCs of mopping up syrup and glass? What do you do first? Is it even possible? *First, sweetheart, calm down.*

Incidentally, Jonah and I did have a plan this morning. After breakfast, we sat down side by side at his therapy table with a yellow legal pad and a box of newly sharpened pencils and made a list of items he and I were going to need to buy to finally make some progress on *More Bad Animals.* We were like a couple of colleagues at a business meeting, kicking ideas around, brainstorming, chewing the fat. Or in Jonah's case chewing the erasers off the pencils. Most days, there isn't an intact pencil anywhere in the house. But I can deal with that. For one thing, it usually means Jonah is focused on the task at hand, that he does, in his own way, mean business. In *The Siege,* Clara Claiborne Park writes about the importance of motivation, how, for a child with autism, it's probably more important than anything else. How when you do find it, it provides a rare glimpse at your wildest dreams coming true. You will see the difference, subtle but dramatic, between your child isolated and your child engaged, your child harnessing his obsession, even his stims. Jonah is something to see when he is on task and focused and, yes, chewing erasers. So much so I leaned over and kissed him as we sat together this morning, though I knew I shouldn't have. We were doing a grownup thing, after all.

His focus didn't last, of course. After a while he kept disappearing into the kitchen to open the refrigerator and make sure the maple syrup I promised him he could have with his lunchtime French toast hadn't somehow vanished. I kept calling him back and yet remained surprisingly calm. *Breathe, sweetheart.* I knew what he was doing. I understood how easy it was to be distracted from the project at hand, how typical it is, under these circumstances, to procrastinate. This is how you begin every daunting story, small or big, by looking for ways to avoid beginning.

So we were starting slow—with a list, perhaps the thing Jonah cares about more than anything else these days. Lists include schedules, calendars, agendas, timetables. Because who could blame Jonah for checking the refrigerator? Who doesn't worry about the maple syrup supply? We all long to know what's next. We all depend on the weather channel. We want assurances and we want them in writing if at all possible. Jonah isn't really asking for anything more than that. He just wants to know what will be required of him and whether, if there are requirements, he will be able to meet them. One day, though not today, not this weekend, not without Cynthia here to back me up, my plan is to talk to my son about the limitations of lists, not to mention the unreliability of the weather channel. I will tell him that sometimes it's wrong and sometimes there isn't enough syrup to go around. I will talk to him about this when I think he's ready to understand his own limitations a little better. We will discuss the importance of going with the flow, rolling with the punches, taking things in stride. I suppose one day I could encourage him to read this so-called memoir of mine, even though I'm not sure, in the end, that it will deliver the right message, that it will convey to Jonah what I want to convey to him most of all: *Don't be so hard on yourself, kid.* But while I'm well aware I may not be the ideal person for this job, this teachable moment, I am his father. If we've proven nothing else this morning it's that we can have a plan and follow through on it. At least until the glass syrup bottle slips out of your hands and hits the hard tile floor.

WHEN IT WAS PUBLISHED in 1967 *The Siege* was the first account of autism written from a parent's point of view—the first "inside" story, as Oliver Sacks has called it. Not coincidentally, it was also one of the first memoirs that let other parents know they were not alone. The ambivalent feelings you have about your child, the love and the anguish, the daily heartbreak and heartbreaking work of living with a child with autism, the anger you harbour for the professionals whose advice can be hit and miss, at best, and cruel, at worst, are all painstakingly documented in *The Siege*. "This is what she did," Park writes of her daughter Elly, "and what we did with her. I have put down almost everything." It reads, in fact, like everything. *The Siege* must have been a gruelling book to write; it's certainly gruelling to read. *The Horse Boy* is, with all its rugged, swashbuckling adventures, a breeze by comparison.

What can feel overwhelming about Park's book is her meticulous account of her hard-earned, incremental accomplishments. *The Siege* is deliberately devoid of highlight moments to put on the cover. There is, instead, a photograph of a very young, very pretty girl looking lost in thought. "We were doing something terribly hard," Park writes, and that is, on every page, indisputable. She and her family were also doing it all alone. Park really was in the wilderness when she began writing *The Siege*, and, at first, everything she and her family did on behalf of her daughter they did without guidance. Her intention, even so, was to find a clearing, if only to enable her to see a few steps ahead. At one point, Park refers to her daughter as having a "strange integrity," and that's as good a description of autism as I've read. It's what you learn about autism eventually; it is always what it is. Park's own "strange integrity" made her unwilling to accept that fact of life with autism. She was indefatigable. She never quit.

If *The Siege* is one of the earliest memoirs written by a parent of a child with autism, *Son-Rise*, by Barry Neil Kaufman, has the distinction of being one of the earliest memoirs written by a father of a child with autism. What the two stories have in common is their protagonists' stick-to-it-iveness. Like Park, Kaufman is fiercely determined to do whatever he has to in order to reach his son Raun, who is diagnosed with autism at just seventeen months. Even at that age, his symptoms—isolation, passivity, lack of eye contact—are unmistakable. Unlike most parents with a child with autism, the Kaufmans have the dubious advantage of knowing, almost from the start, what they're dealing with, knowing, too, that they are dissatisfied with the treatments then available for their son. Kaufman and his wife Suzi, even their babysitters and friends, are way ahead of the curve, and the book has barely begun when Kaufman and Suzi institute a program of their own. It's mostly improvised, mostly a matter of following their gut, and their hippie-style instincts. (*Son-Rise* was published in 1976. And the Kaufmans are nothing if not in tune with their times.) For example, Kaufman and his wife begin their son's self-styled therapy by talking endlessly to each other about their own concerns. All their toxic, negative feelings, as Kaufman puts it, are spewed out in carefully and deliberately planned "rap sessions" wherein emotions run high and the prose runs purple: "We looked at each other through the mist in our eyes ... our ears soaked with our explorations."

"If it is a housecleaning of our feelings, go all the way," Kaufman says of these sessions which often lasted until daybreak. "Fertilize the unhappiness. Get it out. Deal with it so we could be free ... a confrontation with the phantoms of fear." Those phantoms are, admittedly, everywhere—in particular in the advice they receive from professionals and from the literature on autism at the time. This goes hand in hand with the labels they keep hearing applied to their son and his future. Raun, they are told, is "a tragedy. Unreachable. Bizarre ... hopeless.... Unapproachable ... irreversible." But Kaufman, to his everlasting credit, is not undeterred. A new attitude is what they need, he decides, and so, simple as that, he gets himself and his family one. "We would kiss the earth that the literature had cursed," he explains. "We would embrace all the beauty of our son. Raun would become for us a beautiful and enriching journey into our own humanity. We would walk together."

Son-Rise is a story of acceptance, but it's acceptance on a superhuman scale—off the grading chart in other words. What Kaufman never sufficiently explains is how a person is supposed to arrive, admittedly after a few marathon "rap sessions," at this level of acceptance. There are no five stages for Kaufman; he cuts right to the chase. There will be, for his son, "no conditions. No expectations. No judgments. This attitude would be the place to begin with Raun.... His behaviours ... were perfectly okay with us." No embarrassment either? No regrets? No desire to be somewhere, anywhere else? "To love is to be happy with," Kaufman says repeatedly, making the line his custom-made mantra. As if it makes perfect sense. As if all of history, all of the literature dedicated to human beings and their flaws, hasn't taught us the opposite. That we are, in our heart of hearts, ambivalent creatures—never quite satisfied. *To love is to be happy with.* Repeat it to yourself, say it slowly, say it again, then ask yourself: Does that sound the least bit plausible? Never mind that, does that sound anything like love?

Still, if you can get past all the Age-of-Aquarius posturing in *Son-Rise*—and if I can, you can—then there is something surprisingly solid at the book's core. That's the Kaufmans' conviction that they know more about their son than anyone else. They are dedicated; not only that, they are ingenious. Raun's early therapy is one-on-one and intensive—it shares these features with ABA. In the beginning, it consists mainly of Suzi spending all day every day in the bathroom with her son. The bathroom is chosen for having the fewest distractions, the least amount of "interference from audio and visual bombardment." From this point on, though, any planned interaction with Raun diverges dramatically from behaviour modification. Suzi is not modifying Raun's actions and behaviours; she's imitating them. She's spinning plates, flapping her hands, reinforcing his strangeness. All of this is meant to make him feel welcome, to join her in the world, assuming that's what he wants. No conditions, no judgments, remember? As in *The Siege*, gains are hard to come by at first and almost impossible to detect. There are setbacks and infinitesimal miracles. There is vindication. There is, above all, endless patience and faith. There is not, however, any mention by Kaufman of what is perhaps the one piece of mundane information about which every ordinary reader (okay, this ordinary reader) is waiting to be informed. Do the Kaufmans have a second bathroom?

GIVE ME AN A. It took almost an hour, a couple of rolls of paper towels, a change of clothes, for Jonah, then me, but we managed to leave the house with the kitchen floor reasonably clean. A writing teacher told me once that you need to make a mess before you can start to clean it up. *All right*, I used to think, *but then what?* I know better now. You wait for the next mess. They're like buses or shamans. Another one will be along. In the meantime, Jonah and I have our priorities. Buy more syrup. It's on our list.

Earlier, when I was on my knees handing Jonah goo-soaked Scotties to throw in the garbage, he started to mutter about the conspicuous absence of syrup for his unexpectedly delayed lunch. A tantrum seemed imminent.

"Looks like you'll have to have mustard, hot, yucky mustard," I said, raising my head to glance at him. While he grumbled, I waited patiently for him to look at me, to see me smirking, to listen and pick up on my tone of voice. But what was intended to be a pre-emptive joke was a minefield instead. His expression turned sullen, wary. He was gritting his teeth and balling up his fists, and then he caught my eye and understood. It took a moment but he got it.

"Yeah, right!" he said, loudly, though he still glanced at the pantry, worried about the mustard. This was an A+ for both of us. Sarcasm taught, learned, and generalized. I stretched out my fist for him to bump.

So we buy syrup first at the grocery story and then stop at the dollar store to deal with the rest of our list—the one we made specifically for *More Bad Animals*. This trip, according to my original plan, has an additional purpose. It will be a lesson in the simple exchange of goods. Jonah is largely indifferent, for instance, to the idea of receiving an allowance, but this summer we have been giving him one regardless. We do it every week, with the hope that the routine significance of it begins to sink in. Jonah is indifferent to the idea of money too. *We have to teach him everything, sweetheart.* I can't remember him ever asking us to buy him anything in a store, other than food. He will eye a toy sometimes, but he will never take the next step and ask for it or recognize that he has the wherewithal to buy it himself. We will have to teach him this, too, this basic step that is intuitive to all kids who learn instinctively and early on to pester their parents for what they want. We will teach him to be materialistic like all the other little neurotypical consumers.

This is the paradox at the heart of raising Jonah—how much he depends on us to make him independent. Because having protected him for so long, I am also required now to stop protecting him, and having guarded him from failure I am required now to let him fail. Every parent goes through this, I know. But with autism your intuition is continually turned upside down. The counter-intuitive is commonplace. Every decision feels like the wrong one, and the funny thing is, it's supposed to. In many ways, Jonah is like other kids, only reversed. He's not clamouring for toys, at eleven and a half, but he's also not clamouring to be left alone by his hovering parents. Children don't need to be taught to separate from their parents, but Jonah does. He won't, for instance, order me to refrain from kissing him or hugging him when we're out in public. I don't embarrass him because I can't. If anything, he doesn't want me to leave him alone in the dollar store. It's up to me to make that decision—in consultation with Cynthia's voice in my head: *let him try*—and come to the conclusion that the time is right to stand back and dispassionately observe. These days every moment is a teachable moment, and not only for my son.

At the dollar store, Jonah wanders out of line to approach a stranger and launches into a knock-knock joke. It's easy to see that he's not present enough to remember what is required of him next. Next can be a difficult concept for Jonah. It's sometimes hard to say if other people notice how distracted he is, or how odd he is behaving. Or if they just chalk it up to an acceptable amount of childish goofiness or undisciplined behaviour. Cynthia and I have both seen the look from other parents, the one that plainly says: *How did you raise him?*

"Knock knock," Jonah says again.

"Who's there?" the stranger says, reluctantly playing along. Meanwhile, I'm thinking: *Should I intervene? Should I wait?*

"Elk," Jonah says.

"Elk who?"

"Elkaholic."

The stranger, who was mostly ignoring Jonah before, is staring at him now. Then he looks around to see if he can find this kid's parents. He catches my eye and I shrug. When he smiles back the smile comes out crooked. The stranger grabs his own child's hand and walks away. I imagine him whispering something to his son. But I can't imagine what. I'd rather not anyway. I should have intervened. I should have guessed by the look on Jonah's face, the giggly, distracted tone of his voice, that this business of exchanging money for goods had him stumped. All of which is a reminder to me that he should have learned this sort of thing by now, and if he hasn't it's because I haven't taught him, and if I haven't taught him it's because teaching him has required more of me than I was capable of—more patience, more persistence, more hopefulness. Finally, this ordinary trip to the dollar store is a reminder that it's time for all of us to be better, to be different. So rather than do what I am desperate to do, stand next to my son, keep him in line and moving forward, shush him, help him, apologize for him, worry about him, I put my head down, stare at my shoes, and count slowly to ten: *one-steamboat, two steamboats.* I'm hoping now that when I look up (*three steamboats, four steamboats*) in a few seconds Jonah will be at the front of the line (*five steamboats, six steamboats*), the notebook and animal stickers I prompted him to buy for our so-called sequel still in his hand (*seven steamboats*) along with the money required to pay the cashier (*eight steamboats*), and that he will say as loudly and as clearly as he can (*nine steamboats*) what I've coached him, practically word by word and on numerous occasions, to say: "I want to buy this please."

Ten Steamboats. I look up and he is, indeed, standing in front of a young woman at the cash register. All he says is "please," and he mutters that. While she can barely hear him, I can and I'm farther away. She looks puzzled for a moment, but then he hands her the items he's remembered to bring to the cash. He also holds up his five dollar bill, his allowance, and while he doesn't hand it to her, he allows her to take it from him. I exhale and feel a sense of pride out of all proportion with what has just happened. This shouldn't come as a surprise after all these years: a life with autism is a life lived out of proportion, a life lived, at the best of times, slightly askew. The stress involved in going to a family gathering or the corner store or just being out in public can be extraordinary. So, as a consequence, can the feeling of accomplishment that comes when your child does something other children do so matter-of-factly and other parents take so much for granted. There are always a disproportionate number of disappointments to deal with throughout my long day with Jonah, but there are also a disproportionate number of moments when I find myself thinking: *This really is a big deal.* Matter-of-factness is sweet. I'm only sorry it has taken me so long to realize it.

THIS EVENING WHEN Cynthia finally calls from the country I let her message go to voice mail. I'm anxious to know what she thinks of the manuscript, just not right now. Her notes can wait. It's been a long day; though, to be honest, not any longer than usual. I'm overprotected too. My sisters took Jonah swimming in the afternoon. Then his grandparents took him out to dinner. All of this had been arranged by Cynthia before she left. Right now, Jonah is taking a bath—with the assistance of a laminated list of instructions. This is just one of a number of achievements made this summer while I was away. When I returned from Banff, Jonah was selecting his own clothes in the morning and he was getting his own breakfast—juice, toast, and/ or cereal. Cynthia assured me he can bathe on his own, too, but I check in on him periodically to be sure. He's happily reading aloud to himself from his laminated list. "Put shampoo in your hair. Scrub really hard 50 times."

Just before bed, we will finally get around to *More Bad Animals*. In my experience, this isn't the best time to write, but it is the best time to contemplate writing. It's the ideal time to trick yourself into thinking that tomorrow everything will fall into place. It doesn't, of course, but still, the night before, the possibilities seem limitless.

"So how about this, Rooney the Camel drops the biggest ever bottle of syrup on the floor and he gets stuck. When his old friends Deedee the Cow and Moe the Yak try to help him, they get stuck too. They all start shouting and saying lots of bad words. Should we write that down?" I'm drying Jonah's hair with a towel, so I can't see his face. "And then the new characters, remember, the Worst-Monkey-Ever and his father, the Worst-Daddy-Ever argue about what to do next. What do you think should happen next? Go ahead, take a guess. It could be anything, Jonah, there are no wrong answers, okay? It's a story, that's all. See if you can think of something. Use your imagination." When I lift the towel I can see Jonah is frowning; it's a frown I don't think I've ever seen before. How is that possible? He's not angry as much as deeply concerned. *Is he supposed to dry his hair himself? Does he miss his mother? What am I missing?*

"He's not the worst," he whispers.

"What's that Jonesy? What's the matter?"

"It's not true. He's not the worst monkey ever, and not the worst Daddy ever."

"It's just a joke. I thought you'd like those names."

"I don't like them."

"Fair enough. What should we call them? You tell me."

"We should call the monkey Jumpy the Monkey."

"That's a good name for a primate, definitely, I like it. What about his father? What should we call his father?"

"Grumpy the Daddy."

"Yes, and the two of them get into bad trouble. It's just not the worst trouble ever. There are worse things. There are always worse things, I get it. Realism, Jonah, yes, that could work. And they say bad words, like *poop*."

"Like *properly*."

"And they do bad things, like pick their noses." As I talk, I notice Jonah is leaning forward, waiting for me to continue, waiting to hear what comes next and also to add his contribution, and that's when it occurs to me. We are having a simple, ordinary conversation. Okay, maybe not ordinary, but close enough. We also have a story to tell.

"And they eat their boogers," Jonah says.

"Yes, they're definitely booger-eaters. That's perfect. They are irredeemable. Bad guys. Bad characters. I know, just not the worst. Do you know what irredeemable means? It means there's nothing you can say or do that is going to change them. They are who they are."

"Bad animals," he says. "And in the end, they all …"

"All right, tell me, what happens in the end?"

"They all go out to a restaurant for hot dogs and French fries with ketchup."

"And ice cream for dessert."

"Chocolate … in a cone."

"I like it. Yes, I can live with that. I'm telling you, Jonesy, this thing practically writes itself."

SEVENTEEN

August

"Just tell me if you're planning to trick me into saying all sorts of embarrassing, incriminating things."

"About whom?"

"I don't know, all of us. Am I going to have to get up and walk out?" Cynthia asks, glancing at the tape recorder in front of her.

"Like in those old *60 Minutes* interviews, you mean? They don't even do that any more. Besides, where would you go? You live here."

"And what's this for?" she asks, indicating the box of Kleenex next to the tape recorder.

"You never know."

Cynthia and I are sitting side by side at our new dining room table. It was an expensive purchase, a luxury we couldn't afford, but we bought it anyway. You can't put a price on symbolism. This summer we turned Jonah's therapy room back into what it was originally intended to be, a dining room, a place where Jonah can still do his homework and have the occasional therapy session—he'll mostly have a tutor when he starts grade six—and where the three of us can eat together as a family. In *The Blood of the Lamb*, Peter De Vries's autobiographical hero, Don Wanderhope, is obviously not surprised at how overjoyed he is to learn his leukemia-stricken daughter has gone into a brief remission. What surprises him is the reason he's so happy. He hadn't been counting on a miracle, it turns out, only a chance to have things the way they once were. That's miracle enough. Or as Wanderhope says: "The greatest experience open to man then is the recovery of the commonplace." Put another way, we're thrilled about our new dining room table.

Actually, it's only Cynthia and me tonight. Jonah is having a sleepover at my sister's. We're luckier than a lot of people we know who have a child on the spectrum; we have a support system that's dependable and generous with its time. My sisters and Jonah's grandparents are always available to take care of him for a few hours or longer, if necessary. Somehow, they've managed to forgive us for the decision we made early in Jonah's ABA therapy to prohibit them from staying with him unless either Cynthia or I were present as well. We didn't come right out and say that we didn't trust them, but we might as well have.

We didn't think they would be able to impose the proper structure or follow the ABA rules we were then convinced Jonah so desperately required. We were certain any kind of let-up would be disastrous. It was as if our regular meetings with The Consultant had infiltrated the rest of our lives; everyone was looking over everyone's shoulder. We were, in effect, babysitting the babysitters. We had created our own little fascist regime: demoralizing and ultimately unsustainable. *You're exaggerating, sweetheart.* Now, on sleepover nights at my sister's or Friday dinners at his grandparents', pretty much anything goes. Jonah eats whatever he wants, watches whatever videos he wants, stays up as late as he wants. No doubt, he stims to his heart's content. He's like a frat boy on spring break. When he's returned to us the report from all his regular babysitters is invariably the same: he was an angel.

"Should we start with my notes?" Cynthia says, as we clear the dishes from the table. We've had most of the afternoon to deal with those notes, but we decided it might be nice to cook dinner together first, have some wine, make the evening into a kind of working date night. An oxymoron, I suppose, but Harriet would half-approve anyway. Now, however, it's down to business. I warn Cynthia this could last all night and tell her about those "rap sessions" the Kaufmans so enthusiastically endured in *Son-Rise*.

"They explored their innermost feelings, asked and answered the most intimate questions. They gazed into each other's souls. It brought them closer together, apparently."

"Yeah, right!" she says, unprompted. I'm beginning to think wine with dinner might not have been a good idea.

"All right, what do I get wrong?"

"You mean in the book? Well, me, for starters. You make me sound too good. All that stuff about how I sprung into action after the diagnosis. That's not how I remember it. I remember running to the pharmacy to buy those nutritional supplements, those milkshake things in a can. I couldn't eat. I never *can't* eat. I was a mess. I was depressed. You didn't know?"

Cynthia has my manuscript in front of her. It's decorated with pink and blue Post-it notes, providing easy access, I'm guessing, to mistakes and trouble spots. I gasp at the array of colour.

"This includes the parts I liked," she adds quickly, recognizing my need for reassurance. "See all the smiley faces. And those little pencil lines, like rain falling, those are tears."

"All right, let me see."

"Later. First things first: here's what I think you should add."

"Add?"

"You said this was my chapter."

"I did?"

"My Molly Bloom chapter, remember."

"James Joyce's wife didn't actually write that chapter, Joyce did."

"But I bet she had notes. So, here, read this." Cynthia hands me a loose sheet of lined paper, which has as its heading: "Ideas from a

Parent for Educators Who Need to Inform Parents about Children Who Have Developmental Delays."

My first thought is: *I'll have to change that title—maybe something like Let's Talk About Autism.* Underneath the heading, there's a numbered list of suggestions, a well-considered primer on breaking bad news gently, including: "Please do not gang up on and outnumber parents. That is cruel." Or: "Do not be defensive if they have negative comments about your school or daycare. Understand parents need an explanation for the problems with their child. It can take time for parents to come to terms with what might seem obvious to you."

Cynthia is watching me read, and it's taking a while—I get stuck on that phrase "come to terms"—but the moment I look up, she's talking. "I thought this could be useful, you know, for anyone who has to tell a parent about their child having autism. I still wish the daycare people had told us when they first suspected something. I guess they tried. But they didn't know how. Sometimes I think it could have made a difference, a big difference, if we'd known, you know, earlier, if ..."

"I'd rather not think about that," I say and pour myself what's left of the wine. I can't remember if we have another bottle somewhere. Is it too late to go shopping? Neither of us drinks much, though there have been many times in the last seven years when I've wondered why not. Now is one of those times. The idea that there was something that could have been done—something simple—is hard to bear sober.

"I think about it sometimes. About if we'd known a year earlier. And what that might have meant. That's why you should include this—this appendix, you could call it. You see, it doesn't necessarily have to be in the book."

"This isn't really the kind of book that has an appendix."

"Or is useful to anyone?"

"Right. Not that either."

SEQUELS HAVE A momentum of their own. That's not to say Jonah and I have finished *More Bad Animals* or even that we ever will, but in the last month, out walking or in the car, we come back to it every so often. It's taking on the feel of a long-term, ongoing project, one of those things you contemplate for years until it finally starts to make sense and fall into place or until you realize it's going nowhere. In any case, *More Bad Animals* has given us the opportunity to discuss the lives of characters like Deedee the Cow, Moe the Yak, Rooney the Camel, not to mention the monkeys, Jumpy and Grumpy, and how they are required to have an arc. That means they start in one place, I explain to Jonah, and end somewhere else, usually better. Not like people, in real life, who just have their ups and downs and keep on having them.

"Like on a rollercoaster," Jonah volunteers.

"Kind of. But a small rollercoaster, not a fast or scary one."

"Not scary?" He frowns.

"All right, kind of scary, now that you mention it."

Clara Claiborne Park never stopped writing about her daughter Elly, though by the time she got around to adding an epilogue to *The Siege*, fifteen years later, she was using her daughter's real name, Jessy. By then, her concern that Elly might be embarrassed someday by what her mother wrote was no longer an issue. Even at twenty-one, Jessy was immune to embarrassment. She also liked flipping through the pages of *The Siege* and coming across her "book name." By then, Park also realized her daughter was never going to read about herself in a way that might cause her undue hurt. Some twenty years after the epilogue, in 2001, Park wrote a sequel, *Exiting Nirvana: A Daughter's Life with Autism*. Perhaps what is most reassuring about meeting up with Park and Jessy again in *Exiting Nirvana* is the way Park begins the new story. "In bewilderment," she writes, "I think—that's the truest way. That's where we began all those years ago. That's where everyone begins who has to do with autistic children."

Jessy is in her forties in the sequel, living with her parents, and doing well, all things considered. She has improved markedly in certain areas, less so in others. Speech is still a problem, as is social interaction. She is not entirely independent, but she holds down a job in the mailroom at Williams College in Massachusetts where her mother taught English before she retired. Jessy is also a professional artist. She's sold paintings and earned commissions. A few examples of her art are included in the book and are striking for a couple of reasons—the meticulous, geometric rendering of buildings and bridges and the absence of people. "Jessy's life, and life with Jessy, is not all strangeness," Park writes, though she feels compelled to add a little later that there should be no confusion—this is not the story of "a miraculous recovery." Even so, *Exiting Nirvana* serves the purpose every sequel should. It provides its real-life characters as well as its audience with a second opinion, a revised assessment. If you liked how things worked out the first time around, well, here's more of the same. If you weren't satisfied, here's a second chance, a do-over. There is bewilderment here, true enough, but hope, too, in the fact that Jessy goes on learning, and so does Park; that life, even with autism, as Park seems a little amazed to discover, is "less strange every year." Stories continue. Try to stop them.

Of course, if it's something a little more extraordinary you're looking for, there's Barry Neil Kaufman's sequel to *Son-Rise*, which was published in 1994 and unabashedly titled *Son-Rise: The Miracle Continues.* Nothing bewildering here: the foreword is written by Kaufman's son Raun, who is, sixteen years after the first book about him appeared, grateful to his parents for their open-minded attitude. At least as important as being cured, he says, is the fact that his family always accepted him for who he was. He takes some shots at the "experts" in the field of autism and has a good word to say for "false hope." The kind you put in quotation marks—"How in the world can anyone put these two words together?" he writes—the kind Raun is plainly the product of. We also learn, in the foreword, that this young man whom the doctors once called "a tragedy" is in college, on the debating team, reads Stephen King, has a girlfriend, and is politically aware and active. The foreword is, in many ways, a thrilling document. Raun's voice, on the page, is quirky, a little stiff, a little too propped up by self-esteem; nevertheless, this is the voice of a recovered child. Raun is also a poster boy. The aspects of the original memoir which were vaguely irritating, like its author's self-congratulatory style, are less subtle in the sequel. The senior Kaufman appeared to have an agenda or the beginning of one in *Son-Rise*, though it was hard to pinpoint. In *Son-Rise: The Miracle Continues*, it's impossible to miss. The further you read in the sequel the more you realize this is a book-length infomercial for what has turned into a bustling cottage industry. The Kaufmans' trademarked Option Institute offers, according to the dust jacket, "programs for families with special children as well as for adults who come to learn the Kaufmans' self-accepting and empowering process." Today, the Option Institute's website offers seminars and workshops on everything from autism awareness to self-empowerment. You can also order one of Kaufman's twelve bestselling books including *Happiness Is a Choice* and *To Love Is to Be Happy With*. The miracle, indeed, continues.

I googled Clara Claiborne Park recently, hoping that I might be able to get in touch with her, that she might have her own website or an email address where I could contact her. It's so easy to find people today you take it for granted that you can find everyone. I'm not sure what I wanted to say, maybe ask for an update, find out if one more sequel was on the way. In the epilogue to *The Siege*, Park recounts how she never intended to write a book about her then six-year-old daughter. She wanted, instead, to wait and see how the story ended. "Though memory tricks us often enough," she adds, "that memory must be true; I could not possibly have invented words so touchingly, so piercingly naïve. I imagined, then, that the story could have an ending."

What I learned from my internet search was that Park had died a month earlier at the age of eighty-six. Her obituary in the *New York Times* credits her with being a pioneer in raising awareness about autism, in making children with the disorder a little more understood and their parents a little less isolated. It goes some way towards describing a woman with quiet dignity and unrelenting determination. It also provides that update, that sequel, on Park's lifelong subject: "At Williams College, where (Jessy) has been employed since high school, a sign on the door of her workplace says, Jessica H. Park Mailroom." It was good to know. It was also a reminder of what Park once said about true-life stories, how they do not end, how we only stop telling them.

"ALL RIGHT, HERE'S MY idea for another appendix," Cynthia says.

"Another?"

"Should it be appendices? I'm thinking advice for family and friends. I'm thinking about two lists—what's helpful and what's not. For example, not helpful is saying, 'I knew there was something wrong with him.' A lot of people said that."

"Who?"

"Never mind. Also, not helpful: telling me about methods of interventions well into the diagnosis as if you know better, as if I haven't been reading and researching since the moment I got the news. And, oh yes, don't talk to me about vaccines. Not helpful, not interesting.

"Then there are the people who dump you the moment their child says that your child is no fun to play with. Even the nicest people you can imagine. If their three-year-old tells them he or she doesn't want your child at their party, you're suddenly off the party list. I know that kids like Jonah don't act like other kids and I know that makes it difficult. I understand children will say they don't want to play with him because he keeps asking them, 'What's your name? What's your name?' But it shouldn't be up to the children to decide."

"And that happened?"

"I don't want any names mentioned, but there was the time I called a friend, well, you know, one of those friends you make when you have children the same age. We'd had play dates—you know, *before*, just before—and then after I called to invite her son to Jonah's birthday party and she let it slip her son had his party a week earlier. She said, 'Oh well, I thought Jonah wouldn't be comfortable in a big group with so many kids.' Did you ever read the book by Temple Grandin's mother? What's it called?"

"*A Thorn in My Pocket*. No, I haven't gotten to it yet."

"Right, not yet. So Temple's mother talks about Temple growing up in a Boston suburb, a kind of *Leave It to Beaver* environment, and one of the rules of this little community was that everyone was included. Amazing, really, when you think this was the fifties. Temple wasn't exactly an easy kid either. She had tantrums, bad ones. But it didn't matter. The mothers banded together and made sure she was always included.

"I wish people today were that enlightened. The number of times other mothers have ensured that Jonah was included in an activity has been so, so rare. I realized that this summer at the neighbourhood pool. Jonah and I happened to meet the mother of a couple of kids from Jonah's school. She not only told her kids to play with Jonah, she made sure they did. I didn't even ask her. It was very kind of her. I thanked her after and told her how unusual it was.

"What's also helpful: Don't ask what you can do and then forget you asked; follow through. And, oh yes, if you can, give money or cook food or something like that, that means a lot."

"How come I didn't know about the woman at the pool?"

"I told you. Remember, you started to cry."

"TWO PEOPLE CANNOT share unhappiness," De Vries writes in *The Blood of the Lamb*. A second bottle of wine, however, is another matter. Cynthia and I have moved from the dining room table to the living room couch, where it is becoming evident that we will not be exploring our innermost feelings for much longer, certainly not until the sun comes up. It's only ten thirty and we're both yawning. We may have to continue our "rap session" tomorrow and, quite likely, the next day and the day after that until it turns into all it really is, all it ever is—us talking about Jonah.

In the meantime, Jonah is having a ball at my sister's. The report, when we call, is thorough. He went for a swim in the backyard pool, had dinner, then another swim, had dessert, watched the *Madagascar* sequel, *Madagascar: Escape 2 Africa*, and went to bed, though he isn't sleeping yet. I could hear him chattering about something in the background. "Everything is fine," we're assured. "He's reading his new joke book. Do you know what the chicken said to the duck about crossing the road? Give up? Jonah, here, tell Daddy."

Jonah's voice on the phone is always a little fragile, suspicious even, like he's never sure what's going to come back at him from the other end of the line. This time though, the punchline is clear. "The chicken said, 'Don't do it. You won't ever hear the end of it.' Goodbye, daddy."

He hangs up and Cynthia pats me on the back. "I miss him, too," she says. "But this is a good break for everyone. We should probably do this more often. Next time, we'll go to a movie."

"We could even have sex. A movie and sex."

"Yeah, right! Do you ever get the feeling we drive him as crazy as he drives us?"

We're on Appendix III, now, unless I've lost count. This is Cynthia's advice for parents like us—"Well, people who are just recently learning about their child," she says. "First, there's what the woman at the Autism Association said to me when I started investigating our options. She said, 'Do ABA. Do it, even if you have to do it yourself.' I also want to talk about what ABA actually means. I want to make sure people know that it isn't a big mystery. It shouldn't be.

"I mean keep it simple. When your child doesn't understand something, you have to break it down, step by step, into its smallest components, and teach it part by part. Even before we started our home program, I was getting an idea of what I should do from reading about ABA and watching videos. I tried it out by teaching Jonah to count. I bought these toy hippos and he'd count to one and I'd bounce him on the bed or do something else he liked, then we'd count two hippos and do the same thing. Until he understood; until he could … what … what is it?"

"I need a Kleenex."

"You're sweet."

"Seriously."

"Also, respond to behaviours in a way that doesn't make them worse. Why are you looking at me? Don't get paranoid. I'm not talking about you … necessarily."

"Necessarily?" If I wasn't paranoid before, I am now.

"Like I said, it's simple. For example, if your kid hits somebody so he can get a toy and then he gets the toy, that reinforces bad behaviour."

"Isn't that obvious?"

"No, it isn't. People respond to behaviours all the time in ways that make them worse. I met a father at a conference once and he was complaining about his child's tantrums. He kept saying, 'No one can help.' I remember I talked to him afterward. I asked him what he does when his child *isn't* having a tantrum. Because that's the time you can make a difference. Your efforts should be proactive. Play with your child when he's not having a tantrum. Catch them being good, that's what you have to remember. It works for everyone, you know, not just Jonah, not just kids with autism."

"I'll remember that."

"It's classic ABA, sweetheart, reinforce the behaviours you want to see."

"The thing is, this isn't a book about ABA. In a way, it's the opposite. It's about bad behaviour and about what it's like to not have anything to rely on, to hold on to."

"I don't care," Cynthia says. "Second."

"Second? That was five things."

"Second, also do Relationship Development Intervention, or RDI. Which means don't ignore relationships; RDI will help you discover what your role as a parent is. It will also teach your child how to relate to you, first, and then others. In my opinion, there are two great geniuses in terms of treating autism: Lovaas with ABA, and Gutstein with RDI. If you can find a treatment that incorporates the best of both of their programs you're probably on the right track. It's not a coincidence that they have the best critiques of each other. They could team up, of course, but that would make ..."

"Sense?"

"Right, third."

"Third and, finally ..."

"No, not finally," Cynthia continues. "Third, the hardest thing for me, even harder than dealing with autism, is dealing with service providers. I don't really have advice. I hope whoever is reading this is better at it than I am. In our experience the service providers, the school, the hospitals, the government agencies, whoever, are not interested in collaborating with parents. It's a hard job advocating for your child. For me, it's been a huge challenge. So get help. Get advocates. Don't expect it to be easy."

On the subject of unhappiness, De Vries was wrong. It can be shared. In my experience, it is shared every day. It is, in this respect, not very different from happiness.

"Your child might recover and might not; both are possible," Cynthia says, then pauses, choosing her words carefully. "Jonah didn't recover. He hasn't yet. We don't know what kind of life he is going to have. How can we? Who can know? Anything can happen. But we're still aiming high. Yes, *we*. And don't listen to people who say things can't improve. Okay, now I am looking at you. Don't you think I know what *you're* thinking by now? You think your voice isn't in *my* head.

"You know what you said that time, to Harriet, that you underestimate him? Well, you may think you do. But I see you with Jonah every day; I know that's not what you are doing."

"Appendix IV?"

"Don't rush me. I have to talk about the gains. Because even though they may be tiny, they go a long way to make everything worthwhile. Jonah is learning Hebrew. We're learning it together. He knows his fractions. He's going into grade six, on his own. Instead of screaming and having a tantrum every morning like he used to, now he's saying—you've heard him—he's saying, 'Mom, it's seven o'clock.' When we went for a bike ride the other day, he asked me if I was happy. He was interested; I really think he was. Last week, we were waiting in the car at a train crossing and it was a very long train. It must have taken ten minutes to go by. And when it finally did he looked at me and said, 'Thank goodness!' I'd never heard him say something like that, something so ordinary and appropriate. And at that wedding we went to—remember?—he disappeared when we were leaving and I found him saying goodbye to the bride and groom. What now? Are you crying again?"

"Yes, why aren't you?"

She puts her arm around me and kisses me. Meanwhile, I'm thinking rules: *Be proactive. Reinforce behaviours you want to see. Remember to play with him when he's being good.* "Sweetheart, I never expected to be a mother, you know, and now, well, now I am. I mean I wouldn't change anything, not if it meant changing everything, you know. So ..."

"So?"

"That's right, deal with it: lemonade."

"What about Appendix IV?"

"Too sleepy."

"You know you've given advice to everyone, except me."

"Bed, please."

"Just one line, come on."

Cynthia stands and pushes the stop button on the tape recorder. "All right, here it is. Be a good sport," she says, holding out her hand to help me up. "Now will you come to bed already?"

"Yes," I say. "Yes I will."

September

Jonah has a signature move. On the way to the car, he kicks out his right leg, does a stutter step, and then rotates one arm over the other in a kind of tumbling motion. If it's hard to describe accurately, it's even harder to account for. On the one hand, it has the look of being choreographed—like he's a back-up singer for the Temptations. On the other hand, it seems as involuntary as a hiccup. On those rare occasions he gets into the car without doing his move, the lapse will weigh on him to the point where he'll ask me to stop the car. "Please, Daddy," he'll say. "No way, José," I'll counter. Lately, he's been surprisingly sanguine about my flip reply. He hardly even complains. This is a small sign of maturity but an encouraging one nonetheless. Cynthia and I didn't notice Jonah's move at first, not until we compared notes one day and realized it happened whenever he went somewhere. After that, I started watching for it—trying to figure out what comfort it provided, what meaning it might hold for him. Even for Jonah, it was a strange little stim, though endearing, Cynthia and I agreed. Eventually, I stopped analyzing and simply observed him. Now, it's become hard to think of it as strange or even a stim. It's more like a gesture—Jonah being Jonah.

Of course, some things can't be overlooked. A few weeks into grade six and we're already reminded of that. Jonah is also being

Jonah in class, laughing for no reason his teachers or the CCW, the child care worker the school has assigned to him, can make sense of. It doesn't happen all the time, though often enough for him to be a distraction. He's been told, more than once, to stand outside in the hall. We can't help worrying that this has something to do with the fact that he's essentially on his own this year and doesn't have Jessica or someone like her to help him. With Jessica banished, information is spotty, at best. After last year's confrontations, we are not on the best terms with the principal, and so far Jonah's CCW seems to be intent on avoiding us. At the beginning of the year, Cynthia sent her a note asking if they could meet, before or after class to put a face to the name, just say hello. We got a note from the CCW the next day saying she couldn't talk to us. She didn't explain why, though I have a guess. Our reputation as troublemakers precedes us. Now, a meeting is scheduled in a few weeks with the principal and the school board's special-needs consultant to discuss how we can all improve communication and, more to the point, how this very important year got off to a very bad start.

Cynthia believes in talking things out. I believe that will only succeed in making everyone more wary of everyone else and will, in the long run, create more problems than it resolves. This is a reactionary view, I know, but it's not like I don't have the experience to back it up. If there's one thing you learn writing book reviews and having your own books reviewed, it's that the human capacity for holding a grudge and then nursing it is limitless. *You're not getting out of the meeting, sweetheart, if that's what this is about.* For now, we have to make do with Jonah's child care worker grudgingly filling out a short checklist we prepared for her—apparently, filling out checklists, like saying hello, is not part of her job description. In the meantime, Jonah can't seem to keep a straight face when we ask him why he's laughing in class.

AFTER DINNER AND HOMEWORK, we experiment with a new family activity. We all sit down to watch the DVDs of Jonah's baby days that my sisters loaned me almost a year ago. The ones I promised myself I'd never watch. Cynthia and Jonah started watching the DVDs over the summer when I was away and Jonah got a kick out of them. Look at it from his viewpoint: what was there to dislike? He was the star, essentially, of a twelve-hour (so far) one-man show. What's evident in every frame is how the world revolved around Jonah even then—all our worlds—only it did so with a great deal more effortlessness than it does now. When she first watched the DVDs Cynthia's reaction was ambivalent. She knew what she was supposed to be feeling—straightforward, undiluted nostalgia, the kind of emotional response that naturally accompanies the viewing of old home movies of your baby. Except in this case, it was a feeling complicated by hindsight, by signs she might have missed, signs she couldn't help looking for now.

"And what have you noticed?" I asked before agreeing to take part in this latest screening.

"You had more hair and you were happy. A winning combination: want to see?"

So with our eleven-year-old son between us, in constant squirm mode, we learn an important lesson: the past is not a thing of the past. My hairline aside, not as much has changed as you'd think. So while my sisters, who did most of the taping, add a running commentary of adoring baby talk, I come in and out of view, mostly to kibitz with the kid and make a nuisance of myself. Here I am playing peek-a-boo. Here I am making funny faces. Here I am impersonating Winston Churchill giving his famous "We shall never surrender" speech—on the premise that all babies look like the late British prime minister.

I wasn't wrong about Jonah being cute, though he's not quite as faultlessly cute as I remember. He's no Gerber's baby. In some early shots, his skin is blotchy and he's sporting what looks like a comb-over. His scalp was, I'm also reminded, ravaged early by eczema or what the *What to Expect* books called cradle cap. I remember we had to put olive oil on his head every day for months. He was as slippery as a seal and smelled like a chef's salad. Sometimes, he looks jowly— yes, like Churchill—and sometimes gassy, whether he's three months or thirty months. "Women, unlike men, actually notice things," the novelist Richard Russo said, and no doubt, he's right. But if there were lights blinking A-U-T-I-S-M back then, if that's what we were looking for, I swear I can't see it. Instead, what I can't help noticing is a kind of continuity, an unbroken, if not always straight, line between Jonah then and now. If I want a glimpse of a kooky, charming kid I can look at the television screen or at the guy sitting next to me.

JONAH IS STARTING OFF this year the way last year left off, resisting his Read and Respond homework. This time, though, I'm deliberately giving him reason to resist. I've upped the ante and given away our Joy Berry collection of self-help literature. We are going to read a real story instead, a chapter book. On Cynthia's advice, we're going to go slow, no more than two pages at a time, but we're going to stick with it, and, if we do, we should be through the whole thing in a month or so. I've chosen *The Three Musketeers*, the copy I bought before he was born, and since rescued from one of those piles of garage sale junk in the basement.

This abridged version—decimated from some seven hundred pages to barely seventy—is relatively undemanding. Even so, Jonah is having a hard time following the narrative, locating the main idea in a scene, distinguishing between characters. He's not much for swash-buckling, it turns out; or chapter books. There are lots of illustrations, but even so the pages are a bit longer and denser than he's used to. The same goes for the story. When I sense his frustration growing, we take a break and act out a sword-fighting scene. Jonah grabs a plastic baseball bat and I grab an umbrella and we have at it on the trampoline, cursing at each other in fake French. He's d'Artagnan;

I'm Cardinal Richelieu. Cynthia overhears the commotion and comes running, relieved to see we're not actually fighting. She disappears before we can enlist her in the battle. She has work to do; she's researching high school open houses.

"A father is a man who fails every day," Michael Chabon says in *Manhood for Amateurs*. I can only assume his point is, so what? When Jonah and I sit down at the dining room table again, I read one paragraph of *The Three Musketeers* and wait, as patiently as I can, for him to read it over. I've also started encouraging him to take notes, so we stop frequently. Getting through a page this way can take twenty minutes or more. Still, even condensed and slowed down to a crawl, Alexandre Dumas's nineteenth-century tale of seventeenth-century derring-do has some juice to it. It's a story with unrepentant villains and obvious good guys, but even so the good guys, the Musketeers, are flawed. In fact, at the point at which we meet them, you could convincingly argue that they're deadbeats. And while they rise to the occasion, it's not before they've done their share of complaining. They're brave and witty, but also cynical, vindictive, and dissolute. This is apparent, even in a seventy-page adaptation for pre-teens. Dumas's novel was intended to be all about honour, but it ends up being about something else entirely, something smaller but more intimate like fidelity. Like most writers, Dumas didn't have a clue what his story was really about until he got around to telling it.

"And what do they say?" Jonah interrupts, writing a note to himself.

"Tell me. Go ahead. Look." I point to the page, but it's likely I'm over-prompting. He doesn't have to reread it. He remembers the Musketeers' famous unifying motto and says it out loud. "Again," I say, and we shout it together this time, as we wait for his mother to overhear and drop what she's doing.

THE SCHOOL BELL RINGS and I wait for Jonah in the car. A girl from his class who appears, from a distance, to be a pint-sized Oprah gets him in a walking bear hug—she's twice his size—and I watch him try, without success, to wriggle free. On Jonah's checklist the other day his child care worker made a reference to a girl, likely this one, and Jonah behaving "inappropriately" between classes. It seems the two were caught kissing. When I asked Jonah where she had kissed him, he said in the schoolyard. *Good enough.* I admit I probably would have teased Jonah about this if he were a different child. But Jonah, so far, has proven difficult to tease. He either gets mad or is completely unaffected. There's no middle ground. I suppose, with a different kid, I also would have had to resist the clichéd urge to take some obligatory paternal pride in this accomplishment. But with Jonah, a simple playground kiss was, instead, a new and more complicated cause for worry. There was still so much he had to learn, so much he was vulnerable to, so much … okay, who am I kidding? I couldn't be prouder.

Puberty was scary and incomprehensible enough when I went through it, but I can't imagine what it will be like for Jonah. I'd better start, though, because, like it or not, it's here. Last year, Jonah came home from school with a free sample of deodorant in his backpack. This year he's being encouraged to use it. Jonah's homeroom teacher has bluntly suggested to parents they make sure their children bathe regularly and change their clothes. There is, apparently, an odour that hits a peak when kids turn eleven and twelve; in particular, when twenty of them are stuck together for hours in a stuffy classroom. The teachers call it Eau de Sixth Grade.

Jonah is finally free of his, what—girlfriend? stalker?—and he spots me and hops into the backseat. I'm hoping he'll say something about what just happened but he's more interested in where we are having supper. I ignore the question and make up a story about the countless girls who used to hug me all the time when I was his age, but he still doesn't bite. Having had no success at finding out where we'll be eating, he now wants to know what we'll be eating. I start the car and, again, change the subject. I shout, "Shotgun!" Jonah scrambles into the front passenger seat. He's big enough to sit beside me now, and I encourage him to. It makes it easier for us to carry on something closer to a conversation. In fact, Cynthia and I have both noticed he's revealing more about what's happening at school than usual. Not that he's telling us anything useful, anything that will make his homework easier to complete or that will assist us in helping him cope with whatever stresses or pressures he may be feeling. Mostly, it's gossip. Grade six is part *Lord of the Flies*, part reality TV. We have pieced together enough information to know that Stephanie has a crush on James, that Tommy is in trouble for burping in the faces of classmates, and Terrell is relentless in teasing Tyler about his love life. As Jonah explains, "Terrell sings, 'Tyler has a girlfriend; that he'll never see again.'"

This is the good stuff, the reason I like having Jonah beside me in the car. But before we head home I am compelled to at least look through Jonah's backpack to see how much homework he has and what the child care worker has deigned to tell us about his academic day. The news, according to his school agenda, isn't uplifting.

"There seems to be little support in reality for the popular belief that we are mellowed by suffering," Peter De Vries once wrote. "Happiness mellows us, not troubles." If you'd asked me just a year ago if I agreed with this statement, I've no doubt I would have said yes and had good reason to. Ask me now and I'd also say yes. *Be serious, sweetheart.* All right, it has occurred to me this past year that happiness and trouble aren't quite as inseparable as I once thought. What can I say? I have no clue. Which is, coincidentally, *my* signature move.

Jonah is watching me intently as I read the teacher's note in his agenda. I do my best to keep my expression neutral and wait as patiently as I can for him to speak first. He wants to put on "That's Life," but I shake my head and turn off the car engine. Eventually, my old interviewing tactic works. He speaks first and says more than he intends to.

"I laughed today … in school."

"And?"

"I had to stand in the hall outside the class. The teacher said I will have to go see the principal next time."

"And do you want to stand outside? Do you want to go to the principal's office? No? So why do you do it Jonah?"

"My French teacher's name is Miss Melanie and I find it funny to say Miss Shmelanie."

"Jonah?"

"I laugh because it has a *shm* in it for Shmelanie. I have to go out in the hall because I find the *shm* funny." Proving the point, he cracks up, and so, eventually, do I. That's because he's right. It is funny, for the reason he says and, who knows, for a whole lot of other reasons we have yet to figure out.

Selected Bibliography

On Autism

Collins, Paul. *Not Even Wrong: Adventures in Autism*. New York: Bloomsbury, 2004.

Cutler, Eustacia. *A Thorn in My Pocket: Temple Grandin's Mother Tells the Family Story*. Arlington, TX: Future Horizons, 2004.

Grandin, Temple. *Thinking in Pictures: And Other Reports on My Life with Autism*. New York: Doubleday, 1995.

———. *The Way I See It: A Personal Look at Autism and Asperger's*. Arlington, TX: Future Horizons, 2008. This collection of magazine columns has practical advice on everything from dealing with bullying to learning to drive a car.

Grandin, Temple, and Maureen S. Scariano. *Emergence: Labelled Autistic*. New York: Warner Books, 1986.

Grinker, Roy Richard. *Unstrange Minds: Remapping the World of Autism*. New York: Basic Books, 2007.

Gutstein, Stephen E. *The RDI Book: Forging New Pathways for Autism, Asperger's and PDD with the Relationship Development Intervention Program*. Houston: Connections Center Publishing, 2009. Just so you know, I've made it to page seventy-five.

Haddon, Mark. *The Curious Incident of the Dog in the Night-Time*. Toronto: Anchor Canada, 2004.

Hornby, Nick. *Songbook*. New York: Riverhead Books, 2003. Hornby's collection of essays on his favourite songs includes "Puff the Magic Dragon," on Hornby's son Danny, who has autism.

Howard, Cori (ed.). *Between Interruptions: 30 Women Tell the Truth about Motherhood*. Toronto: Key Porter, 2007. This anthology includes Estée Klar's essay about her son.

Isaacson, Rupert. *The Horse Boy: A Father's Quest to Heal His Son*. New York: Little, Brown, 2009.

Kaufman, Barry Neil. *Son-Rise*. New York: Harper and Row, 1976.

———. *Son-Rise: The Miracle Continues*. Tiburon, CA: H.J. Kramer, 1994.

Lord, Cynthia. *Rules*. New York: Scholastic Press, 2006. A charming novel about a twelve-year-old girl and her younger brother who has autism; it's intended for grades four to seven.

Lovaas, O. Ivar. *Teaching Individuals with Developmental Delays: Basic Intervention Techniques*. Austin, TX: Pro-Ed Inc., 2003. This ABA manual is appropriately dedicated to "all parents of children with developmental delays in recognition of the heavy burdens they carry and the models they provide for all parents to follow."

Moon, Elizabeth. *The Speed of Dark*. New York: Random House, 2003. This is a science-fiction novel which features a hero with autism.

Nazeer, Kamran. *Send in the Idiots: Stories from the Other Side of Autism*. London: Bloomsbury, 2006.

Page, Tim. *Parallel Play: Growing Up with Undiagnosed Asperger's*. New York: Doubleday, 2009.

Park, Clara Claiborne. *The Siege: A Family's Journey into the World of an Autistic Child*. Boston: Little, Brown, 1982.

———. *Exiting Nirvana: A Daughter's Life with Autism*. Boston: Little, Brown, 2001.

Picoult, Jodi. *House Rules*. New York: Atria Books, 2010. This is an engaging if formulaic novel by a bestselling author who takes on topical themes. In this case, one of the novel's main characters has Asperger's and is also a murder suspect.

Sacks, Oliver. *Anthropologist on Mars: Seven Paradoxical Tales*. Toronto: Knopf Canada, 1995.

Tammet, Daniel. *Born on a Blue Day: A Memoir of Asperger's and an Extraordinary Mind*. London: Hodder and Stoughton, 2006. Tammet's sequel, *Embracing the Wide Sky: A Tour across the Horizons of the Mind*, was published in 2009.

Williams, Donna. *Nobody Nowhere: The Extraordinary Autobiography of an Autistic*. Toronto: Doubleday Canada, 1992. This is one of the early insider memoirs. Williams wrote three more memoirs: *Somebody Somewhere*, *Like Color to the Blind*, and *Everyday Heaven*.

Other Sources

Berry, Joy. *Let's Talk About Complaining*. Danbury, CT: Grolier, 1982.

Brown, Ian. *The Boy in the Moon: A Father's Search for His Disabled Son*. Toronto: Random House Canada, 2009. This memoir isn't specifically about autism, but it is a bravely written book about being the father of a son with special needs.

Chabon, Michael. *Manhood for Amateurs: The Pleasures and Regrets of a Husband, Father, and Son*. New York: HarperCollins, 2009.

De Vries, Peter. *The Blood of the Lamb*. Boston: Little, Brown, 1961.

Dyer, Geoff. *Out of Sheer Rage: In the Shadow of D.H. Lawrence*. London: Abacus, 1997.

Elkin, Stanley. *The Living End*. New York: E.P. Dutton, 1979.

Fitzgerald, F. Scott. *The Crack-Up*. New York: Charles Scribner's Sons, 1931.

Geisel, Theodor. *Horton Hears a Who!* New York: Random House Books for Young Readers, 1954.

———. *Green Eggs and Ham*. New York: Beginner Books, 1960.

Gilmour, David. *The Film Club: A True Story of a Father and a Son.* Toronto: Thomas Allen, 2007. This is a frank and charming father–son love story.

Humphreys, Josephine. *The Fireman's Fair.* New York: Penguin, 1991. I also recommend Humphreys's earlier novels, *Dreams of Sleep* and *Rich in Love.*

Joyce, James. *Ulysses.* London: Penguin Classic, 2000 (New Edition).

Kingsley, Jason, and Mitchell Levitz. *Count Us In: Growing Up with Down Syndrome.* Orlando, FL: A Harvest Book, 1994. This is the book co-written by the son of Emily Perl Kingsley, author of "Welcome to Holland."

Menaker, Daniel. *A Good Talk: The Story and Skill of Conversation.* New York: Twelve, 2010.

Pinker, Susan. *The Sexual Paradox: Extreme Men, Gifted Women and the Real Gender Gap.* Toronto: Vintage Canada, 2008.

Roth, Philip. *Patrimony: A True Story.* New York: Simon and Schuster, 1991.

Schwartz, Lynne Sharon. *Ruined by Reading: A Life in Books.* Boston: Beacon Press, 1996.

Shields, Carol. *Unless.* Toronto: Random House, 2002.

Acknowledgments

Excerpts from *Bad Animals*, in somewhat different form, appeared in *Maisonneuve Magazine* (Spring 2008) as well as *The Malahat Review* (Winter 2008) and the anthology *In Other Words: New English Writing from Quebec* (Véhicule Press, 2008). An early version of the chapter "What You Need" was also broadcast on CBC Radio's *Cinq à Six*. I gratefully acknowledge the support of the Canada Council and Quebec's Conseil des Arts. Special thanks to the Quebec Writers' Federation, especially Lori Schubert, as well as to my colleagues in the Literary Journalism Program at The Banff Centre, in particular to my editors there, Marni Jackson and Don Gillmor.

If it doesn't exactly take a village to raise a child, it takes a lot of people working hard. I am grateful to all of Jonah's therapists and teachers over the years. As well, my thanks to the Friendship Circle and Mrs. Rudski at Kumon. Our families—in particular Cynthia's parents and my sisters—have had our backs, as always. And Sybil Kramer remains an inspiration. My thanks to the friends who have listened to me whine about this book pretty much forever; they are numerous, but a few should be singled out for their occasionally contradictory mix of good sense and encouragement. A few have made more of a difference than they probably know: Mark Abley, Julie Bruck, Bryan Demchinsky, Dawn Rae Downton, David Homel, Elaine Kalman Naves, Scott Lawrence, and Monique Polak.

Helen Reeves has provided invaluable assistance in helping me give shape to this story. Everyone at Penguin has been a pleasure to work with. John Pearce, at Westwood Creative Artists, has provided expert guidance and judgment. Finally, this book is dedicated to my wife and my son, but that hardly does justice to their part in its writing—their constant and sometimes unsuspecting collaboration. What's best in *Bad Animals* I owe to them.